Samuel Johnson and Moral Discipline

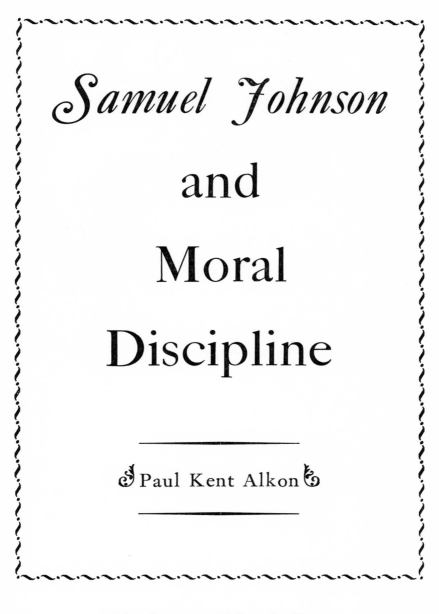

Samuel Johnson

and

Moral

Discipline

⚜ Paul Kent Alkon ⚜

Northwestern University Press

MCMLXVII

*Paul Kent Alkon is Assistant Professor
of English at the University of California
at Berkeley.*

TO SHELDON SACKS

❧ Contents ❧

❦ Preface ❧

A STRIKING FEATURE of Johnson's prose is the relative infrequency of imperative sentences: the great moralist seldom commands. Yet, he acknowledges in the final *Rambler* essay that he had assumed the task of providing "dictatorial instruction," and he is famous if not notorious for his role as stern preceptor. Nor is this fame unjustified. It is entirely appropriate that Becky Sharp was made to throw a copy of Johnson's *Dictionary* into Miss Pinkerton's garden as a symbolic renunciation of authority, and it is equally appropriate that Miss Jemima was nearly shocked into silence by that gesture. What is less fitting is the twentieth-century scholar's surprise upon discovering that Johnson's moral essays are at once less hortatory and more flexible—in a word, more "modern"—than they had been supposed. Yet we have hardly begun to break our own silence in order to express and properly qualify our appreciation of this fact. Too little work has been done on the problem of evaluating and understanding Johnson's methods of providing dictatorial instruction. His views on politics, lexicography, literary criticism, and the profession of journalism have been discussed in reasonably satisfying detail; there have been careful assessments of his own achievements as political pamphleteer, lexicographer, poet, dramatist, "novelist," editor, parliamentary reporter, and literary critic. But we have not yet looked closely enough at Johnson's endeavor as a moralist.

In this book I have undertaken part of that task by analyzing the controlling assumptions of Johnson's moral writings in order to show the nature of those assumptions and how they are related to a few important but neglected or misunderstood aspects of their intellectual backgrounds. For this purpose everything that Johnson wrote is in one way or another relevant, because he attempted to breathe moral instruction into all his works in an effort to make them (as he made the *Rambler*) "exactly conformable to the precepts of Christianity, without any accommodation to the licentiousness and levity of the present age." He even notes in his diary, for example, a hope that the *Lives of The Poets* had been written "in such a manner as may tend to the promotion of Piety." But the great moral essays and apologue of the 1750's are central. In the *Rambler*, the *Adventurer*, the *Idler*, and *Rasselas* are found Johnson's most considered ethical opinions as well as the literary forms which he thought best suited to the end of moral instruction. I have therefore drawn chiefly upon these works for evidence of Johnson's methods as a public moralist. Earlier and later statements amplify the moral stance assumed by Johnson during the fifties, but they do not substantially modify it. Although by no means inflexible, he was remarkably consistent throughout his career. His moral outlook may therefore be studied as a finished whole rather than as a series of shifting stages leading to a final synthesis. For this reason I occasionally base my analysis upon statements written before or after the 1750's.

But in order to avoid a serious methodological confusion I have avoided inferences based upon Johnson's conversation. This limitation is designed to forestall the dangers attending on overhasty attempts to interpret purely personal statements—often uttered while talking for victory—in the light of literary works or vice versa. The result of such enterprise is too often circular reasoning that blurs some important distinctions between these discrete areas of Johnson's activity. This variety of confusion has been greatest in those studies which have regarded Johnson's publications mainly as keys to his personal experience or primarily as expressions of that experience.

Of course no careful biographical study of Johnson needs any apology or deserves any reproach. Yet I have preferred to leave biogra-

phy in other hands while here examining Johnson's works in themselves and in relation to their intellectual milieu. Surely even critics
sailing on this tack will ultimately come about and find themselves
closer to the biographer's goal of understanding a remarkable human
being. Not that any study of Johnson's works can ignore the man. But
it should be useful to look steadily at what he wrote and endeavor to
see it as a whole before trying finally to synthesize the spoken and
written records. A rather unexpected picture, for example, emerges
from the periodical essays and *Rasselas* if we momentarily stop reading them as the inevitable statements of an individual who suffered
from an abnormally exaggerated preoccupation with death. The role
of justice and reason in man's relationship with God then looms
larger than the question of divine retribution and the emotion of fear
which plagued Johnson's own life.

For the purpose of looking steadily at what is most characteristic of
Johnson's methods as a moralist I have divided this study into six
parts. In the first two chapters I discuss Johnson's view of human
nature and what he called "the anatomy of the mind." Because Johnson's works are clearly grounded upon a consistent set of assumptions
about the mechanism of the mind and its relationship to behavior, it is
enlightening to outline systematically the underlying pattern of psychological theory that is woven throughout and to a great extent
determines the method of his periodical essays. Such analysis not only
reveals how Johnson thought the mind actually does work but also
suggests a good deal about the rationale of his effort as a moralist.
Chapter III discusses the relationship between Johnson and Locke
in order to dispel the misleading view that Johnson was opposed to
naturalistic description of human nature. To misunderstand him
on this point is to misread his works and underrate their originality. In
Chapter IV Johnson's views on the consequences, forms, causes, and
cures of self-delusion are closely examined in order to show how he
approached the more prescriptive aspects of what he calls in the
Rambler, No. 47, "the arduous province of preserving the balance of
the mental constitution." Chapter V traces in detail Johnson's purely

normative advice on what he terms "the moral discipline of the mind." By analyzing this most hortatory part of his "dictatorial instruction," it is possible to understand how his accomplishment as a moral psychologist is shaped by his religious convictions. Chapter VI, finally, turns to the question of why Johnson's best works, though deeply religious, avoid falling into the dreariness of the typically homiletic.

In organizing my book so that attention is drawn first to the descriptive and then to the prescriptive aspects of Johnson's work, I have remembered Coleridge's maxim: "The office of philosophical disquisition consists in just distinction; while it is the privilege of the philosopher to preserve himself constantly aware, that distinction is not division." It has seemed useful to distinguish so extensively between the descriptive and prescriptive sides of Johnson's writing only because to draw that distinction is simultaneously to suggest that there is no corresponding division in his works. Johnson's achievement is not fragmented in ways that analysis of it must necessarily be. And this difference reflects a major source of Johnson's greatness.

It is a pleasure to acknowledge the help I have received. Old debts not forgotten are owed to Gavin I. Langmuir and John M. Bullitt. Gwin J. Kolb and Arthur Friedman gave sound advice while setting high standards of scholarship and generosity that I hope I can live up to some day. Encouraging criticism was provided by Bertrand H. Bronson, Ralph W. Rader, Donald J. Greene, Stephen W. Booth, and Jay Ludwig. Special thanks are due to Jean H. Hagstrum for rendering assistance far beyond the ordinary call of Johnsonian duty.

P. K. A.

Samuel Johnson and Moral Discipline

Chapter I

Appetites and Passions

LOOKING BACK over the preceding two years during which he had persisted in "the anxious employment of a periodical writer," Johnson stated in the final number of the *Rambler* that it had been his "principal design to inculcate wisdom or piety." That design governed his literary career. An endeavor to encourage virtue among people whose attention was usually given to other matters informed almost all of his writing, from the early translation of Father Lobo's *Voyage to Abyssinia* to the *Lives of the Poets*. In fact, Johnson's own work as translator, dramatist, poet, essayist, biographer, lexicographer,

3

"novelist," journalist, and literary critic provides a perfect illustration of his firm conviction that "the end of writing is to instruct." Even when assigned as parliamentary reporter for the *Gentleman's Magazine,* he employed the rough notes supplied by Cave's assistant to reconstruct workaday political oratory in such a way that, as one critic has put it, "the emphasis is not on the arguments themselves but on the great questions which embrace those arguments. Johnson always brings the particular within the frame of the general and so gives the *Debates* universality." [1] Not only as a reporter but whenever he picked up his pen, Johnson sought to achieve universality, hoping thereby to accomplish his primary design more effectively, since "he that writes upon general principles, or delivers universal truths, may hope to be often read, because his work will be equally useful at all times and in every country." [2] In Johnson's view, anyone who aims to "inculcate wisdom or piety" is obliged to avoid statements that are merely topical and particular in order to achieve the widest results, because universal truths comprise the most useful form of profane knowledge, while, in the realm of moral discourse, it is equally axiomatic in his view that "right and wrong are immutable." [3] It is impossible to overlook Johnson's explicit assumption that all systems of "wisdom or piety" must ground their utility upon a bedrock of immutable truth.

Yet it is necessary to realize that Johnson numbered in his role of

1. B. B. Hoover, *Samuel Johnson's Parliamentary Reporting* (Berkeley and Los Angeles, 1953), p. 141.

2. *Idler,* No. 59 (Samuel Johnson, *The Idler and The Adventurer,* ed. W. J. Bate, John M. Bullitt, and L. F. Powell [The Yale Edition of the Works of Samuel Johnson; New Haven, 1963], Vol. II). (Quotations from the *Idler* and the *Adventurer* will be taken from this edition. Other subsequent references to Johnson's writing, except for his *Diaries, Prayers, and Annals,* ed. E. L. McAdam, Jr. with Donald and Mary Hyde [Yale Edition; New Haven, 1958], Vol. I, and his *Poems,* ed. E. L. McAdam, Jr. with George Milne [Yale Edition, New Haven, 1964], Vol. VI, will be to *The Works of Samuel Johnson, LL.D.* [9 vols.; Oxford, 1825], cited hereafter as *Works.*)

3. *Adventurer,* No. 95.

immutable truths the fact that we live in a world of continual flux. "Sublunary nature" was, in his opinion, the sphere of "mutability . . . corruption and decay."[4] Man, as a part of that sphere, is "a transitory being"—"a being from whom permanence and stability cannot be derived." Johnson was keenly aware of "the mutability of mankind" and urged writers to "observe the alterations which time is always making in the modes of life." He also pointed out that no man is ever wholly immune from the influence of those manifold changes to which the mercurial world subjects him and to which he often subjects himself. It is not only that "we see men grow old and die at a certain time one after another, from century to century," but, what is perhaps more noteworthy, "human characters are by no means constant; men change by change of place, of fortune, of acquaintance." In discussing Johnson's view of man it is essential to keep in sight the backdrop of mutability against which he projected various universal truths for our guidance. It is also necessary to recall that he acknowledged the existence of striking individual differences in response to the same event: "No man can exactly judge from his own sensations, what another would feel in the same circumstances." Unless these attitudes are kept firmly in mind, it is easy to misunderstand the implications of Johnson's well-known conviction that "human nature is always the same."[5]

One source of misunderstanding on this issue is Johnson's profound conservatism. He certainly distrusted change and believed that "there is in constancy and stability a general and lasting advantage." But he also realized that "novelty is the great source of pleasure" in life as well as in literature.[6] At no time, moreover, did Johnson entirely ignore change. On the contrary, he always took it into account, and nowhere more thoughtfully than in his deliberate and long-continued

4. "Preface to the English Dictionary" (*Works*, V, 46).

5. *Idler*, No. 4; *Plan of an English Dictionary* (*Works*, V, 12); *Adventurer*, No. 95; "Preface to the English Dictionary" (*Works*, V, 46); "Life of Pope" (*Works*, VIII, 293); *Rambler*, No. 128; *Adventurer*, No. 99.

6. "Preface to the English Dictionary" (*Works*, V, 27); "Life of Prior" (*Works*, VIII, 18).

endeavor, as he put it, to "analize the mind of man." [7] That endeavor, in fact, was largely an attempt to delineate the complex interrelationship between the immutable aspects of human nature and the kaleidoscopic patterns of individual human character.

Within a month after the appearance of the first number of the *Rambler*, Johnson pointed out that his purpose was "to consider the moral discipline of the mind, and to promote the increase of virtue rather than of learning." He regarded this purpose as in some measure a novel venture into what he later referred to as "the unexplored abysses of truth" and observed that "this inquiry seems to have been neglected," although "many acute and learned men" have set out to discover how "the understanding is best conducted to the knowledge of science." [8] In his *Dictionary* Johnson defines *science* as "1. Knowledge . . . 2. Certainty grounded upon demonstration . . . 3. Art attained by precepts, or built upon principles . . . 4. Any art or species of knowledge . . . 5. One of the seven liberal arts, grammar, rhetorick, logick, arithmetick, musick, geometry, astronomy." This definition makes it clear that when Johnson refers to science in the *Rambler* he means primarily the liberal arts or other species of secular knowledge rather than what he sometimes explicitly identifies (as in the *Dictionary* definition of *theological*) as "The science of divinity." It is significant that in opposing his essays to the work of those who had been concerned with "the knowledge of science" Johnson was taking an early occasion to dissociate his own chosen field of inquiry from the area of merely secular learning.

Less than two months afterwards, he remarked in the *Rambler*, No. 24, that "the great praise of Socrates is, that he drew the wits of Greece, by his instruction and example, from the vain pursuit of natural philosophy to moral inquiries, and turned their thoughts from stars and tides, and matter and motion, upon the various modes of virtue, and relations of life." Thus, at the outset of his career, John-

7. *Adventurer*, No. 95.
8. *Rambler*, No. 8; *Rambler*, No. 137.

son explicitly and implicitly associated himself with the long tradition of Socratic humanism rather than with the concerns of the liberal arts or the newer branches of mechanical science, whose pursuit he regarded as interesting and often necessary but still "less suitable to the state of man" than consideration of the moral discipline of the mind.[9]

It must be emphasized, however, that Johnson did not merely consider himself the guardian of an ancient body of knowledge. He regarded his own work as a contribution that was definitely novel in method. The reason why "this inquiry seems to have been neglected," he asserts, is simply the *"want of remembering, that all action has its origin in the mind, and that therefore to suffer the thoughts to be vitiated, is to poison the fountains of morality."* Implicit in this reminder is a conviction that although there is no shortage of advice on proper moral conduct, a good deal of such advice is vitiated in practice for lack of considering the antecedent mental dispositions bearing on our ability to behave as we all know we ought to behave. It was this deficiency that Johnson consciously sought to remedy by taking up the anxious employment of a periodical writer in addition to the lexicographer's harmless drudgery. He clearly recognized— and evidently believed himself singular in recognizing—that *"it is no vain speculation to consider how we may govern our thoughts, restrain them from irregular motions, or confine them from boundless dissipation"* [italics added].[10]

But in order to achieve this goal it was first necessary to have a

9. *Rambler*, No. 24. In *Philosophic Words: A Study of Style and Meaning in the "Rambler" and "Dictionary" of Samuel Johnson* (New Haven, 1948), W. K. Wimsatt, Jr. has brilliantly illustrated Johnson's wide familiarity with the new science and the manner in which he adapted its terminology and concepts to suit his own ends by applying them "to psychology in a metaphoric way." Wimsatt also notes that "Johnson's *Rambler*s, as a plausible outcome of the very abstraction, simplification, and systematization of the world seen by the mechanical science, exhibit perhaps the most concentrated use in English literature of mechanical imagery turned inward to the analysis of the soul" (pp. 101, 104).

10. *Rambler*, No. 8.

coherent picture of how the mind does operate. Johnson believed that such knowledge had only been actively sought after—and systematized—during the latter part of the seventeenth century and in his own lifetime. Before Shakespeare's death,

> Speculation had not yet attempted to analyze the mind, to trace the passions to their sources, to unfold the seminal principles of vice and virtue, or sound the depths of the heart for the motives of action. All those inquiries, which from that time that human nature became the fashionable study, have been made sometimes with nice discernment, but often with idle subtilty, were yet unattempted.[11]

Thus, in Johnson's opinion, the new speculations about human nature provided a fund of knowledge that could be of supreme importance to the moralist, although it was still necessary to winnow out useful information and then apply it. Only in this way would it be possible to prescribe rules for properly governing thoughts and thereby achieve a method of dealing with the moral discipline of the mind.

The first step, therefore, was to discern those aspects of human nature that remain immutably the same in every mind and through all time. It was in reference to these more static elements of the mind that Johnson, possibly remembering Burton, adopted an uncomplicated but very striking metaphor to explain a fundamental premise. "The anatomy of the mind," he noted in the *Adventurer*, No. 95, "as that of the body, must perpetually exhibit the same appearances; and though by the continued industry of successive inquirers, new movements will be from time to time discovered, they can affect only the minuter parts, and are commonly of more curiosity than importance." It follows from this basic assumption that before any moralist can hope to minister to a mind diseased, he must understand the structure of our mental anatomy in its healthy state. It also follows that, with some slight exceptions, such understanding is well within the realm of present knowledge. Johnson evidently assumed, in fact, that he need not go out of his way on every relevant occasion to sketch in his view

---

11. "Preface to Shakespeare" (*Works*, V, 130–31).

of this subject because such information, having recently become "the fashionable study," would be vaguely familiar to all his educated readers. He most often writes about our mental anatomy as though it were more a question of reminding his audience of a neglected consideration than of persuading them to accept a radically novel outlook.

This may partly account for a common misconception, shared by even so perceptive a critic as Jean Hagstrum, who has written that

when Johnson referred to "the general system" of nature . . . he also referred to the permanence and immutability of human nature, whose elementary passions have always been the same and have always operated in essentially the same way. Such moral and psychological universals Johnson found within nature. But he never explained or clarified them fully. They always remain general and basic. They are the simple assumptions of common sense, without which there could be neither morality, language, nor art.[12]

Johnson did, in fact, explain and clarify the constant aspects of human nature almost as fully as they could be explained given his concept of their structure, although it is easy to overlook his statements because they are closely woven into the fabric of discussions on other topics and are seldom announced with any fanfare. No issue of the *Rambler* or the *Idler*, for example, is devoted solely to their consideration.

The *Rambler*, No. 49, however, does contain a very full treatment of "mental anatomy" serving as introduction to a consideration of the ethical value of that longing for fame—the "fever of renown" as Johnson calls it in *The Vanity of Human Wishes*—which motivates so much human behavior. In this treatment Johnson clarifies many aspects of the more static elements of the mind by describing the genesis and nature of man's basic appetites and passions.

❧ 2 ☙

At the most fundamental level are the "animal appetites" which are "the first motives of human actions" and which "Providence has

12. Jean H. Hagstrum, *Samuel Johnson's Literary Criticism* (Minneapolis, 1952), p. 71.

given to man in common with the rest of the inhabitants of the earth." These are hunger, thirst, and the need of sleep—the "wants of nature" which we share with all animate creation. In his *Dictionary* Johnson defines *appetite* as "The natural desire of good; the instinct by which we are led to seek pleasure . . . the desire of sensual pleasure." It is plain that he regarded the instinctive attraction towards whatever is physically necessary and pleasant as responsible for our most basic impulses.

At the next level of mental organization are the passions "immediately arising" from animal appetites. These elemental passions are "hope and fear, love and hatred, desire and aversion." They are called into being by the mind's "power of comparison and reflection." In the *Rambler*, No. 49, Johnson does not spell out precisely how the six fundamental passions are *first* brought into existence by our innate ability to compare and reflect, although his conception of that process is certainly implicit in his explanation of how they "extend their range wider, as our reason strengthens, and our knowledge enlarges":

At first we have no thought of pain, but when we actually feel it; we afterwards begin to fear it, yet not before it approaches us very nearly; but, by degrees, we discover it at a greater distance, and find it lurking in remote consequences. Our terrour in time improves into caution, and we learn to look round with vigilance and solicitude, to stop all the avenues at which misery can enter, and to perform or endure many things in themselves toilsome and unpleasing, because we know by reason, or by experience, that our labour will be over-balanced by the reward, that it will either procure some positive good, or avert some evil greater than itself.

This analysis of the part played by reason and experience in extending the range of our six primary passions implies a straightforward theory of their origin. Physical necessities create appetites which are disturbing while unsatisfied. The mind is somehow aware of such disturbances by its power of reflecting on its own experience, and that awareness is sufficient to set in motion the passions differentiated by the terms *love, desire, hope, fear, hatred,* and *aversion.*[13] These passions, in turn, evidently serve the purpose of initiating action designed to remove the unpleasant situations giving rise to them, because when the scope of such passions is extended we begin to take steps that will "either procure some positive good, or avert some evil" similar to "pain when we actually feel it," albeit looming as a future prospect rather than acting as a present annoyance.

Johnson's conception of the purposes served by the primary passions is further exemplified by his *Dictionary* definitions of *love, desire, hope, fear, hatred,* and *aversion. Hatred* is defined as "The passion contrary to love," and equated with the roughly synonymous terms *hate, ill-will, malignity, malevolence, dislike, abhorence, detestation,* and *abomination.* But Johnson's meaning is made most clear by an illustrative quotation from Locke's *Essay Concerning Human Understanding:* "*Hatred* is the thought of the pain which any thing present or absent is apt to produce in us" (*Essay,* II, xx, 5). Johnson defines *desire* as "Wish; eagerness to obtain or enjoy" and illustrates this definition by quoting from the next paragraph of Locke's *Essay:* "Desire is the uneasiness a man finds in himself upon the absence of any thing, whose present enjoyment carries the idea of delight with it." After thus defining *desire* Locke observes "by the by, it may

---

13. Johnson uses the term "reflection" in the same sense that John Locke did when he defined it in Book II, Chap. i, par. 4 of his *Essay Concerning Human Understanding,* ed. A. C. Fraser (2 vols.; New York, 1959), I, 124. (Subsequent references to Locke's text will cite book, chapter, and paragraph of Locke's *Essay* rather than the page numbers of the Fraser edition.) "By reflection," Locke wrote, "I would be understood to mean, that notice which the mind takes of its own operations, and the manner of them, by reason whereof there come to be ideas of these operations in the understanding." In his *Dictionary,* Johnson defines the verb *to reflect,* in its third sense, as meaning "To throw back the thoughts upon the past or on themselves." The fifth meaning of *reflection* is "The action of the mind upon itself" and is illustrated by Locke's phrase, "*Reflection* is the perception of the operations of our own minds within us, as it is employed about the ideas it has got." (All citations from Johnson's *Dictionary* are taken from the fourth edition, 1773.)

perhaps be of some use to remark, that the chief, if not only spur to human industry and action is *uneasiness*. For whatsoever good is proposed, if its absence carries no displeasure or pain with it, if a man be easy and content without it, there is no desire of it, nor endeavour after it." In this matter, as in so many others, Johnson's ideas are in close agreement with, and doubtless partially derived from, those of Locke. Fraser observes that "pleasure and pain . . . play a supreme part in Locke's ethical system, as *motives* for conforming to moral relations that are themselves acknowledged by him to be immutable and eternal"; and this observation applies equally well to Johnson's ethical system.[14]

Johnson defines *hope* as "Expectation of some good; an expectation indulged with pleasure," and illustrates his meaning by a quotation from Book II, Chapter xx, paragraph 9 of Locke's *Essay:* "Hope is that pleasure in the mind which every one finds in himself, upon the thought of a profitable [Locke's *Essay* reads "probable"] future enjoyment of a thing which is apt to delight him." The *Dictionary* definition of *fear* as "Dread; horrour; painful apprehension of danger" is illustrated from the tenth paragraph of the same chapter in Locke's *Essay: "Fear* is an uneasiness of the mind, upon the thought of future evil likely to befal us." Finally, *aversion* is defined merely as "Hatred; dislike; detestation, such as turns away from the object," while *love* is shown in many different senses ranging from "The passion between the sexes" to "Fondness; concord," and including "Kindness; good-will; friendship; courtship; tenderness; parental care; liking; inclination to; lewdness"; and "Unreasonable liking"; but the root meaning of *love* is made most clear by the definition of its opposite, *hatred*. All these definitions, four of which are illustrated from Locke's *Essay,* amplify and make more explicit the view of primary passions implicit in the *Rambler,* No. 49.

In the analytical context of that essay *good* and *evil* are synonymous with *pleasure* and *pain,* as they always are when Johnson is

---

14. *Essay,* I, 302, n. 1.

speaking as mental anatomist rather than moral disciplinarian. In reading his works it is necessary to bear in mind the difference between these two roles in order to understand him clearly. He is, for example, sitting in the chair of mental anatomy and not pronouncing from the throne of moral discipline, when he refers, in the *Rambler*, No. 1, to "the desire of good and the fear of evil" as "the two great movers of the human mind" and also when he defines appetite as "the natural desire of good." He means not ethical good and evil but simply pleasure and pain, both physical and mental. This would no doubt be plain enough to anyone reading these particular statements, but in other contexts the distinction is not so apparent.

Yet if we misread Johnson on this issue we may seriously underrate his estimate of the importance of pleasure and pain as determinants of human motives. Walter Jackson Bate, for example, while correctly noting Johnson's opposition to the doctrine of determinism, remarks that Johnson was also antagonistic "to any form of the belief, such as that popularized by Hobbes a century before, that human motives are determined by a mechanical, inner calculus of pleasure that ministers to our own egos." [15] In fact, however, Johnson seems to have grounded his thought on the assumption that the six primary passions, which motivate so many of our actions, are indeed based on just such an "inner calculus": attraction towards pleasure and aversion from pain are "the two great movers of the human mind." In the *Idler*, No. 18, he asserts that "the mind is seldom quickened to very vigorous operations but by pain, or the dread of pain. . . . He that is happy, by whatever means, desires nothing but the continuance of happiness." And it is significant that he illustrates the meaning of *motive* ("That which determines the choice; that which incites the action") in his *Dictionary* by quoting Locke's statement that "the *motive* for continuing in the same state is only the present satisfaction in it; the *motive* to change is always some uneasiness." [16] It would

15. *The Achievement of Samuel Johnson* (New York, 1961), p. 144.
16. *Essay*, II, xxi, 29.

therefore be more accurate to say that Johnson was realistic enough to look squarely at the means whereby primary passions are called into being, extend their range, and initiate cautionary actions designed to "procure some positive good or avert some evil." Johnson accepted this somewhat mechanical process for what it is and only asserted that human conduct need not—and should not—always follow the bidding of our primary passions and appetites. He knew that we cannot help being thirsty at times but insisted that we ought never to drink from a poisoned well.

❧ 3 ☙

The primary passions, however, were only one side of the coin. Johnson continues in the *Rambler*, No. 49:

As the soul advances to a fuller exercise of its powers, the animal appetites, and the passions immediately arising from them, are not sufficient to find it employment; the wants of nature are soon supplied, the fear of their return is easily precluded, and something more is necessary to relieve the long intervals of inactivity, and to give those faculties, which cannot lie wholly quiescent, some particular direction. For this reason, new desires and artificial passions are by degrees produced; and, from having wishes only in consequence of our wants, we begin to feel wants in consequence of our wishes.

Johnson here makes an important distinction between the six primary or natural passions and a spectrum of artificial passions which are less immediately related to "the wants of nature" and which are not uniformly found in every human being. It is this distinction which provides a high degree of flexibility to an analytical schema of the mind which many readers have persistently regarded as rigid, over-generalized, and hopelessly behind the times. By carefully distinguishing the six natural passions that are universal constants in human nature from the artificial passions that do not necessarily appear or play the same part in everybody, Johnson opens the door to a system that can take flexible account of both individual differences within the same society and variations of character created by differing social climates.

The flexibility of Johnson's outlook is apparent in his further explanation of how artificial passions are created:

We persuade ourselves to set a value upon things which are of no use, but because we have agreed to value them; things which can neither satisfy hunger, nor mitigate pain, nor secure us from any real calamity, and which, therefore, we find of no esteem among those nations whose artless and barbarous manners keep them always anxious for the necessaries of life.

It is somewhat surprising to discover that Johnson does not refer primarily to material objects when he uses the word "things" in this context. Obviously, an isolated group of Hottentots scratching out a meager subsistence will not naturally desire to own monogrammed snuff boxes, because they will not know that such things exist. Johnson must have expected his readers to accept this kind of cultural difference as self-evident and certainly not important enough to waste ink and quills upon. He refers, rather, to less tangible "things" which we learn to value according to the dictates of society and not the promptings of nature. He lists these intangibles as avarice, vanity, ambition, envy, curiosity, friendship, and love of fame. They are the artificial or "adscititious" passions.[17] The list is striking in itself and because of what it implies. If primitive man living an "artless and barbarous" existence is not prey to the meaner feelings of envy, avarice, and vanity, neither is he impelled to display curiosity or friendship. We know that Johnson regarded curiosity as "the thirst of the soul . . . one of the permanent and certain characteristics of a vigorous intellect." He also believed that "life has no pleasure higher or nobler than that of friendship."[18] Clearly, Johnson agreed with

---

17. In the *Dictionary* Johnson defines *adscititious* as "That which is taken in to complete something else, though originally extrinsick; supplemental; additional." No example of its use is given.

18. *Rambler*, No. 103; *Idler*, No. 23.

Hobbes in believing that the life of man in a state of nature is solitary, poor, nasty, and brutish.

It is also plain from Johnson's discussion in the *Rambler*, No. 49, that the artificial passions, as he conceived of them, are entirely determined by social custom and individual circumstance. Unlike the elemental emotions of love, hatred, desire, aversion, hope, and fear, which will be found playing their parts in every person whether civilized or savage, an artificial passion such as avarice—or friendship—may never be found in many people, although the *capacity* for both natural and adscititious passions is a universal constant in human nature. When Johnson remarks that "human nature is always the same," he means that it remains the same because the natural passions are never absent. But the proportion of artificial passions may vary in each individual, and such variation determines what Johnson labels *character*. In the *Life of Savage*, for example, he refers to "the different combinations of passions, and the innumerable mixtures of vice and virtue, which distinguish one character from another." [19] In the *Dictionary* he defines *character* as "The particular constitution of the mind." The particular configuration of artificial passions in each person determines his mental character and ultimately, in Johnson's opinion, his moral character as well.

Our artificial desires, Johnson goes on to explain in the *Rambler*, No. 49,

arise from the comparison of our condition with that of others. He that thinks himself poor because his neighbour is richer; he that, like Caesar, would rather be the first man of a village, than the second in the capital of the world, has apparently kindled in himself *desires which he never received from nature*, and acts upon *principles established only by the authority of custom* [italics added].

Society—not nature—is thus the source not only of many noble feelings but also of a demonic roll call of baser desires that flourish "only by the authority of custom." In itself, therefore, civilization is re-

19. *Works*, VIII, 125.

garded as fundamentally ambiguous. If the primitive state of nature seemed appalling to Johnson, civilization was evidently no unmixed blessing in his eyes; civil society is necessary for the noblest human passions to flourish, but it can also open a Pandora's box of unnaturally vicious behavior. Johnson's efforts as a moralist are largely directed at forestalling the latter possibility. Consequently, his works are primarily concerned with the realm of artificial passions and unnatural depravity.

Yet once artificial passions have been called into being and are maintained by the authority of custom, they operate in the same manner universally, though with different objects and outward symptoms in different societies. This was also in Johnson's mind when he observed that human nature is always the same. He remarks in the *Adventurer*, No. 95, for example, that the influence of the passions "is uniform, and their effects nearly the same in every human breast: a man loves and hates, desires and avoids, exactly like his neighbour; resentment and ambition, avarice and indolence, discover themselves by the same symptoms, in minds distant a thousand years from one another." In this statement Johnson includes the natural passions—love, desire, aversion, and hatred—as well as the artificial passions—ambition, resentment, and avarice. They are alike in uniformity of effect, although very different in origin. That is, if it is present at all, each passion operates uniformly within every person by initiating the same kind of impulse on each occasion: avarice never prompts a man to fling coins out of his coach window, nor does anyone feel aversion for an unpleasant object and want to move closer to it. Thus human nature is uniform insofar as each passion has "nearly the same" results "in every human breast." But this is no more than to say that if an emotion is not marked by some similarity of inward effect when it is roused in different people, it is not present in each. No one—least of all a modern anthropological relativist—would deny this truism, because it is merely the assumption we have to make when using the same word in reference to situations that are "nearly the same." Johnson is only saying that a given term has, by definition, the same denotation whenever it is employed correctly. This is certainly a simple assumption of common sense without which language could not exist. However, it is not Johnson's only assumption.

As the foregoing discussion has shown, he also assumed that each individual may have a different slate of artificial passions. What is equally important, Johnson assumed not that any one passion would always manifest itself externally by "the same symptoms" but rather, that each passion invariably initiates the same *inner* impulse, even *"in minds distant a thousand years from one another."* The outward symptoms, however—modes of conduct—might vary enormously through the ages and from culture to culture. Recognition of this possibility, as of the distinction between natural and artificial passions, enormously increases the scope and flexibility of Johnson's anatomy of the mind by allowing him to take full account of the diversities in human behavior without sinking to mere enumeration of individual eccentricities. Thus, for example, he explains in the *Adventurer*, No. 95, that

love is uniform, but courtship is perpetually varying; the different arts of gallantry, which beauty has inspired, would of themselves be sufficient to fill a volume; sometimes balls and serenades, sometimes tournaments and adventures have been employed to melt the hearts of ladies, who in another century have been sensible of scarce any other merit than that of riches, and listened only to jointures and pin-money. Thus the ambitious man has at all times been eager of wealth and power; but these hopes have been gratified in some countries by supplicating the people, and in others by flattering the prince: honour in some states has been only the reward of military atchievements, in others it has been gained by noisy turbulence and popular clamours. Avarice has worn a different form, as she actuated the usurer of Rome, and the stock-jobber of England; and idleness itself, how little soever inclined to the trouble of invention, has been forced from time to time to change its amusements, and contrive different methods of wearing out the day.

In Johnson's view, human nature is universally the same in some ways, but individual conduct and social customs provide an infinite variety that is, moreover, mirrored within the mind. "If we analize the mind of man," he goes on to observe, we shall discover that "all the pleasures and pains that we see and hear of" are produced by only a handful of passions,

but those few agitated and combined, as *external causes shall happen to operate, and modified by prevailing opinions and accidental caprices*, make such frequent alterations on the surface of life, that the show while we are busied in delineating it, vanishes from the view, and a new set of objects succeeds, doomed to the same shortness of duration with the former [italics added].

Thus, far from believing that there is nothing really new under the sun, Johnson is keenly aware of the eternal flux in which all mankind is involved.

What is even more important, however, is the fact that he is well aware of how responsive human character is to the molding influence of its fluctuating social environment. In the *Dictionary* Johnson defines *passion* as "Any effect caused by external agency; susceptibility of effect from external action; violent commotion of the mind." [20] This definition, as well as his observations in the *Adventurer*, No. 95, reveals Johnson's conviction that the individual pattern

20. Johnson's definition of *passion* may be compared with the definitions provided by some earlier lexicographers. Edward Phillips, *The New World of Words: or a General English Dictionary* (3d ed.; London, 1671), defines *passion* as "Suffering: also an affection of the mind; also in Poems, and Romances, it is more particularly taken for the passion of love." The fifth edition of *The New World of Words* (London, 1696) states that "Passion is opposed to Action; also suffering, enduring; said also of the different Agitations of the Soul according to the various Objects that present themselves to the Senses. But in Poems and Romances it is more particularly spoken of the Passion of Love." This revised definition contains a statement that is similar to Johnson's definition of *passion* as "Any effect caused by external agency." However, John Kersey, in *A New English Dictionary* (London, 1702), merely defines *passion* as "Suffering, or anger" and *the passions* as "Affections of the mind." In the fifth edition of *A New English Dictionary* (London, 1748), the definition of *passion* is expanded to "Transport of Mind, Love, Anger, Suffering; pain in the Body," and the definition of *the passions* is expanded to "The Affections of the Mind; as Love, Hatred, &c." Kersey's definitions are similar to those provided by Nathan Bailey, whose *Universal*

taken by the handful of passions available to every person is most
often determined, not by free choice—however desirable that would
be—but rather by the capricious "external causes" that "shall happen
to operate." Thus "prevailing opinions" in a man's nation usually
determine whether he will peacefully open shop to amass "jointures
and pin money" or belligerently set out in quest of "tournaments and
adventures" in order to win a wife. Everybody is stirred by the
primary passion of love, but prevailing local customs may seize on this
emotion to mold an individual into a peaceful trader or else transform
him into a bellicose adventurer. The mentality in each case is surely
quite different, and that difference, Johnson implies, is socially—not
naturally—created. Johnson was violently opposed to the notion that
men are born governed by some "ruling passion." Instead, he believed that *"most minds are the slaves of external circumstances, and*

Etymological English Dictionary (6th ed.; London, 1733) defines *passion* as
"Affection, transport of Mind, Anger, Suffering; [Among Physicians] Pain or
Uneasiness of the Body" and *the passions* as "[Among Humanists] The
Affections of the Mind, as Love, Hatred, &c." Finally, Thomas Dyche and
William Pardon, *A New General English Dictionary* (3d ed.; London,
1740), define *passion* as "Any strong emotion of mind, inclination, or desire
for, or aversion against a thing; so anger, love, joy, &c. are called *passions* of
the soul or *mind*."

These definitions show that Johnson's definition of *passion* is not altogether
original. However, the range of definitions provided by Phillips, Kersey,
Bailey, Dyche, and Pardon also reveals that an area of choice was sometimes
open to Johnson even when a word had been previously defined by several
lexicographers. For this reason, we are safe in assuming in such cases that
Johnson's definition represents his own considered opinion of the word's
meaning. Even in those cases where Johnson merely reiterates what had by
then become the traditional definition of a word, such reiteration implies his
agreement with that definition, since he was always free to provide a novel
definition if he wanted to. Therefore, throughout this study I have simply
taken for granted that Johnson's *Dictionary* is our best source of information
about what he took to be the meaning of any particular word. For a general
discussion of the relationship between the *Dictionary* and earlier lexicographical tradition, see James H. Sledd and Gwin J. Kolb, *Dr. Johnson's Dictionary*
(Chicago, 1955), pp. 1–45.

conform to any hand that undertakes to mould them, roll down any torrent of custom in which they happen to be caught, or bend to any importunity that bears hard against them" [italics added].[21] To Johnson's way of thinking, such slavery to "external circumstance" is deplorable because it amounts to a kind of social determinism against which the average individual is powerless. Johnson saw men as for the most part helplessly pitched and tossed upon mountainous waves of "prevailing opinion." But he did not relish the spectacle.

❧ 4 ❧

Joseph Wood Krutch has observed that Johnson's *Rambler,* No. 114, on prisons, hanging, and the question of capital punishment for robbery, is "one of the relatively rather rare occasions when even he deals with what we should call a sociological rather than a moral subject." [22] This is certainly true, and perhaps it is now possible to understand more clearly why Johnson avoided dealing with what we think of today as sociological problems. He was not unaware of such problems and was even personally involved in many of them during his long, arduous climb from Grub Street to Streatham. His early and middle life was hardly a sheltered one. Yet, by the same token, he realized how difficult it was to change the world around him: "He who has so little knowledge of human nature, as to seek happiness by changing any thing but his own dispositions, will waste his life in fruitless efforts, and multiply the griefs which he purposes to remove." [23] Moreover, his years as a parliamentary reporter for the *Gentleman's Magazine* had given him a firsthand knowledge of the practical "social science" of his day. By elaborating theoretical discussions on both sides of such issues as import duties and navigation laws, regulation of drinking and alcoholism, bills for "the encouragement and increase of seamen," and "punishment of mutiny and desertion,"

21. *Rambler,* No. 70.
22. *Samuel Johnson* (New York, 1944), p. 39.
23. *Rambler,* No. 6.

maintenance of a standing army, and "cleansing and paving the city of Westminster," Johnson must have seen how easy it is to propose speculative answers to social problems—and how little assurance there is that such speculation or legislation will in fact have much real effect in alleviating widespread distress. Measures imposed upon the mass of men from outside will all too often be smashed to bits against a coral reef built up of immovable individual dispositions. Therefore, the greatest hope for social improvement, he must have reasoned, rests in altering individual attitudes and teaching men how to swim against the currents of prevailing opinion when necessary. Consequently, Johnson's moral essays are his way of dealing with sociological issues.

But those moral essays would have been impossible if Johnson had not rejected the doctrine of the "ruling passion." It was not until he wrote the "Life of Pope," however, that his rejection of that theory was explained in detail. In the moral essays themselves, he merely states his disapproval of the theory and suggests that it is untenable. In the *Rambler*, No. 43, for example, he caustically refers to "some that imagine themselves to have looked with more than common penetration into human nature" and who "have endeavoured to persuade us that each man is born with a mind formed peculiarly for certain purposes, and with desires unalterably determined to particular objects, from which the attention cannot be long diverted, and which alone, as they are well or ill pursued, must produce the praise or blame, the happiness or misery of his future life." This, in sum, is the doctrine of the ruling passion, which Johnson goes on to dismiss by remarking that "if the doctrine of innate ideas be itself disputable, there seems to be little hope of establishing an opinion, which supposes that even complications of ideas have been given us at our birth, and that we are made by nature ambitious, or covetous, before we know the meaning of either power or money." [24] This dismissal,

24. In the "Life of Pope," Johnson provides a similar definition, explaining that the theory of the ruling passion postulates "an original direction of desire

although only grounded explicitly upon an improbability arising from the dispute over innate ideas, is actually a corollary of the distinction between natural and artificial passions. Having accepted that distinction—which he explained at length in the *Rambler*, No. 49, three weeks after No. 43 was published—Johnson clearly could not agree that passions such as avarice or ambition, encouraged and molded as they are by prevailing opinions in particular societies, are inborn. Later, in the "Life of Pope," he was more explicit.

The first reason given in that work for doubting the theory of the ruling passion is drawn from experience: "Human characters are by no means constant; men change by change of place, of fortune, of acquaintance; he who is at one time a lover of pleasure, is at another a lover of money." This observation of the inconstancy of character, as I have noted, was one of Johnson's fundamental assumptions in working out his distinction between natural and artificial passions. That distinction, in fact, was evolved largely to explain the mechanism

---

to some particular object; an innate affection, which gives all action a determinate and invariable tendency, and operates upon the whole system of life, either openly, or more secretly by the intervention of some accidental or subordinate propension" (*Works*, VIII, 293).

Even though Johnson rejects the idea that men are born with a particular (and inescapable) mental character, he clearly recognizes that after environmental influences have done their work, there do "seem to be some souls suited to great, and others to little employments; some formed to soar aloft, and take in wide views, and others to grovel on the ground and confine their regard to a narrow sphere." He does not, however, make it altogether clear whether temperamental differences of this sort are in some measure innate. Probably he believed that there is a degree of inborn disposition towards wide-ranging, even reckless, capability in some people and narrow, timid incompetence in others. But I doubt whether he regarded these differences as very significant. The discussion in the *Rambler*, No. 43, warning reckless souls against the dangers of hasty decisions and over-confidence and advising them to be more persevering and cautious in estimating difficulties, implies that the crucial matter is whether or not a man understands his own temperament and is prepared to take proper measures in guarding against the mistakes to which it renders him most liable.

whereby men do change. Since they do, Johnson argued, we cannot sensibly suppose them subject to any one "ruling passion." However, to ward off a possible objection, he offers an alternative theory explaining why outstanding men are most frequently active in only one field.

Those, indeed, who attain any excellence, commonly spend life in one pursuit: for excellence is not often gained upon easier terms. But to the particular species of excellence men are directed, not by an ascendant planet or predominating humour, but by the first book which they read, some early conversation which they heard, or some accident which excited ardour and emulation.[25]

Johnson thus asserts that a man's area of interest is determined not by any innate internal cause ("predominating humour") or by some remote external influence ("an ascendant planet") but rather by a chance and immediate event. He does not deny that, *once excited*, a passionate interest will profoundly influence the course of a man's life, even to the point of becoming a kind of obsession in some cases—but he refuses to concede that such influence is either inescapable or predetermined.

In his discussion of how men's governing interests arise, Johnson again shows his lively awareness of the crucial effects of early surroundings. But the profound importance of early environment, to Johnson, is that it determines the range of possibilities open to the *freely choosing* individual, who picks one from among the available goals competing for his attention and "ardour." Johnson goes on with more than a hint of sarcasm:

It must be, at least, allowed, that this "ruling passion," antecedent to reason and observation, must have an object independent on human contrivance; for there can be no natural desire of artificial good. No man, therefore, can be born, in the strict acceptation, a lover of money; for he may be born where money does not exist: nor can he be born, in a moral sense, a lover of his country; for society, politically regulated, is a state contradistinguished from a state of nature; and any attention to that coalition of interests which makes the happiness

25. "Life of Pope" (*Works*, VIII, 293).

of a country, is possible only to those whom inquiry and reflection have enabled to comprehend it.[26]

In Johnson's view, no civilized pursuit is necessarily chosen by any process "antecedent to reason and observation." Nor does he conceive the environment as molding any individual in the Freudian sense of acting to create unconscious needs that relentlessly shape the pattern of future choices. Professor Bate has rightly observed that "few classical moralists are closer to Freud than Johnson." [27] But while applauding Johnson's modernity, we must not lose sight of the very real differences between his concepts and the twentieth-century images of man. His significance for us resides as much in those differences as in his similarities to our own outlook, for we can only learn what we are by discovering what we are not.

Johnson's final reason for rejecting the theory of the ruling passion is that

this doctrine is, in itself, pernicious as well as false; its tendency is to produce the belief of a kind of moral predestination, or overruling principle which cannot be resisted; he that admits it is prepared to comply with every desire that caprice or opportunity shall excite, and to flatter himself that he submits only to the lawful dominion of nature, in obeying the resistless authority of his ruling passion.[28]

Thus Johnson saw in the theory of the ruling passion a grave danger to society. By acquiescing to any such scheme of "moral predestination," an individual can find a ready excuse for giving up all pretense of self-control and, instead of trying to guide his own conduct, can merely allow himself to be swayed by desires welling up capriciously within his mind or excited from without. Such acquiescence is one of many reasons why most men are inescapably swept along "down any torrent of custom in which they happen to be caught." Johnson does not minimize the difficulty of resisting social pressure. On the contrary, he believed that resistance can be successful only if men

26. *Ibid.*
27. *The Achievement of Samuel Johnson*, p. 67. See also pp. 93–94.
28. "Life of Pope" (*Works*, VIII, 293–94).

recognize the difficulties and make a strenuous effort to overcome them. But he rejected the doctrine of the ruling passion because when it is accepted all strenuous efforts to overcome immoral impulses or evil customs soon end. Moreover, social progress becomes impossible if that doctrine is accepted, because individual mortality—which is founded upon energetic opposition to unlawful customs and passions—is the key to collective improvement.

It is plain that a series of essays devoted to the moral discipline of the mind can only be undertaken if such discipline is really possible. But if any "kind of moral predestination, or overruling principle which cannot be resisted" exists, that possibility vanishes, and such essays become farcical, for one cannot teach others how to discipline thoughts that are beyond all control. Therefore, rejection of the theory of the ruling passion and other explicitly deterministic doctrines was essential before Johnson could even begin to consider the moral discipline of the mind. Throughout his moral essays, as elsewhere, he insists that we can be free if we will trouble to understand the difficulties that confront us and endeavor to overcome them. But he also insists that if we fail to do so, our freedom will be lost and we shall become (as most minds do become) *the slaves of external circumstance.*

Johnson opposes the theory of the ruling passion on two grounds: first, because it is false, and second, because it is pernicious. The order of attack is highly significant because it demonstrates a characteristic aspect of Johnson's thought. He usually endeavored to discover the truth, no matter how unpleasant, *before* passing moral judgment upon the facts in question. Hence he is most often able to "analyze the mind of man" as objectively and amorally as Hobbes or Machiavelli ever did. And the results are often startling, for, like them, he frequently confronts us with aspects of human nature that we are usually content to leave comfortably out of sight.

Johnson believed that "right and wrong are immutable" but that human character is not. He never confused the two. He might censure someone's conduct as morally indefensible in the light of Christian ethics, but he seldom dismissed it as outside the pale of human nature. He had, in fact—despite many blind spots—an ability, rare in any age, to understand what lay behind conduct that he felt obliged to disapprove of. Moralists too often respond to proscribed behavior as they would to a python: fire your shotgun at it, they seem to say, and never mind how such a disagreeable beast ever came here in the first place. Johnson's attitude, on the contrary, is more like that of a calm naturalist studying a creature's habits in order to trace its breeding place and remove it at the source if necessary, at the same time warning everyone of the danger. The wonder is not that Johnson had blind spots and prejudices, as he assuredly and sometimes amusingly had, but that, in an age of prevailing absolute standards, he was able to enlarge his sympathies so impressively. It is that sympathetic enlargement of understanding, and not Johnson's blind spots, that ultimately gives his work enduring importance.

However, Johnson's immense reach of sympathetic understanding has not yet been sufficiently appreciated. He is too frequently regarded, even among our graduate students of literature, as the supreme example of narrow insularity: an eccentric but entertaining Old Tory who disliked the Scots, thought any three Englishmen equal to sixteen hundred Frenchmen, looked askance at romantic poetry, and refused to understand the democratic aspiration of American colonists, not to mention John Wilkes. It has been the task of modern scholarship to remove the misconceptions responsible for that distorted image of Johnson, and to a considerable extent this has been accomplished, even though much still remains to be done. It is especially necessary to see precisely why Johnson was able to transcend so many of his own limitations—limitations so real, and so apparent, that throughout the nineteenth century they almost completely overshadowed his amazing ability to rise above them. Those limitations, of course, are more evident in his conversations than in his works, and that is one reason why he has been misrepresented. But we have at last put Boswell back on the shelf long enough to take down Johnson's own volumes for examination. They are even being printed

again. Although progress in revaluating Johnson has been slow, it
has been very sure in recent years.

Donald J. Greene, for example, has brilliantly exploded the myth
of Johnson's obstinate and inflexible Toryism. He has also observed
what inevitably impresses any but the most casual reader: "The vast
range of Johnson's interests is perpetually astonishing." Even more
noteworthy, Greene has accurately characterized a fundamental aspect of Johnson's view of human nature. Noting the contrast between
Johnson's preface to his translation of Father Lobo's *Voyage to
Abyssinia* and the contents of the book itself, Greene observes that
"the customs contrary to the laws of nature, which shock the Jesuit,
Johnson is prepared to subsume under the normal 'mixture of vice
and virtue.' It is," Green continues, "a remarkably liberal attitude,
closer to that of the modern scientific anthropologist than to those of
either the seventeenth-century missionary or the eighteenth-century
Rousseauist." [29] On the whole, this observation may be extended to
Johnson's entire outlook on human conduct. More often than not, he
is indeed "closer to . . . the modern scientific anthropologist" than to
the popular attitudes of the eighteenth century. And in the light of
the foregoing discussion of appetites and passions, it is now possible to
understand more clearly why Johnson was able to maintain such a
"remarkably liberal attitude." But to understand him fully, it will be
helpful to examine two other characteristic instances of Johnson's
wide reach of sympathetic insight.

Shakespeare's *King Lear* and *Macbeth* were both grounded upon
behavior that seemed highly improbable to many eighteenth-century
playgoers. Lear creates the situation that ultimately destroys him by
giving over control of his kingdom on terms that would hardly have
occurred to George II or Louis XV. Macbeth decides to turn against
Duncan and then to continue his bloody course, partly as a result of
encounters with the Weird Sisters. His treacherous impulses are thus
strengthened by influences which are very unlike those that

29. *The Politics of Samuel Johnson* (New Haven, 1960), pp. 67–68.

prompted, say, Sir John Fenwick to engage in the Jacobite plot of 1696 against King William. The treason might be viewed as almost equally shocking in both cases, but Fenwick's conduct was at least more understandable to Johnson's contemporaries because it was not given impetus by any supernatural agency. Johnson, however, was able to bring both Lear and Macbeth into meaningful relationship with the more familiar world of George II, Louis XV, and the Old Pretender. Thus Johnson remarks in his general observations on the play:

On the seeming improbability of Lear's conduct, it may be observed, that he is represented according to histories at that time vulgarly received as true. And, perhaps, if we turn our thoughts upon the barbarity and ignorance of the age to which this story is referred, it will appear not so unlikely as while we estimate Lear's manners by our own. Such preference of one daughter to another, or resignation of dominion on such conditions, would be yet credible, if told of a petty prince of Guinea or Madagascar.[30]

Johnson no more regards Lear's conduct as unnatural than he does that of the Abyssinians described by Father Lobo or the behavior of eighteenth-century chieftains in Guinea and Madagascar. He may not approve of its "barbarity and ignorance," but he is nevertheless prepared to encounter such behavior in lands where less civilized customs and opinions prevail. Johnson is keenly aware that we cannot estimate another culture's "manners by our own," if we hope to understand the rational foundation of individual conduct within that society. He also observes, in the "Life of Milton," that "those who have no power to judge of past times, but by their own, should always doubt their conclusions." [31] This kind of judgment, or "estimation," as Johnson usually calls it, is in his view different from—and antecedent to—moral judgment.

He is like modern scientific anthropologists in objectively examining

30. "General Observations on King Lear" (*Works*, V, 173).
31. *Works*, VII, 107.

the underlying motivations created by "prevailing opinion" within an alien culture and then—on the basis of that examination—"estimating" how normal, "credible," or "unlikely" any particular action is in the light of the standards accepted by that society itself. Johnson is unlike most modern anthropological relativists primarily because he goes ahead to pass explicit moral judgment upon the alien standards by invoking his own values as superior. In our age the emphasis is most frequently upon "estimation," and we are reluctant to speak up in behalf of what we hold dear.

To be sure, it is possible to make a more thorough description if one specializes in that alone and gives over all attempt at passing moral judgment upon whatever one is describing. Such specialization has certainly been the means of amassing an unprecedented wealth of accurate information that could hardly have been gathered in any other way. But what is gained in accuracy may be at the expense of human significance. This is the great danger of mere objectivity, however necessary that virtue might be. In his "Life of Milton," for example, Johnson complained—and the complaint has not diminished in urgency over the intervening years—that "the innovators whom I oppose . . . seem to think, that we are placed here to watch the growth of plants, or the motion of the stars." At the close of his career, as at its outset, Johnson was careful to dissociate himself explicitly from total commitment to the amoral outlook of natural science, preferring to place himself on the side of Socrates, who "was rather of opinion, that what we had to learn was, how to do good, and avoid evil." [32]

It is, however, to Johnson's credit that, although refusing to regard it as an end in itself, he never completely rejected a central aspect of the new scientific method: namely, its focus upon objective description and comparative valuation or "estimation." His acceptance of that method is perhaps most striking in the moral essays, for there one least expects to find dispassionate analysis and estimation. Yet it is

32. *Works*, VII, 77.

precisely a note of calm objectivity which sets the prevailing tone of Johnson's endeavor as a moralist. The same note sounds throughout his literary criticism, where Johnson attempted "to reduce those regions of literature under the dominion of science, which have hitherto known only the anarchy of ignorance, the caprices of fancy, and the tyranny of prescription." [33] The most important critical result of this attempt is the kind of historical approach to literature found in his remarks on *King Lear*.

That approach was announced as early as 1745, when Johnson stated in his *Miscellaneous Observations on the Tragedy of Macbeth*, that "in order to make a true estimate of the abilities and merit of a writer, it is always necessary to examine the genius of his age, and the opinions of his contemporaries." Later, in the "Preface to Shakespeare," Johnson again affirmed that "every man's performances, to be rightly estimated, must be compared with the state of the age in which he lived, and with his own particular opportunities." This historical principle of evaluation provides a major touchstone for Johnson's famous defense of Shakespeare's achievement and underlies Johnson's explanatory comments on each individual play as well. In the *Lives of the Poets*, this principle results in a similar emphasis upon biographical and historical considerations. In *Rasselas*, through Imlac, Johnson generalizes the historical method of estimation to include all human affairs: "To judge rightly of the present," Imlac observes, "we must oppose it to the past." It should be emphasized that in Johnson's practice, such judgment is antecedent to his *final* verdict upon the moral (or other) worth of the objects or conduct in question. A poem may be condemned as lackluster and yet still may be appreciated as remarkable in view of the circumstances under which it was created. So may any other object. "The palaces of Peru or Mexico," Johnson observes, "were certainly mean and incommodious habitations, if compared to the houses of European monarchs; yet who could forbear to view them with astonishment, who

33. *Rambler*, No. 92.

remembered that they were built without the use of iron?" [34] Whatever the final verdict, Johnson insists upon the importance of examining conduct or creative effort on its own terms to see how—and why—it came into being, as well as what its most distinctive characteristics are, *before* proceeding to pass final sentence upon it. Without such anterior appraisal, Johnson implies, no truly useful judgment can ever be reached.

One may, it is true, pronounce an accurate judgment—as when, for example, one condemns belief in witchcraft as a wicked and absurd superstition. But this accurate condemnation may often be useless

34. *Works*, V, 55; V, 124; I, 264; "Preface to Shakespeare" (*Works*, V, 124). Johnson's observation on the palaces of Peru and Mexico is reminiscent of Mandeville's remark that "It is said by some men of reputation, that the *Americans* in *Mexico* and *Peru* have all the signs of an infant world; because when the *Europeans* first came among them, they wanted a great many things, that seem to be of easy invention. But considering, that they had no body to borrow from, and no iron at all, it is amasing which way they could arrive at the perfection we found them in" (Bernard Mandeville, *The Fable of the Bees*, ed. F. B. Kaye [Oxford, 1924], II, 319–20). Although *The Fable of the Bees* is not cited in the *Dictionary*, Johnson had read Mandeville's work while still very young. Replying to Miss Seward during a conversation that took place on April 15, 1778, he criticized Mandeville's failure to define vices and benefits but then went on to remark: "I read Mandeville forty, or, I believe, fifty years ago. He did not puzzle me; he opened my views into real life very much" (James Boswell, *The Life of Samuel Johnson*, ed. G. B. Hill, rev. L. F. Powell [Oxford, 1934–50], III, 292).

There are several striking similarities between Johnson and Mandeville. Both stress the importance of pride and the longing for superiority as guiding principles in human nature. Both, like Locke, emphasize fear of pain as a most important motive. Both emphasize the importance of custom and environment in molding individual character. Finally, Mandeville, like Johnson, stresses the importance, in analyzing human nature, of "separating what is acquired from what is natural, and distinguishing between them" (*The Fable of the Bees*, II, 301). But even though Mandeville's distinctions between what he calls "real" or "natural" passions and appetites and what he calls "artificial" or "acquired" passions is similar to Johnson's distinction between "primary" or "natural" and "artificial" or "adscititious" passions, Mandeville does not provide the same list of natural and artificial passions which Johnson does, nor is Mandeville quite as consistent as Johnson in working out his scheme of distinctions.

without some prior estimation of the rational grounds for such belief. It would certainly be useless in evaluating the artistic integrity of *Macbeth*—which Johnson defends by explaining why the central action of the play was made to hinge upon Macbeth's belief in witchcraft and the acceptance of false prophecies. To explain why Macbeth's belief in the three Weird Sisters must not merely be dismissed as absurdly improbable, Johnson shows in great detail how widespread the belief in witchcraft had been, from remote antiquity up to, and even beyond, Shakespeare's day. It was, Johnson observes, a belief shared not only "by the common people," but "by the learned themselves." Then, in the light of his survey, Johnson concludes that "upon this general infatuation Shakespeare might be easily allowed to found a play, especially since he has followed with great exactness such histories as were then thought true; nor can it be doubted that the scenes of enchantment, however they may now be ridiculed, were both by himself and his audience thought awful and affecting." [35] Johnson thus reminds his readers that no matter how silly and improbable Macbeth's credulity may seem to them, it must, in view of the prevailing opinions in Shakespeare's age, be taken seriously as providing an important, credible, and therefore historically valid part of Macbeth's motivation.

In this reminder, there emerges the same characteristic pattern of thought which is evident in the comments upon *King Lear* and other plays, in the *Lives of the Poets*, and throughout the moral essays. Johnson, though fully sharing the values of his own age, nevertheless realizes that his judgment as an eighteenth-century Englishman must be held in abeyance while he first explores the rational grounds of seemingly improbable or even morally pernicious conduct. In the case of Macbeth those grounds are fully recovered and explained, although Johnson firmly believed that "a poet, who should now make the whole action of his tragedy depend upon enchantment, and produce the chief events by the assistance of supernatural agents, would

35. *Miscellaneous Observations on the Tragedy of Macbeth* (*Works*, V, 59).

be censured as transgressing the bounds of probability; he would be banished from the theatre to the nursery, and condemned to write fairy tales instead of tragedies." [36] Here, and throughout Johnson's work, one finds an impressive readiness to suspend final judgment long enough for objective examination and estimation. Johnson believed, of course, that judgment is the ultimate duty of the critic as well as the moralist. He never evades that obligation. But neither does he make it serve as a substitute for the equally necessary and arduous task of dispassionate analysis.

It is, as Professor Hagstrum has emphasized, "important to be fully aware of the extent to which one who was primarily a judicial critic accepted the soundest insights of the eighteenth-century school of literary historians." [37] The range of Johnson's interest in various aspects of history and the depth of his historical sense have been increasingly remarked by scholars over the past twenty-five years.[38] As Hagstrum has also emphasized, "One of the most important respects in which he differed from his predecessors, the great literary Augustans of the earlier part of the century, lay in his staunch allegiance to modern learning and investigative technique." [39] Johnson's extensive use of the historical approach to literature—of which his comments on *Lear* and *Macbeth* are typical—represents only one aspect of that allegiance. Another aspect, less frequently noted, is manifest in the objective quality of his endeavor to "analyze the mind of man" before proceeding to prescribe rules for ethical conduct. Johnson, like Machiavelli, Hobbes, and the modern anthropologists, tries to look

36. *Ibid.*, p. 55.

37. *Samuel Johnson's Literary Criticism*, p. 22.

38. See, for example (in addition to Hagstrum's book on Johnson's literary criticism), René Wellek, *The Rise of English Literary History* (Chapel Hill, 1941), pp. 140–42; J. W. Krutch, *Samuel Johnson*, p. 329; Godfrey Davies, "Doctor Johnson on History," *Huntington Library Quarterly*, XII (1948–49), 1–21; and W. J. Bate, *The Achievement of Samuel Johnson*, p. 31.

39. *Samuel Johnson's Literary Criticism*, p. 22.

closely and calmly at the way human motives are actually formed. His usual rhetorical strategy throughout the *Rambler*, for example, is first to provide some generalization about man's mental constitution, then to show how that knowledge is helpful in our effort to achieve morally permissible conduct: he does not merely state how we *ought* to conduct ourselves. Johnson's ability to attain a high degree of objectivity—and accuracy—in those generalizations, as well as his ability to maintain a "staunch allegiance to modern learning and investigative technique" in practically all his literary criticism, are both different facets of his impressive capacity for transcending the prevailing opinions of his own century even while sharing many of them.

That impressive capacity, in turn, could not have been realized so extensively if Johnson had not allowed for a wide range of individual and cultural diversity by sharply limiting the role assigned in his system to natural passions, while at the same time stressing the importance of what he calls artificial passions. This distinction is central to his thought because it lies behind, and goes far to explain, his ready acceptance of attitudes that are thought of as peculiarly modern. If Johnson had been more rigid in his insistence that "human nature is always the same," he could neither have adopted the historical method of literary criticism nor could he have been so quick to appreciate the role played by environment in shaping individual character and conduct.

Johnson has been partially misunderstood because readers have not clearly grasped the relationship between his postulation of natural and artificial passions on the one hand and his distinction between unchanging human nature and variable human character on the other. D. J. Greene, for example, has accurately observed Johnson's "remarkably liberal attitude," but he has incorrectly accounted for it. He notes Johnson's "refusal to believe that human nature varies greatly from one part of the world to another" but then adds that "the importance to Johnson's political thinking of this belief in the essential homogeneity of human motivation—a radical egalitarianism, one is justified in calling it—can hardly be stressed too much." [40] Now it is certainly true that Johnson believed in the uniformity of human nature, and his opinion on this matter is indeed important in every area of his thought. However, that opinion cannot be equated with a "belief in the essential homogeneity of human motivation," because it was precisely in the area of *motivation* that Johnson accepted the widest possible diversity. When he said that human nature is everywhere the same, he meant only that all men share the natural appetites and passions, together with a capacity for entertaining diverse artificial passions. But such capacity is a far cry from "essential homogeneity of human motivation" since Johnson did not expect all men to be motivated by the same slate of artificial passions.

That is why he never expected to find—despite their common nature—any necessary similarity in the motives governing the conduct of, say, his own sovereign, a petty prince in Guinea or Madagascar, and King Lear. Johnson not only opposed natural desires to desires "never received from nature" which lead us to act "upon principles established only by the authority of custom," but he was also aware of the melancholy fact that "the greatest part of mankind have no other reason for their opinions than that they are in fashion." He also stressed the fact that customs and fashions vary not only from society to society but even from age to age within the same society. "The inhabitants of the same country," he observes in the *Rambler*, No. 122, "have opposite characters in different ages." Johnson never

40. *The Politics of Samuel Johnson*, pp. 67–68. A possible source of confusion is Johnson's somewhat misleading assertion in the *Rambler*, No. 60, that "we are all prompted by the same motives, all deceived by the same fallacies, *all animated by hope*, obstructed by danger, *entangled by desire*, and *seduced by pleasure*" [italics added]. If, as I believe is the case, the italicized phrases are in apposition to "we are all prompted by the same motives," then Johnson is merely suggesting that all men are moved by the same natural passions and only in this limited sense motivated alike. If the italicized phrases are not intended to clarify by spelling out in more detail the meaning of "prompted by the same motives," then the sentence is one of the rare instances in his writings where Johnson contradicts his usual views about human nature.

forgot that man is "a being from whom permanence and stability cannot be derived."[41]

Therefore he was prepared—as Father Lobo was not—to recognize that neither the goals proposed by men nor the force of their motivation towards such goals will inevitably remain homogeneous in all parts of the world and through all time, even though human nature remains the same everywhere to the extent that all men are driven by the same roster of natural appetites and passions. For, in Johnson's opinion, the area of conduct shaped by these universal constants is rather small—smaller, certainly, than most critics have realized— while the area subject to the controlling influence of time and place plays a role at least equally important in Johnson's thought. It is Johnson's flexible conception of human character that accounts for his closeness to the prevailing outlook of our own age. We feel at home with his image of man because it allows for rich variety without losing sight of a comforting thread of underlying uniformity.

Johnson's central distinction between natural and artificial passions provides us with a key to another hitherto puzzling chamber of his mind. Bate remarks that "Johnson's continual concreteness, his empirical grasp of the immediate problem or occasion, is probably unparalleled in the history of moral thought."[42] Krutch has observed that

it may seem at first odd that Johnson, whose name the popular mind commonly associates with sonorous generalities, should insist so strongly upon the exclusive importance of the specific character and the individual trait. Yet he was, as the *Rambler* will demonstrate, an early champion of realistic prose fiction as well as of picturesque biography, and his own best writing is by no means the tissue of large generalities it is sometimes assumed to be.[43]

The seeming oddity of Johnson's insistence upon "the exclusive importance of the specific character and the individual trait" vanishes,

41. *Miscellaneous Observations on the Tragedy of Macbeth* (*Works*, V. 58); *Works*, III, 82; *Plan of an English Dictionary* (*Works*, V, 12).

42. *The Achievement of Samuel Johnson*, p. 31.

43. *Samuel Johnson*, p. 76.

however, when we realize that his encouragement of prose fiction and detailed biography was unquestionably strengthened greatly, if not made inevitable, by his belief that every individual's moral character is largely formed by the interplay of various artificial passions—such as avarice, vanity, ambition, envy, and friendship—with prevailing local opinions and circumstances.

That interplay, in Johnson's opinion, produces wide diversity of interests and standards even within the same society. "So much are the modes of excellence settled by time and place," he observes in the *Rambler*, No. 201, "that men may be heard boasting in one street of that which they would anxiously conceal in another. The grounds of scorn and esteem, the topics of praise and satire, are varied according to the several virtues or vices which the course of life has disposed men to admire or abhor." But since "the end of writing is to instruct," it is necessary to appeal somehow to such widely varying interests and standards in order to capture attention and thereby lead men closer to recognition—and acceptance—of universally valid standards of moral excellence. And, as Johnson remarks in the *Rambler*, No. 60 (which is devoted to considering the utility of biography),

parallel circumstances . . . to which we readily conform our minds, are, above all other writings, to be found in narratives of the lives of particular persons; and, therefore, no species of writing seems more worthy of cultivation than biography, since none can be more delightful or more useful, none can more certainly enchain the heart by irresistible interest, or more widely diffuse instruction to every diversity of condition.

Clearly, if it were not for the great "diversity of condition," detailed biography would lose its position of paramount utility and could be replaced by abstract discussions of universal truth. Johnson, however, was opposed to any such replacement because he understood that the ways in which men differ from one another are as important as the ways in which human nature remains invariable at all times and in all places. Therefore, Johnson's belief in the essential diversity of human character and circumstances led him to emphasize the "exclusive importance of the specific character and the individual trait." One notable result of that encouragement, of course, is Boswell's *Life of Samuel Johnson.*

❧ 5 ❧

Before leaving Johnson's analysis of the passions and proceeding to discuss his conception of the other areas of the mind, it is necessary to consider one passion that is, in his view, neither natural nor artificial. The *Rambler,* No. 60, devoted to emphasizing the importance of detailed biography, opens with an assertion that

All joy or sorrow for the happiness or calamities of others is produced by an act of the imagination, that realizes the event, however ficti- tious, or approximates it, however remote, by placing us, for a time, in the condition of him whose fortune we contemplate; so that we feel, while the deception lasts, whatever motions would be excited by the same good or evil happening to ourselves.

This "act of the imagination" which allows us to share vicariously for a moment another person's situation is the mechanism of sympathy, or compassion—which Johnson defines in his *Dictionary* as "Pity; commiseration; sorrow for the sufferings of others; painful sympa- thy."

Johnson's view of the mechanism whereby compassion is aroused closely parallels the explanation provided by Hobbes in his *Levia- than.* "Grief for the calamity of another is pity," Hobbes observes, and he then goes on to assert that it "ariseth from the imagination that the like calamity may befall himself; and therefore is called also compassion, and in the phrase of this present time a fellow-feeling." [44] Evidently Johnson accepted this Hobbesian explanation of the man- ner whereby compassion operates within the mind, although he does

44: Thomas Hobbes, *Leviathan: or the Matter, Forme and Power of a Commonwealth Ecclesiasticall and Civil,* ed. Michael Oakeshott (Oxford, 1946), p. 37.

not explicitly refer to him in the *Rambler,* No. 60. Nor does he mention Hobbes in the *Idler,* No. 89, where he points out that compassion is the emotion responsible for the impulse towards charitable action: "We are incited to the relief of misery," Johnson remarks, "by the consciousness that we have the same nature with the sufferer, that we are in danger of the same distresses, and may sometime implore the same assistance." Despite his omission of any reference to the *Leviathan,* however, Johnson was plainly in agreement with Hobbes, if not indebted to him, on this issue. They both elaborate essentially the same explanation of a very important passion.

But Johnson explicitly parted company with the Hobbesian school of thought when he considered more fully, in the *Idler,* No. 4, the nature and source of institutionalized charity. Johnson first asserts that "charity, or tenderness for the poor, which is now justly considered, by a great part of mankind, as inseparable from piety, and in which almost all the goodness of the present age consists, is, I think, known only to those who enjoy, either immediately or by transmission, the light of revelation." This assertion is given substance by Johnson's observation that the nations of classical antiquity, despite their wise political institutions and glorious "examples of patriotism . . . have yet left behind them no mention of alms-houses or hospitals, of places where age might repose, or sickness be relieved." The largess distributed by Roman emperors is discounted because it was designed for the merely selfish—and immediate—purpose of achieving popularity. After thus reinforcing his initial assertion by historical evidence, Johnson alludes—without naming names—to the Hobbesian explanation of pity by remarking that "compassion is by some reasoners, on whom the name of philosophers has been too easily conferred, resolved into an affection merely selfish, an involuntary perception of pain at the involuntary sight of a being like ourselves languishing in misery." At first glance, this rough dismissal of "some reasoners on whom the name of philosophers has been too easily conferred" has all the earmarks of that ill-considered dogmatism which the popular mind associates with the Old Tory at work smashing away with the butt end of his pistol. Johnson's own explanation of compassion, after all, is not so very different from that put forward by "some reasoners."

But a closer consideration of Johnson's discussion dispels that first impression. He continues his analysis of compassion by stating that any "affection merely selfish," such as that postulated by some reasoners, "if ever it be felt at all from the brute instinct of uninstructed nature, will only produce effects desultory and transient; it will never settle into a principle of action, or extend relief to calamities unseen, in generations not yet in being." Thus Johnson questions whether compassion ever really arises naturally in human beings through the operation of any "instinct of uninstructed nature" in the way that appetites and the natural passions such as fear, hatred, aversion, or desire presumably do. Johnson adds that even if that should happen, the results would hardly be lasting. He does not, however, reject the underlying Hobbesian assumption that human nature is basically selfish but rather views unselfish behavior as, in a good sense, unnatural by going on to remark emphatically that "the devotion of life or fortune to the succour of the poor, is a height of virtue to which humanity has never risen by its own power."

This remark eliminates society and prevailing opinion as the first cause of charity; and instinct has been ruled out of the picture as well. Thus it is the Hobbesian attempt to explain the *source*—not the nature—of compassion in human terms which Johnson rejects. He rejects it by vigorously affirming, in effect, the Hobbesian assumption that unselfish action is indeed foreign to humanity, which is surely to hoist the Hobbists with their own petard.[45] Johnson thereby

45. Bate observes that "Johnson does not, like Shaftesbury, Rousseau, or other romantics, simply deny Hobbes's arguments that man is basically selfish. Instead, he takes them for granted. Where Johnson differs from Hobbes is in supplementing these arguments with other considerations which Hobbes overlooks or disregards. He does this especially by recurring always to the nature of desire itself, as an activity inherent in a living creature 'whose motions are gradual'" (*The Achievement of Samuel Johnson*, p. 69).
Robert Voitle has suggested that in the *Idler*, No. 4, Johnson "seems to be

demonstrates that a Hobbesian analysis of man, while perhaps correct so far as it goes—and it undeniably goes a good way in his view—nevertheless does not provide an adequate explanation for sustained and systematic philanthropy in terms of rational self-interest or even irrational identification with the suffering of fellow creatures. Therefore, there must be another explanation. And because one can assume that human nature has remained constant throughout the ages, it follows that we ourselves would be as little disposed to charity as the Romans, were it not for some new influence acting upon us. In Johnson's view, that new influence was evidently not the mere "authority of custom" as in the case of our artificial passions, which are grounded upon self-interest, but was rather "the light of revelation."

Thus compassion, which seemed inexplicable on rational grounds, was treated by Johnson as a divinely irrational impulse playing an important social role unique to the Christian era by leading to the creation of institutionalized philanthropy. The pity which inclines men systematically to help their fellows arises not because of what men are, but because God, through "the light of revelation," has enabled man to transcend his own nature at times. It is clear why Johnson, holding this view, found the Hobbesian materialistic analy-

---

answering" Mandeville (*Samuel Johnson the Moralist* [Cambridge, Mass., 1961], p. 54). But Voitle neither points out that Mandeville's explanation of compassion echoes that provided by Hobbes nor comments on the parallel which I have noted above between the *Rambler*, No. 60, and the explanation of compassion in the *Leviathan*. Moreover, Johnson refers to "some reasoners, on whom the name of philosophers has been too easily conferred" rather than to any single reasoner, and this plural reference suggests that he had more than one person in mind when he set about refuting the Hobbesian explanation of charity and compassion. The problem is therefore complex, although it is probably true enough that Mandeville was one of those whom Johnson was answering in the *Idler*, No. 4. There seems at present to be no way of settling this question, for while we know that Johnson had read Mandeville (see n. 34 above), he may have read the *Leviathan* also. Therefore, since Hobbes is the more important, as well as the earlier, of the two most prominent advocates of the explanation of compassion which Johnson attacks, I have identified that explanation as Hobbesian in my text.

sis doubly unsatisfactory, for in his opinion it failed to explain charity adequately on the basis of its own exclusively rationalistic assumptions, while also failing to provide any other explanation. Hence, it is no wonder Johnson complained that "the name of philosophers has been too easily conferred" upon such thinkers. This complaint, properly seen in its context of his own complex view of the issue in question, is hardly the casually dogmatic condemnation that it appears at first sight. Johnson could well afford to cast a philosophical stone at the Leviathan.

Chapter II

Higher Faculties

PITY IS IN JOHNSON'S VIEW the only emotion explicitly associated with a supernatural source and thereby is given the highest possible sanction. In the *Rambler*, No. 59, Johnson observes that it brings comfort to many people "in hopeless distresses, as it contributes to recommend them to themselves, by proving that they have not lost the regard of others; and *heaven seems to indicate the duty even of barren compassion, by inclining us to weep for evils which we cannot remedy*" [italics

44

added].[1] The phrasing of this remark is unusual in Johnson's works because it implies that one duty, at least, is not only set before us by revelation but is made easier to comply with by divine inspiration: heaven inclines us actually to respond as it teaches us we *ought* to respond when we see our fellows in distress.

Most of Johnson's moral essays are written as though predicated upon the assumption that Christianity imposes obligations but does not ease the great difficulty we encounter in meeting them. Johnson is primarily concerned with showing us ways of circumventing our weaknesses and putting limited natural abilities to work for the ends of religion. He counsels self-knowledge and active endeavor, rather than passive faith in divine assistance, as the surest pathway to moral conduct and eternal happiness, although he never completely rules out the pleasant possibility of "those irradiations from above, the hope of which," as he remarks in the *Rambler*, No. 7, he has "no intention to withdraw from the sincere and the diligent." It is striking, however, that compassion—"even barren compassion"—is the only widespread realization of that hope which Johnson observed in his extensive survey of mankind. For the rest, in matters relating to this world and the next, he saw man acting through the doubtful agency of his own weak nature.

But Johnson does assert in the *Rambler*, No. 7, that "our senses, our appetites, and our passions, are our lawful and faithful guides, in most things that relate solely to this life." Thus, for many earthly transactions at least, the "sensitive faculties"—senses, appetites, and passions—are adequate, if not wholly satisfactory, guides, provided, of

---

1. Cf. Hooker's observation that "There is no kind of faculty or power in man or any other creature, which can rightly perform the functions allotted to it, without perpetual aid and concurrence of that Supreme Cause of all things" (Richard Hooker, *Of the Laws of Ecclesiastical Polity* [Everyman Edition; London, 1958], I, 185). Although Johnson may have agreed with this observation (which he quotes in his *Dictionary* to illustrate one meaning of *faculty*), he does not emphasize so strongly the importance of continual divine assistance for the proper functioning of our mental powers.

course, that they are not disordered. Animals, for example, apparently get along well enough without any of the higher faculties which are thought of as man's prerogative. "We know not," Johnson observes in the *Idler*, No. 24, "how much the brutes recollect of the past, or anticipate of the future; what power they have of comparing and preferring; or whether their faculties may not rest in motionless indifference, till they are moved by the presence of their proper object or stimulated to act by corporeal sensations." In the *Rambler*, No. 41, Johnson had made this point even more emphatically:

We have no reason to believe that other creatures have higher faculties, or more extensive capacities, than the preservation of themselves, or their species, requires; they seem always to be fully employed, or to be completely at ease without employment; to feel few intellectual miseries or pleasures, and to have no exuberance of understanding to lay out upon curiosity or caprice, but to have their minds exactly adapted to their bodies, with few other ideas than such as corporal pain or pleasure impress upon them.

If man had been destined only to act out his part on the small stage of this world, Johnson implies, our mental endowment might not be more highly elaborated than that discernible in brute creation. But religion teaches us that as we have a higher destiny and act upon a far wider stage, we have been endowed with faculties which enormously increase our capacity for good and evil.

The precise nature of that destiny, however, remained an impenetrable mystery for Johnson—one of those "first and fundamental" questions about the nature of man which lie beyond the scope of human knowledge and which he had severely reproached Soame Jenyns for not approaching in a more suitable spirit of "humble acquiescence and fervent adoration." Johnson himself always approached such matters without attempting to plumb unknowable first causes. He preferred merely to state the issues involved in terms that are completely understandable and therefore useful. Thus he would go no further in explaining the nature of man's ultimate destiny than to stress the fact that it partakes of eternity. Unlike the animals, our existence is not confined to this world. Consequently, "the great task of him who conducts his life by the precepts of religion, is to make the future predominate over the present." ² Since every man is enjoined to obey the precepts of religion, it follows that we have been endowed with faculties for "making the future predominate over the present." This, for Johnson, is the real *raison d'être* of the higher faculties and the key to their nature and proper function: reason, memory, imagination, judgment, and will all enable man to transcend the immediate moment and conduct his life by the precepts of religion—if he cares to do so.

Naturally everyone should do so, if only because, as Johnson asserts in the *Rambler*, No. 80, "it is unworthy of a reasonable being to spend any of the little time allotted us, without some tendency, either direct or oblique, to the end of our existence." Thus a reasonable being—that is, according to the *Dictionary*, one "Having the faculty of reason; endued with reason; acting, speaking, or thinking rationally"—should always act to help further the ultimate purpose for which he was uniquely endowed. Johnson defines that purpose as precisely as he ever cared to when he goes on to observe that although "every moment cannot be laid out on the formal and regular improvement of our knowledge, or in the stated practice of a moral or religious duty, yet none should be spent so as to exclude wisdom or virtue, or pass without possibility of qualifying us more or less for the better employment of those which are to come." To achieve wisdom and virtue is to achieve the two highest goals of this life—and of the two, Johnson, of course, considered virtue supreme. In the "Life of Blackmore," for example, he refers to "the promotion of religion" as "the highest and noblest purpose." ³ The ultimate purpose of a rational being, in other words, is to follow "the precepts of theology." These, in turn, "have no other tendency than to enforce a life of faith; a life regulated not by our senses but our belief." ⁴

2. *Rambler*, No. 7.

3. *The Works of Samuel Johnson, LL.D.* (9 vols.; Oxford, 1825), VIII, 43–44. (Cited hereafter as *Works*.)

4. *Rambler*, No. 178.

Thus a moral life presupposes a high degree of control over the senses no less than over the passions set in motion by external agencies acting through the medium of the senses. In the *Idler*, No. 89, Johnson explains that "Godliness, or piety, is elevation of the mind towards the supreme being, and extension of the thoughts to another life. The other life is future, and the supreme being is invisible." Our senses, however necessary in lesser matters, must be controlled and often discounted because they can never directly convey the most important knowledge of all: knowledge of God. Consequently, the supreme task of our higher faculties is to free us from improper bondage to the present moment and to the world in which we are temporarily placed. Johnson suggests this most clearly in the *Rambler*, No. 41, after first observing that

so few of the hours of life are filled up with objects adequate to the mind of man, and so frequently are we in want of present pleasure or employment, that we are forced to have recourse, every moment, to the past and future for supplemental satisfactions, and relieve the vacuities of our being, by recollection of former passages, or anticipation of events to come.

This grim observation leads Johnson on to the sanguine affirmation that he "cannot but consider this necessity of searching on every side for matter on which the attention may be employed, as a strong proof of the superior and celestial nature of the soul of man." The faculties giving rise to our continual dissatisfaction with the influx of immediate sensory impressions must therefore be the most truly distinctive aspects of human nature. Johnson's affirmation also implies a hierarchy of existence stretching above—to what is celestial—as well as below mankind.

Yet in his review of Soame Jenyns' *A Free Enquiry into the Nature and Origin of Evil* Johnson took particular issue with the widely accepted concept of the chain of being, which he claimed to "have demonstrated to be raised by presumptuous imagination, to rest on nothing at the bottom, to lean on nothing at the top, and to have vacuities, from step to step, through which any order of being may sink into nihility without any inconvenience, so far as we can judge, to the next rank above or below it." [5] But when seeking to define the nature of man in his own writings, Johnson always agreed that men, while certainly no part of any infinite gradation of beings ranging from nonentity to God, were nevertheless placed in a middle state between animals and the heavenly orders of existence. He usually tried to view the various aspects of human nature—especially in the sphere of mental anatomy—in relation to these polar opposites. Consequently, he was concerned not merely with showing how we differ from the beasts but, what is far more important, with how closely we approach—or fail to approach—the divine attributes. Thus, in the *Rambler*, No. 162, he asserts that "reason is the great distinction of human nature, the faculty by which we approach to some degree of association with celestial intelligences."

Though this assertion reveals much about Johnson's conception of the mind and something about his understanding of God, it throws most light on the rhetorical strategy of his moral essays. To say that reason is the great distinction of human nature is to imply that other faculties are rightly ordered only when they cooperate to induce rational behavior; and to say that celestial intelligences share with us the one faculty of reason is to suggest an attribute of God. But it would be wrong to conclude that reason is therefore, in Johnson's view, God's most important characteristic. Yet this conclusion is forced upon any attentive reader of Johnson's secular prose.

In the periodical essays, *Rasselas*, and the *Lives of the Poets*, Johnson seldom speculates upon the nature of God. The subject is largely avoided, and when it is touched upon Johnson mostly supplies brief, impersonal adjectives or phrases. In the *Rambler*, No. 6, he refers to God as "infinite Goodness." Similarly, God is referred to in the *Rambler*, No. 184, as "Omnipotent Goodness." In the "Life of Waller" Johnson mentions the traits of omnipotence, infinity, and perfection before negatively characterizing God as "a being without

5. *Works*, VI, 59.

passions." [6] There is a slightly more extensive discussion in the *Rambler*, No. 110, where Johnson asserts:

That God will forgive, may, indeed, be established as the first and fundamental truth of religion; for, though the knowledge of his existence is the origin of philosophy, yet, without the belief of his mercy, it would have little influence upon our moral conduct. There could be no prospect of enjoying the protection or regard of him, whom the least deviation from rectitude made inexorable for ever; and every man would naturally withdraw his thoughts from the contemplation of a Creator, whom he must consider as a governor too pure to be pleased, and too severe to be pacified; as an enemy infinitely wise, and infinitely powerful, whom he could neither deceive, escape, nor resist.

Although this passage affirms the existence of a more comforting attribute than omnipotence, infinity, or perfection, Johnson suggests in the *Rambler*, No. 185, that even the mercy of God is grounded upon dispassionate assessment of every individual's conduct: "Of him that hopes to be forgiven, it is indispensably required that he forgive. It is therefore superfluous to urge any other motive. On this great duty eternity is suspended, and to him that refuses to practice it, the Throne of mercy is inaccessible, and the Saviour of the world has been born in vain." Here God's mercy is again mentioned, but only to point out the condition under which it may become "inaccessible."

Such emphasis throughout the moral essays upon God's role as dispassionately rational and therefore just judge would be misleading

6. *Works*, VII, 213–14. In his article on "The Impassibility of God," F. L. Cross, *The Oxford Dictionary of the Christian Church* (London, 1961), notes that "In Christianity there is an acute tension between the Greek and the Hebrew conceptions [of God]. On the one side there is the immutability, perfection and all-sufficiency of God which would seem to exclude all passion, and this has been the basis of the traditional emphasis among theologians. But on the other side there is the central Christian conviction that God in His essence is love, that His nature is revealed in the Incarnate Christ and not least in His Passion, and that He 'sympathizes' with His Creatures. . . . Perhaps the problem is akin to that of the admitted coexistence of justice and mercy in God and the truth lies in the recognition that both aspects must be preserved in a way that is beyond the competence of human reason to exhibit."

were it not for the survival of the sermons which Johnson wrote for his friend Dr. Taylor. In these more formally homiletic works Johnson is inclined to depreciate or at least minimize the importance of what he refers to in Sermon IV as "fallible reason." [7] He consistently stresses God's mercy, compassion, and affection for mankind in ways that make these amiable attributes loom larger than they do in his secular prose. He states in Sermon II, for example, that God's "mercy is ever made the chief motive of obedience to him; and with the highest reason inculcated, as the attribute which may animate us most powerfully to an attention to our duty." [8]

While this remark is in no way logically incompatible with the discussion of God's mercy extracted above from the *Rambler*, No. 110, the rhetorical appeal is very different. In the sermon Johnson proposes consideration of God's mercy as an inducement to obedience, whereas in the moral essay the fact of God's mercy is presented in order to remove a philosophical difficulty that would, if allowed to remain, stifle impulses to moral conduct and force each man to "withdraw his thoughts" from further consideration of God. There is a great emotional if not logical difference between "that which may animate us most powerfully" and that which merely prevents us from turning away.

Moreover, the statement in Sermon II is preceded by a passage which eloquently amplifies the point made with such concise logic in the *Rambler*, No. 110:

That God is a being of infinite mercy; that he desires not the death of a sinner, nor takes any pleasure in the misery of his creatures; may not only be deduced from the consideration of his nature, and his attributes; but, for the sake of those that are incapable of philosophical inquiries, who make far the greatest part of mankind, it is evidently revealed to us in the Scriptures, in which the supreme Being, the Source of life, the Author of existence, who spake the word, and the world was made, who commanded, and it was created, is described as looking down from the height of infinite felicity, with tenderness

7. *Works*, IX, 320.
8. *Ibid.*, p. 301.

and pity, upon the sons of men; inciting them by soft impulses, to perseverance in virtue, and recalling them, by instruction and punishment, from errour and from vice. He is represented as not more formidable for his power, than amiable for his mercy; and is introduced as expostulating with mankind upon their obstinacy in wickedness; and warning them, with the highest affection, to avoid those punishments, which the laws of his government make it necessary to inflict upon the inflexible and disobedient.[9]

Here Johnson not only stresses the "tenderness and pity" of God more emphatically than he does in the moral essays, but he obliquely calls attention to the nature of this striking difference of emphasis. By remarking that the scriptural portrait of God is designed for a particular (if widespread) audience, Johnson implicitly reminds us that the sermon does lean most heavily upon biblical allusion rather than upon the emotionally different appeal of "philosophical inquiries" into the divine attributes. In Johnson's view there was clearly a choice open between two rhetorical strategies that differ widely even though they are not always mutually exclusive.

Sermon XVI makes even more clear the nature (though not the grounds) of this choice so far as it bears on any form of discourse involving consideration of the attributes of God. Johnson asserts that "the two great attributes of our Sovereign Creator, which seem most likely to influence our lives, and, by consequence, most necessarily to claim our attention, are his justice and his mercy." [10] Here Johnson explains why any practical moralist must be concerned primarily with pointing to God's justice and mercy, though he does not suggest any grounds for concentrating upon one attribute more heavily than upon the other. Nor does the consideration in Sermon II of how moral discourse may be adapted to differing audiences provide a priori grounds for weighting such discussion on one side or the other. Perhaps insofar as exhortations are freed from the necessity of depending upon biblical authority and thereby may lean towards purely philosophical argument, there will inevitably be some tendency to

9. *Ibid.*, pp. 300–301.
10. *Ibid.*, p. 435.

concentrate upon the rational workings of divine justice rather than upon the more appealing emotional operations of God's mercy, tenderness, pity, and affection for mankind. In any case, the range of choices considered available by Johnson is clear, and so is the noteworthy fact that his moral essays do stress the most rational attribute of God and consequently invite men to guide themselves by "reason . . . the faculty by which we approach to some degree of association with celestial intelligences." [11]

2

One result of Johnson's rhetorical strategy is frequently deplored. It is quite evident that he grounded his moral essays upon an extended appeal to the most fundamental form of self-interest: the desire for personal happiness. To be sure, he invariably emphasized enlightened, rational self-interest because he was "always afraid of determining on the side of envy or cruelty" and was therefore opposed to all happiness that could only be achieved by inflicting suffering upon others.[12] His Oxford toast to the next insurrection of slaves in the West Indies is universally applauded. But when the applause for such liberal opinions fades away, voices are often raised to

11. In his prayers no less than in his sermons Johnson frequently refers to God in ways that emphasize His mercy. See, e.g., *Diaries, Prayers, and Annals,* ed. E. L. McAdam, Jr., with Donald and Mary Hyde (New Haven, 1958), pp. 37, 38, 40, 41, 43–46, 49, 55, and *passim.* The formulaic phrase "Almighty God, merciful Father," or slight variations of it ("Almighty and most merciful Father"), is used more than fifty times. Johnson relies less frequently on such other epithets as "heavenly Father," "Giver of Wisdom," "Creator and Judge," and "Almighty and Everlasting." But the fact that Johnson does sometimes use epithets that do not call attention to God's mercy shows that he might have done so more frequently. The alternative terms were available and not improper. But in his prayers Johnson preferred to use epithets emphasizing God's mercy.

12. "Review of *A Free Enquiry into the Nature of Good and Evil*" (*Works,* VI, 57).

reproach Johnson for his calculating approach to morality. Many are repelled by what is to their way of thinking a Machiavellian argument in favor of paying for happiness in the coin of virtuous conduct. Perhaps C. S. Lewis has stated the case against Johnson's outlook most concisely by observing that "Christianity is in constant danger of relapsing into theological hedonism" and then adding that "it had so relapsed in the eighteenth century when Boswell could say (without contradiction from Johnson) that the doctrine of future rewards and punishments was its very essence." [13]

It is certainly true that Johnson agreed with Boswell on the importance of future rewards and punishments. He did not confine his expression of that accord to silent acquiescence. In the *Rambler*, No. 178, for example, Johnson asserts that theology encourages "a life in which pleasures are to be refused for fear of invisible punishments, and calamities [are] sometimes to be sought, and always endured, in hope of rewards that shall be obtained in another state." However, while Johnson assuredly stresses eternal happiness as an ultimate goal, he also hopes thereby to accomplish the immediate task of freeing us from excessive dependence upon the senses during this life. That hope has been the dream of moralists since antiquity. As Hagstrum observes, Johnson

felt that the Christian revelation was given not to annihilate pagan morality but to complete it by adding to it the doctrine of immortality and of future rewards and punishments. Those doctrines gave ultimate sanction to morality, but they did not destroy its rational foundations. . . . To Johnson, as to Locke and most thinkers of the period, religion and reason were not antithetical but complementary.[14]

13. *English Literature in the Sixteenth Century, Excluding Drama* (Oxford, 1954), p. 189.

14. Jean H. Hagstrum, *Samuel Johnson's Literary Criticism* (Minneapolis, 1952), p. 69. See also Chap. XLVIII of *Rasselas* (*Works*, I, 308) in which Imlac, speaking of the soul, asserts: "That it will not perish by any inherent cause of decay, or principle of corruption, may be shown by philosophy; but philosophy can tell no more. That it will not be annihilated by him that made it, we must humbly learn from higher authority." This assertion is one

Since reason, which facilitates emancipation from the chains of appetite and passion, was presented by Johnson as man's most godlike attribute, he asserted that rational conduct—including exercise of rational self-interest on the highest plane—is the most noble form of behavior available to man. Far from being shamefully self-centered, considerations of ultimate advantage—which often force us to refuse present pleasure and accept a good deal of immediate discomfort—seemed to Johnson the highest possible foundation of morality.

Moreover, he did not rule out other considerations. Johnson saw love of virtue for its own sake as a desirable goal. The distinguishing mark of Johnson's moralizing is not that he denied the desirability of that love—which he never did—but rather that he regarded it as following in the wake of rational considerations, and he therefore emphasized the role of reason because of the practical nature of his task. He makes clear in the *Rambler*, No. 70, that he is a "moralist, whose precepts are intended chiefly for those who are endeavouring to go forward up the steeps of virtue, not for those who have already reached the summit." He was not writing primarily for those who already loved virtue for its own sake. Those happy few would need no explanations, while for the rest it was most important to enlist self-interest upon the side of virtue because, as Johnson explained:

It may easily happen, and, in effect, will happen, very frequently, that our own private happiness may be promoted by an act injurious to others, when yet no man can be obliged, by nature, to prefer, ultimately, the happiness of others to his own; therefore, to the instructions of infinite wisdom, it was necessary that infinite power should add penal sanctions. That every man, to whom those instructions shall be imparted, may know, that he can never, ultimately, injure himself by benefiting others, or, ultimately, by injuring others benefit himself; but that, however the lot of the good and bad may be

example of the way in which Johnson describes reason and religion as complementary rather than antithetical; "higher authority" does not contradict "philosophy" but instead provides information which we cannot discover merely by the exercise of reason.

huddled together in the seeming confusion of our present state, the time shall undoubtedly come, when the most virtuous will be most happy.[15]

Furthermore, because of the divine nature of reason, it is not only desirable but altogether fitting that man's highest faculty be enlisted in the service of moral conduct for the purpose of restraining short-sighted impulses towards the infliction of suffering upon others for the sake of some momentary pleasure. Johnson even viewed that enlistment as in some degree inevitable, because "he that thinks reasonably must think morally." Yet Johnson also believed that *"all reasonable beings naturally love justice"* [italics added].[16] He seldom dwells at length upon the intrinsic charm of virtue because he considered it well-known to those who respond reasonably and incapable of demonstration to those who do not. After a man has been persuaded to act rationally—and therefore morally—by appealing to his self-interest, he will in due course come to love virtue. Before he does so, it is senseless to make an appeal that will have little or no meaning for him. Therefore, Johnson, who was primarily concerned with the practical part of religion, most often confined his discussion to the first and more crucial stage of the process whereby we set out to court happiness only to find ourselves falling in love with virtue.

But it is misleading to dismiss Johnson's entire religious outlook as mere "theological hedonism" simply because he usually emphasized the "lowest" level of Christianity—its doctrine of rewards and punishments—in order to appeal most strongly to his countrymen's sense of rational self-interest and their desire for personal happiness. We must remember that such an appeal was often made with more dignity in the eighteenth century than it usually is at present and that Johnson knew he was far from alone in regarding reason as the most celestial faculty of man and enlightened self-interest as a perfectly valid

15. "Review of *A Free Enquiry into the Nature and Origin of Evil*" (*Works*, VI, 71–72).

16. "Preface to Shakespeare" (*Works*, V, 115); "General Observations on King Lear" (Works, V, 174).

foundation for morality. John Locke, for example, asserts in his *Essay Concerning Human Understanding* that "the highest perfection of intellectual nature lies in a careful and constant pursuit of true and solid happiness." He also asserts that "God Almighty himself is under the necessity of being happy; and the more any intelligent being is so, the nearer is its approach to infinite perfection and happiness." [17] Both of these opinions were undoubtedly as familiar, and as acceptable, to the vast majority of Johnson's educated readers as they were to Johnson himself. No one who accepted such notions would have been offended by a moralist who endeavored to demonstrate that "the time shall undoubtedly come when the most virtuous will be most happy." On the contrary, they would have agreed with Locke that pursuit of such true and solid happiness is an entirely praiseworthy means of approaching infinite perfection.

Rational pursuit of happiness was in fact regarded as more than praiseworthy. It was regarded as an obligation that men have no right to neglect, for, as Locke goes on to observe, "he that will not be so far a rational creature as to reflect seriously upon *infinite* happiness and

17. *An Essay Concerning Human Understanding*, ed. A. C. Fraser (2 vols.; New York, 1959), Book II, Chap. xxi, pars. 51, 52. (Subsequent references to Locke's text will cite book, chapter, and paragraph of Locke's *Essay*.) In the *Dictionary* Johnson illustrates the third meaning of *to act* by citing the sentence immediately preceding the one I have quoted from par. 51 and illustrates the fourth meaning of *to suspend* by citing the first sentence of par. 53. On Johnson's general use of Locke in the *Dictionary*, see Chapter III. On his extensive use of Book II, Chap. xxi, see below, n. 47.

Another important thinker with whose work Johnson was familiar was Bishop Richard Cumberland, who asserted that "we must do all we can, That, we must act the best, in order to secure and lead an happy Life: And This, by the Bye, *is the one only Rule*, which Moral Philosophy or Practical Right Reason lays down, for the Regulation and Conduct of all our Behaviour and Practice" (*A Philosophical Enquiry into the Laws of Nature*, trans. John Towers [Dublin, 1750], p. 370). For an account of Johnson's familiarity with the Towers translation of *De legibus naturae* as well as an extensive discussion of some significant parallels between the views of Cumberland and Johnson, see Robert Voitle, *Samuel Johnson the Moralist* (Cambridge, Mass., 1961), pp. 61–76, 100, 108–9, 115, 147.

misery, must needs condemn himself as not making that use of his understanding he should." [18] Having been given the talent of reason, it is our duty to make the fullest possible use of it. Whenever we shirk that responsibility, we fail ourselves and our creator as well. This attitude, though foreign to our own outlook, was not unusual during the eighteenth century. It is even reflected in two of the quotations chosen by Johnson to illustrate his *Dictionary* definition of *rational*. The first, taken from Hammond, is a simple statement: "God decreed to create man after his own image, a free and *rational* agent." The second, taken from Law, is in the form of a premise and conclusion: "If it is our glory and happiness to have a *rational* nature, that is endued with wisdom and reason, that is capable of imitating the divine nature; then it must be our glory and happiness to improve our reason and wisdom, to act up to the excellency of our rational nature, and to imitate God in all our actions to the utmost of our power." Both of these remarks, together with those from Locke's *Essay* (with which Johnson was thoroughly familiar), suggest, if not the sources, at least a more than sufficient and by no means contemptible sanction for Johnson's extensive appeal to our sense of rational self-interest and our longing for personal happiness.

Another extensive discussion of the moral worth of those virtuous actions which are done primarily in order to achieve personal happiness in the hereafter is found in Henry Hammond's *Practical Catechism*, a work which Johnson cites forty-three times in Volume I of his *Dictionary*.[19] Hammond carefully answers the question, "If there be an eternal reward proposed by God to the vertuous liver, will not this . . . make the vertuous liver uncapable of reward, who, it appears, doth all for the love of that reward, and not for the love of vertue?"

In the first place, Hammond observes in reply to this question, the

18. *Essay*, II, xxi, 72.
19. Lewis Freed, "The Sources of Johnson's Dictionary" (diss., Cornell University, 1939). See also Henry Hammond, *A Practical Catechism* (7th ed.; London, 1662), pp. 355–59.

rewards proposed by God are either "such . . . as might be most desireable to vertuous mindes," and thus tempting only to those who love virtue for its own sake, or else rewards that are only bestowed upon people who are inclined to love virtue for its own sake once they have been tempted out of their sinful ways by the prospect of eternal rewards. In the second place, Hammond observes, the eternal rewards proposed by God are so distant and uncertain (for we must accept on faith the fact that there will be such rewards) that they are not really a strong present temptation. Hence, on these grounds as well it remains true that

none but a vertuous person that apprehends pleasure in present vertue, and hath his love of vertue for itself, to assist the arguments on that side, would ever part with all carnal pleasures and profits (and life it self) in pursuit of it: and accordingly this is observable in the world, that as we easily believe that which we wish, and more hardly that which we have less minde to; so the lover of vertue doth easily come to believe that eternal promise of a spiritual holy life, whereas they that are lovers of pleasures, &c. do either not believe, or not consider it.

Thus Hammond equates ready belief in the prospect of future rewards with love of virtue for its own sake by asserting that only those who do love virtue will be disposed to act virtuously in expectation of a future reward. He thereby suggests that the distinction between interested and disinterested conduct is not nearly so important as the distinction between conduct motivated by "that eternal promise of a spiritual holy life" and conduct motivated by a desire for "carnal pleasures and profits." In his view, self-interested action is only immoral if it is directed towards the wrong goal.

Later in his discussion, for example, Hammond observes that

he that loves vertue for its own sake, and would doe so though there were never an Heaven hereafter, hath nothing to be objected against him, and yet must be acknowledged to doe what he doth for the sake of the present pleasure in vertue, satisfaction of conscience, &c. the perferring of which before more vigorous sensitive pleasures is the vertue in him rewardable, and not the no-pleasantness of it. And consequently, there will be no more reason to prejudge the love of vertue in him that loves it for Heavens sake.

This passage makes it clear that in Hammond's opinion the kind of pleasure we pursue is more important than the question of whether we are pursuing pleasure. He distinguishes between immediate carnal or "vigorous sensitive pleasures" on the one hand and, on the other hand, a range of higher and therefore permissible pleasures extending from the immediate satisfactions we may derive from acting virtuously to the distant rewards that will be granted to those who have lived virtuously. It is this distinction, and not the distinction between acting virtuously because we love virtue and acting virtuously in expectation of future benefits, which Hammond views as crucial.

Moreover, he concludes his discussion by observing that

if (to acknowledge the utmost imaginable) the loving vertue for the reward be less excellent, and less rewardable, then [*sic*] loving it for it self, yet being still good and rewardable in a lower degree, it was still fit for God to propose these promises to men, because by that means many are and will be attracted and brought in love with vertue, which would not otherwise have been attracted; and so that infinite number of Christians so attracted will recompense that defect of perfection which arises from the hope of the reward. And this withall tends much to the glory of God (which may justly be designed the end of all) which is most illustrated by this means, That men acknowledge to owe to him the all that ever they receive.

Hammond's remarks are significant not only because they provide ample justification for Johnson's strategy as a moral essayist and because Johnson was familiar with Hammond's work but also because the *Practical Catechism* was an extremely important and widely read Anglican document: first published in 1645, it went through fifteen editions by 1715. The popularity of the *Practical Catechism* may possibly explain why Johnson did not bother to repeat Hammond's arguments in detail but instead chose to write moral essays which, by extensively appealing to our sense of rational self-interest and our longing for future personal happiness, were in effect a practical application of Hammond's arguments in defense of those who act virtuously in expectation of eternal benefits. By the outset of the eighteenth century it was widely, if not universally, accepted in Anglican homiletics that such an appeal "tends much to the glory of God."

Moreover, rational self-interest was a very different matter from *selfishness*, which Johnson defined as "Attention to his own interest, without any regard to others; self-love." Enlightened consideration of his own eternal happiness—or everlasting punishment and misery —teaches every man *"that he can never ultimately injure himself by benefiting others, or ultimately by injuring others benefit himself."* Consequently, truly rational self-interest abolishes selfish conduct. God has created us in such a way that "no man can be obliged by nature to prefer ultimately the happiness of others to his own." Therefore, the establishment of unselfish conduct on this earth must depend upon an appeal to every man's desire for eternal pleasure and his fear of eternal punishment. Johnson does not attempt to explain why this should be so. But since it is so, in his opinion, there can be nothing disgraceful in an attempt to bring that longing for pleasure under the guidance of reason in order to induce men to follow God's commandments. This is hardly "theological hedonism." Anybody who actually guided his conduct according to such a principle would surely be regarded as a remarkably austere, unselfish, and saintly person.

It is not so much that Christianity had relapsed into theological hedonism as that Christendom had fallen away from even professing its religion, much less practicing it. Johnson, who lived in an increasingly secular age, was therefore compelled to present those aspects of Christianity which had the most immediate appeal. Moreover, he had a lively awareness of how the individual mind progresses towards increasingly higher and more sophisticated pleasures and responses. In the *Rambler*, No. 7, for example, he observes that "the senses have not only that advantage over conscience, which things necessary must always have over things chosen, but they have likewise a kind of prescription in their favour. We feared pain much earlier than we apprehended guilt, and were delighted with the sensations of pleasure, before we had capacities to be charmed with the beauty of rectitude." [20] This observation suggests that Johnson probably would have stressed the "lower" aspects of Christianity even if he had shared our fine modern tendency to look upon an appeal to rational self-interest as a shameful expedient.

For he realized that because fear of pain and love of pleasure are powerfully established as habitual responses very early in life and increase as we grow older, no appeal which ignores this most fundamental level of mental anatomy can hope for as much—or as ready—success as an invitation which takes into account our persisting drive towards sensual pleasure. Only such basic invitations will have the great advantage of "a kind of prescription in their favour." Holding this view, Johnson could hardly have avoided emphasizing the great and lasting pleasure to be derived from accepting, and acting in accord with, the precepts of Christian revelation. He recognized, however, that we ascend from naïve expectation of an eternity of sensual pleasures to a more sophisticated appreciation of the pleasures inhering in virtue itself: eventually we develop our latent "capacities to be charmed with the beauty of rectitude" and discover that moral conduct is not only reasonable in view of the pleasant rewards it

20. Johnson's phrase "the beauty of rectitude" is reminiscent of Hooker's observation that "there is also in rectitude, beauty; as contrariwise in obliquity, deformity" (*Of the Laws of Ecclesiastical Polity*, I, 175). In his *Dictionary*, Johnson defines *obliquity* as "1. Deviation from physical rectitude; deviation from parallelism or perpendicularity. 2. Deviation from moral rectitude." The second definition is illustrated by Hooker's observation. Thus, like Hooker, Johnson affirmed that what is good is also beautiful. But neither man asserted that everyone, in all cases, will respond to that beauty: Johnson only affirms that we all develop "capacities to be charmed with the beauty of rectitude." In the *Rambler*, No. 76, however, Johnson does remark that most of our self-deceptions are "incited by that conviction of the deformity of wickedness, from which none can set himself free." This remark seems to imply that even though we are not always attracted by the beauty of rectitude we are at least always repelled by the ugliness of vice, if only to the extent of concealing from ourselves the nature of our vicious actions when we do not reform them.

can bring but that it is inherently beautiful. Duty then becomes pleasure.

Lewis has acutely observed "that morality or duty . . . never yet made a man happy in himself or dear to others." He goes on to remark that

it is shocking, but it is undeniable. We do not wish either to be, or to live among, people who are clean or honest or kind as a matter of duty: we want to be, and to associate with, people who like being clean and honest and kind. The mere suspicion that what seemed an act of spontaneous friendliness or generosity was really done as a duty subtly poisons it. In philosophical language, the ethical category is self-destructive; morality is healthy only when it is trying to abolish itself. In theological language, no man can be saved by works.[21]

The emphasis of Johnson's moral essays is clearly upon works, although he never argued that works alone, however necessary, were sufficient to insure salvation: he described religion, for example, as "animated only by faith and hope." [22] Nor was he unaware of "the beauty of rectitude" or of the fact that mere time-serving performance of duty is hardly endearing. Thus, in the *Rambler*, No. 188, Johnson points out that "it is always necessary to be loved, but not always necessary to be reverenced." And he realized with evident relief that his century was largely free from "the sour solemnity, the sullen superstition, the gloomy moroseness and the stubborn scruples of the ancient puritans." [23] In fact, it is safe to assume that Johnson felt free to concentrate upon the importance—and advantages—of works because he not only realized that a healthy morality should abolish itself but was confident that it will inevitably do so. He implies, in any case, that if our inescapable longing for pleasure is satisfied by a rational expectation of future happiness, we shall be free to develop our appreciation of the beauty of rectitude and will

21. *English Literature in the Sixteenth Century*, p. 187.
22. "Life of Milton" (*Works*, VII, 115).
23. "Life of Butler" (*Works*, VII, 153).

eventually behave as we ought because we truly want to be virtuous, not merely because we know it is expected of us.

But however important Johnson may have considered our "capacities to be charmed with the beauty of rectitude," there was a final reason for not discussing them at greater length and, indeed, for avoiding any elaboration of the higher and more elusive pleasures of Christianity. In the "Life of Waller," he observes that poetry cannot deal successfully with piety although didactic verses might adequately describe "the motives to piety" or might treat, not God Himself, "but the works of God." The reason why poetry cannot often touch satisfactorily upon religious feeling is very clear: "Of sentiments purely religious, it will be found that the most simple expression is the most sublime. . . . The ideas of Christian theology are too simple for eloquence, too sacred for fiction, and too majestick for ornament." [24] This statement plainly applies to prose as well and explains why Johnson would probably have confined himself to the most elementary ideas of Christian theology, even if he had not considered rational emphasis upon the doctrine of future rewards and punishments thoroughly dignified and rational pursuit of happiness an obligation imposed upon all creatures endowed with the celestial faculty of reason. If Johnson avoided elaborating upon the higher and more "unselfish" religious sentiments in his moral essays as well as in his poetry, it was not because he never recognized their existence and compelling beauty but rather because he believed that comment was superfluous. No statement, in his opinion, could even remotely convey the final grandeur—and ultimate appeal—of Christianity. Therefore, his pen could add nothing to any man's appreciation of the beauty of rectitude although, as a moralist, he might well hope to demonstrate the folly of vice or explain the importance of striving to remain "a free and rational agent."

24. *Works*, VII, 213–14.

❧ 3 ❧

Because he viewed reason as our most celestial faculty, Johnson vigorously reaffirmed the classical doctrine that reason ought to predominate over imagination at all times and, with the possible exception of the divinely irrational impulse towards compassion, over the passions as well—over, in other words, "those passions which now produce all our pains and all our pleasures." Clearly, Johnson never regarded the achievement of such predominance as an easy matter, however necessary it might be. But it is supremely necessary, because "he . . . that would govern his actions by the laws of virtue, must regulate his thoughts by those of reason." [25] Convinced of this necessity, Johnson devoted a major portion of his effort as a moralist to the delineation of those conditions under which—and only under which—reason *can* play its proper part in guiding our conduct in this life and preparing us for the next.

Johnson considered it essential to define the limitations which our state imposes upon the power of reason in order to avoid the mistake of setting impossible tasks and also to avoid pointless accusations, because "that error cannot be justly reproached which reason could not obviate, and prudence avoid." [26] His satiric portrait of the stoic sage in *Rasselas* illustrates the limitations imposed by Providence upon even the most resolute attempts at conducting human affairs wholly by the light of reason. In *The Vision of Theodore* those limitations are explained allegorically. [27] Reason is the figure charged with conducting those who receive her laws to Religion, "a better Guide." Reason only has power "to advise, not to compel." Unless it is supplemented by faith, the dangers created by appetites, passions, and bad habits cannot be eluded. Lust and Vanity are described as

25. *Rambler*, No. 8.
26. *Rambler*, No. 63.
27. *The Vision of Theodore, The Hermit of Teneriffe* (*Works*, IX, 162–75).

having "the greatest Success upon the Followers of Reason"—that is, upon those who follow only Reason, to the exclusion of Revelation. It is Religion that teaches Reason the right path, although, once taught, Reason may enable men to perceive the rectitude of the instructions. Yet if Faith is indispensable, so, despite its limitations, is Reason. It is characterized in the allegory as "of all subordinate Beings the noblest and the greatest." Neglect of Reason is chastized in the *Vision* as a "Crime." No more inclined to fideism than to deism, Johnson saw many circumstances in which men's highest faculty is powerless or insufficient, yet he also believed that human conduct can and should be far more rational than it usually is.

He was therefore at some pains to explain how men can make fullest use of their capacities for rational behavior. Johnson knew that the line dividing us from animals will vanish if we forget (or never learn) how to put our unique endowments to their proper use. As he pragmatically observes in the *Rambler*, No. 162, "Not to have reason, and to have it useless and unemployed, is nearly the same." He devoted less time, however, to the ancillary business of merely outlining a static picture of the higher faculties, partly because he assumed that most of his readers would be more or less familiar with the various tasks performed by reason, memory, will, imagination, and judgment. Moreover, Johnson was reluctant to regard those aspects of the mind as altogether separate entities, although he sometimes had to write as though they were in order to underscore a point more vividly or make his meaning more explicit. But even when momentarily considering a mental power in isolation, Johnson most often proceeds to recall its relationship with some other aspect of the mind to show the interrelated bearing of both powers on human conduct. He seldom leaves his readers persuaded that the mind is a mere storage house of useful but unrelated mechanisms.

Johnson was not alone, of course, in avoiding that dangerous oversimplification. John Locke, for example, warned the readers of his *Essay* that faculties are "not real beings."

The ordinary way of speaking is that the understanding and will are two *faculties* of the mind; a word proper enough, if it be used, as all words should be, so as not to breed any confusion in men's thoughts, by being supposed (as I suspect it has been) to stand for some real beings in the soul that performed those actions of understanding and volition. For when we say the *will* is the commanding and superior faculty of the soul; that it is or is not free; that it determines the inferior faculties; that it follows the dictates of the understanding, &c.,—though these and the like expressions, by those that carefully attend to their own ideas, and conduct their thoughts more by the evidence of things than the sound of words, may be understood in a clear and distinct sense—yet I suspect, I say, that this way of speaking of *faculties* has misled many into a confused notion of so many distinct agents in us, which had their several provinces and authorities, and did command, obey, and perform several actions, as so many distinct beings; which has been no small occasion of wrangling, obscurity, and uncertainty in questions relating to them.[28]

Johnson, who had carefully read this statement, seems to have remembered its warning; at least, he avoided the kinds of confusion and obscurity that Locke refers to. Surely, it is more than coincidental that Johnson chose the first phrase of this particular passage to illustrate his definition of *faculty* in the *Dictionary*. The term means, according to Johnson, "Powers of the mind, imagination, reason, memory," as in the phrase "in the ordinary way of speaking, the understanding and will are two *faculties* of the mind." This illustration shows the common meaning of *faculty* to any casual reader and also recalls a useful caution to those familiar with Locke's *Essay*.

Bate has observed that "we should also note how frequently Johnson prefers to use the word 'mind' rather than terms that express separate faculties." [29] This is quite true, though perhaps most applicable to Johnson's discussions of the higher faculties. He is usually willing enough to consider appetites and passions as distinct entities

28. *Essay*, II, xxi, 6.
29. Walter Jackson Bate, *The Achievement of Samuel Johnson* (New York, 1961), p. 208.

set in opposition to, or cooperating with, the combined operations of the higher faculties; and he frequently singles out imagination to accuse it, in effect, of acting in league with the emotions against a beneficent confederacy of will, memory, reason, and judgment. These latter, however, are treated as though they were four carriage wheels upon whose cooperation we depend for every useful motion: if the operation of any one is impaired, Johnson frequently implies, the others will no longer be able to carry out their proper tasks, and we shall veer dangerously away from our proper course.

Nevertheless, it is possible to observe throughout Johnson's writings a consistent set of assumptions about how each of the higher faculties goes about its business when it is free to do so. The role of memory, for example, is considered crucial in our moral as well as in our mental life. "It is, indeed," Johnson observes in the *Rambler*, No. 41, "the faculty of remembrance, which may be said to place us in the class of moral agents." [30] The ultimate significance of memory, however, resides in its ability to provide reason with material upon which to operate: "Memory is the purveyor of reason, the power which places those images before the mind upon which the judgment is to be exercised, and which treasures up the determinations that are once passed, as the rules of future action, or the grounds of subsequent conclusions." [31] Since without memory reason would be almost powerless, memory is therefore, as Johnson observes in the *Idler*, No. 44,

the primary and fundamental power, without which there could be no other intellectual operation. Judgment and ratiocination suppose something already known, and draw their decisions only from experience. Imagination selects ideas from the treasures of remembrance, and produces novelty only by varied combinations. We do not even

30. Memory places us in the class of moral agents, Johnson goes on to explain, because "if we were to act only in consequence of some immediate impulse, and receive no direction from internal motives of choice, we should be pushed forward by an invincible fatality, without power or reason, for the most part, to prefer one thing to another, because we could make no comparison but of objects which might both happen to be present."

31. *Rambler*, No. 41.

form conjectures of distant, or anticipations of future events, but by concluding what is possible from what is past.

The primacy of memory, however, does not imply superiority any more than the importance of the harpsichord implies its supremacy over the musician. *Memory* in Johnson's *Dictionary* is defined as "The power of retaining or recollecting things past." That definition is illustrated by Locke's statement that *"memory* is the power to revive again in our minds those ideas which after imprinting have disappeared, or have been laid aside out of sight." [32] In the *Idler*, No. 44, Johnson also explains that "the two offices of memory are collection and distribution; by one images are accumulated, and by the other produced for use." Thus the importance of memory, like that of an artist's palette, arises from its utility in the service of operations which it is itself incapable of performing. Memory alone is no more—or less—important than the colors available to the artist: everything depends upon the use to which those paints are put, just as the value of memory finally resides in the way its accumulated images and ideas are handled by the powers of imagination, judgment, and reason.

Imagination *"selects* ideas from the treasures of remembrance, and *produces novelty* only by varied combinations." In the "Life of Butler" Johnson points out that "Imagination is useless without knowledge: nature gives in vain *the power of combination,* unless study and observation supply materials to be combined" [italics added].[33] These statements suggest that rearranging and combining memories of originally disparate sensory impressions is the second of two fundamental tasks performed by the imaginative faculty. The first major task is clearly selection and representation and is

32. *Essay,* II, x, 2. Johnson has altered the order of Locke's statement and condensed it.
33. *Works,* VII, 151. See also the *Rambler,* No. 151, in which Johnson refers to fancy as "busied in arranging" images and combining "them into pleasing pictures with more resemblance to the realities of life as experience advances, and new observations rectify the former."

emphasized in the *Dictionary* by Johnson's definition of *imagination* as "Fancy; the power of forming ideal pictures; the power of representing things absent to oneself or others." Plainly, the formation of an *ideal*—that is to say, "Mental; intellectual; not perceived by the senses"—representation of some real object (which is not before our eyes as we do so) is barely distinguishable from *memory*, "The power of retaining or recollecting things past." Therefore, insofar as accurate representations of reality are concerned, imagination (or fancy) is hardly more than the active aspect of memory and might be thought of as the process whereby recollections are crystalized into distinct ideas and images. *To imagine* is "To fancy; to paint in the mind." And *fancy* is "Imagination; the power by which the mind forms to itself images and representations of things, persons, or scenes of being." Such portrayal "of things, persons, or scenes of being" as they really are is certainly, in Johnson's opinion, the least distinctive—and least dangerous—aspect of imagination, even though it is the aspect that he chose to emphasize in the *Dictionary*.

The second major task of imagination is *invention*—"The act or power of producing something new." Sometimes, as in "The Life of Pope," Johnson distinguishes invention as a separate faculty and confines *imagination* to the meaning stressed in the *Dictionary*. Thus he remarks:

Pope had, in proportions very nicely adjusted to each other, all the qualities that constitute genius. He had invention, by which new trains of events are formed, and new scenes of imagery displayed, as in the Rape of the Lock; and by which extrinsick and adventitious embellishments and illustrations are connected with a known subject, as in the Essay on Criticism. He had Imagination, which strongly impresses on the writer's mind, and enables him to convey to the reader, the various forms of nature, incidents of life, and energies of passion, as in his Eloisa, Windsor Forest, and Ethick Epistles.[34]

However, it is plain from his statements in the *Idler*, No. 44, and in "The Life of Butler" that Johnson more often subsumed invention

34. *Works*, VIII, 342–43.

under the imaginative faculty, because by its ability variously to combine and rearrange ideas selected from the storehouse of memory, imagination "produces novelty." Thus someone long ago combined his recollection of a horse with that of a man by an act of the imagination and thereby created the centaur, an imaginary beast. In the *Dictionary*, *imaginary* is defined as "Fancied; visionary; existing only in the imagination." Johnson's distrust of the visionary and fanciful is well-known. Certainly the most distinctive—and potentially dangerous—aspect of imagination, in Johnson's opinion, is its power of creating novel images and ideas that exist *only* in the mind.

Such images must be of two kinds: those that are not capable of actual realization and those that are. Both kinds may be characterized by the adjective *fantastic*, which Johnson defines in his *Dictionary* as "1. Irrational; bred only in the imagination. 2. Subsisting only in the fancy; imaginary." The *irrational* inventions of the imagination have no accurate relationship to the world of reality and therefore preoccupation with such fantastic notions is highly dangerous. In *Rasselas*, for example, the Prince is suspicious of the artisan's project for enabling men to fly: " 'I am afraid,' said he . . . 'that your imagination prevails over your skill, and that you now tell me rather what you wish, than what you know.' " Those suspicions prove only too well-founded: after an unsuccessful attempt at flight the inventor "in an instant dropped into the lake." In this case, imagination encourages a dangerous attempt at the impossible. Johnson thus associates the imaginative faculty with unworkable schemes, whereas he seldom if ever gives it credit for useful and feasible designs.

There is no mention of imagination in connection with one of the same artisan's more practical inventions. The Prince "came one day to amuse himself in his usual manner, and found the master busy in building a sailing chariot; he saw that the design was practicable upon a level surface, and, with expressions of great esteem, solicited its completion." In the case of this happier project, the artisan has confined his imagination within the bounds of probability and has thereby avoided irrational and dangerous action of the kind that his impossible scheme of flight involved him with. His career provides an apt illustration of Imlac's observation that "no man will be found, in whose mind airy notions do not, sometimes, tyrannize, and force him to hope or fear beyond the limits of sober probability." Imlac goes on to assert that "all power of fancy over reason, is a degree of insanity." It is plain that Johnson viewed reason as the primary source of feasible conduct, while blaming unchecked imagination for hopeless endeavors to put into effect schemes that are intrinsically "beyond the limits of sober probability."

However, Johnson did view imagination as the breeding ground of one very important kind of perfectly practical, though utterly pernicious, action. The nature of that action is amply suggested by a quotation from *Macbeth* chosen by Johnson to illustrate the second meaning of *fantastic*, namely, the sense of "Subsisting only in the fancy; imaginary" (notice that the qualifying term *irrational*, with its implication of impossibility, is not included in this sense of the word). The illustration is from one of Macbeth's soliloquies:

> Present fears
> Are less than horrible imaginings:
> My thought, whose murther yet is but *fantastical*,
> Shakes so my single state of man, that function
> Is smother'd in surmise; and nothing is
> But what is not.

Thus fantastical *imaginings* can lead towards murder and other crimes. Johnson thought of reason, insofar as it serves to check the imagination, as the guardian of morality. Indeed, he illustrates the meaning of *reason* by quoting—undoubtedly with complete approval— Hooker's assertion that "the laws of well doing are the dictates of right reason." Truly rational conduct, as opposed to visionary and impractical schemes on the one hand or possible but depraved projects on the other, is above all else moral conduct. Reason, in Johnson's opinion, impels us not only towards what is practical, but towards what is ethical: *"He that thinks reasonably must think morally."*

Imagination, however, is usually seen by Johnson as the hand-maiden of illusion, impossibility, and evil. In one of the earliest numbers of the *Rambler*, Johnson explained at length the process whereby unchecked imagination can lead even the most well-intentioned people to commit crimes not unlike the murder of Duncan:

> In futurity chiefly are the snares lodged, by which the imagination is entangled. Futurity is the proper abode of hope and fear, with all their train and progeny of subordinate apprehensions and desires. In futurity, events and chances are yet floating at large, without apparent connexion with their causes, and we therefore easily indulge the liberty of gratifying ourselves with a pleasing choice. To pick and cull among possible advantages is, as the civil law terms it, *in vacuum venire*, to take what belongs to nobody; but it has this hazard in it, that we shall be unwilling to quit what we have seized, though an owner should be found. It is easy to think on that which may be gained, till at last we resolve to gain it, and to image the happiness of particular conditions, till we can be easy in no other. We ought, at least, to let our desires fix upon nothing in another's power for the sake of our quiet, or in another's possession for the sake of our innocence. When a man finds himself led, though by a train of honest sentiment, to wish for that to which he has no right, he should start back as from a pitfall covered with flowers. He that fancies he should benefit the publick more in a great station than the man that fills it, will in time imagine it an act of virtue to supplant him; and as opposition readily kindles into hatred, his eagerness to do that good, to which he is not called, will betray him to crimes, which in his original scheme were never proposed.
>
> He, therefore, that would govern his actions by the laws of virtue, must regulate his thoughts by those of reason.[35]

Thus, by indiscriminately letting our imagination *image*—that is, "Copy by the fancy; imagine"—"the happiness of particular conditions," and then by allowing it to persist in the contemplation of such imaginings "till we can be happy in no other" circumstance, we may be led "to crimes" just as Macbeth was, even though our intentions may have been far more honest to begin with. We shall then in time

35. *Rambler*, No. 8.

find ourselves prey to illicit desires and hatreds that will irresistibly
sweep us into criminal conduct as the passions, unleashed by imaginative preoccupation with some remote possibility, usurp control of our
behavior. Unhappily, this plunge down the slope of imagination into
a bottomless pit of sin is as easy as it is dangerous. Johnson's lively
fear of this particular "pitfall covered with flowers" is one of the most
important, although least remarked, reasons for his well-known distrust of the imagination.

The most frequently discussed reason for Johnson's distrust of the
imagination is its insidious power to enervate or even paralyze the
will, thereby preventing all action and weakening or destroying our
grasp of reality as well. As R. D. Havens has pointed out, Johnson
feared the ease with which unchecked imagination leads us to spend
time in mere "day-dreaming—escaping reality and avoiding action by
withdrawing into the ideal world or to a fairyland of beauty, love,
and adventure." [36] The classical example in Johnson's works of such
"dangerous prevalence of the imagination" is the astronomer in *Rasselas* who had by degrees indulged his daydreams to the extent that
he eventually believed himself in control of the weather over the
entire earth. Johnson explains that such obsessions arise because after
protracted solitude "in time, some particular train of ideas fixes the
attention . . . and . . . By degrees the reign of fancy is confirmed
. . . Then fictions begin to operate as realities, false opinions fasten
upon the mind, and life passes in dreams of rapture or of anguish."
Thus the unchecked "reign of fancy" may cause us to waste life in idle
and passive "dreams of rapture or of anguish." In Johnson's view
such delusions do not necessarily make us miserable, although they
may. It is, in fact, the seductively pleasant quality of many escapes
from reality into the lotus-land of illusion which renders such states
very difficult to cure.

As Johnson observes in the *Rambler*, No. 207, "Such is the pleasure of projecting, that many content themselves with a succession of

36. "Johnson's Distrust of the Imagination," *ELH*, X (1943), 243–55.

visionary schemes, and wear out their allotted time in the calm amusement of contriving what they never attempt or hope to execute." Whenever fancies produce rapture instead of anguish, there is no incentive to break away from our preoccupation, because, as Johnson asserts emphatically in the *Idler*, No. 89, "None would fix their attention upon the future, but that they are discontented with the present. If the senses were feasted with perpetual pleasure, they would always keep the mind in subjection. Reason has no authority over us, but by its power to warn us against evil." By "evil" Johnson here means physical or mental pain, of course. This assertion explains why, in his view, reason is often powerless against the enervating quality of imagination once we have been captivated by "the pleasures of projecting": pain is the only begetter of rational conduct. If we were not dissatisfied with our present state we should never pay the slightest attention to reason. Unchecked imagination, in other words, may undermine all incentive to action by creating pleasures that destroy the authority of reason.

Thus, a fivefold conception of imagination underlies Johnson's literary criticism, creative writing, and moral essays. As the faculty responsible for such pleasing literary fictions as the Rosicrucian sylphs and gnomes in Pope's *Rape of the Lock* and also for vivid descriptions of "the various forms of nature, incidents of life, and energies of passion, as in his Eloisa, Windsor Forest, and Ethic Epistles," Johnson saw imagination as a useful source of harmless pleasure—pleasure that might be pressed into the service of instruction. In the "Life of Milton" poetry is defined as "the art of uniting pleasure with truth, by calling imagination to the help of reason." Moreover (as I have explained in Chapter I), it is an "act of the imagination" which allows us to empathize with others and which therefore provides a necessary, though not sufficient, condition for the exercise of compassion. But the other three roles performed by the imagination are more sinister because of the dangerous consequences attendant on excess: if unchecked by reason and the demands of reality, beguiling fancies may become delusive obsessions which utterly paralyze the will and lead to pernicious inaction; or else imagination may suggest irrational and impractical schemes that, if attempted, may be quite as harmful as the more passive forms of self-destruction; or, finally, imagination may inspire designs that are feasible enough, but immoral, as in the case of Macbeth.[37] It is therefore no wonder Johnson asserted that unless reason keeps "a constant guard over imagination . . . we have otherwise no security for our own virtue." [38]

The role of judgment is more limited: it prevents mistakes. Consequently it cannot create either as much harm or as much good as imagination can. But despite this limitation we cannot get along without judgment because "as laws operate in civil agency not to the

37. In "Johnson's Distrust of the Imagination," R. D. Havens observes that "Johnson seems to have ascribed to the imagination at least six closely related functions: (1) The power of representing to one's self things absent, of evoking on one's own volition images of things previously seen. (2) The power of representing to one's self things described by others which they have seen, i.e., of responding, by evoking images, to the descriptions of others. These two are relatively passive; the following require a more active, unusual gift. (3) The power of representing to one's self on one's own initiative objects, persons, places, or actions which one has never seen or never seen pictures of, i.e., 'imagining' a Caliban, a phoenix, a battle . . . a tropical forest, or life in Athens in the days of Pericles. This is done by combining and changing what we know, have seen, or have seen pictures of. (4) This is only an extension of the view of the imagination Johnson frequently expressed: that it is the faculty whereby we form concepts of characters, plots or problems for plays or stories, ideas for poems and the like. . . . (5) The power of evoking such objects, places, or actions as are mentioned in (3) when they are described by another. (6) Empathy—Johnson also used 'imagination' as we do today, in the sense of empathy, the 'imaginative projection of one's own consciousness into another being' (Webster's Dictionary)." After establishing this useful classification of the various functions ascribed by Johnson to the imagination, Havens concludes that Johnson, "viewing imagination chiefly as 'a licentious and vagrant faculty, unsusceptible of limitations, and impatient of restraint,' as the father of daydreaming, of extravagant conceptions, and impossible adventures," conceived a strong distrust of that faculty. While correct so far as it goes, this conclusion is incomplete because it does not take into account Johnson's distrust of the corrosive moral effects of unchecked imagination.

38. *Rambler*, No. 8.

excitement of virtue, but the repression of wickedness, so judgment in the operations of intellect can hinder faults, but not produce excellence." [39] Thus it serves, along with reason, to create necessary restraints upon excesses originating in other areas of the intellect.

In his *Dictionary* Johnson defines *judgment* as "The power of discerning the relations between one term or one proposition and another . . . the quality of distinguishing propriety and impropriety; criticism." The first meaning is illustrated by three quotations. The first, from Shakespeare's *Julius Caesar*, suggests how closely judgment is allied with reason, in Johnson's view: "Judgment! thou art fled to brutish beasts, / And men have lost their reason." The second, taken from Locke's *Essay Concerning Human Understanding*, makes clear the distinction between judgment and reason: "The faculty, which God has given man to supply the want of certain knowledge, is judgment, whereby the mind takes any proposition to be true or false, without perceiving a demonstrative evidence in the proofs." [40] Thus, when there is insufficient evidence to enable reason to provide a demonstrative and indisputable proof of the truth or falsehood of any assertion, we must fall back upon judgment. Reason may lead us onward through successive stages of a discursive analysis, but judgment, in Johnson's view, can only pronounce sentence upon particular propositions as they are advanced for consideration. In matters of conduct as well as in literature, judgment enables us to distinguish "propriety and impropriety." In life, as in art, this is its most important function.

However, the third illustration of the first meaning of *judgment* (taken from Watts) does suggest an ancillary power that is by no means unimportant: "Judgment is that whereby we join ideas together by affirmation or negation; so, this tree is high." Thus, judgment is the means of determining certain matters involving comparisons, as well as the faculty that enables us to decide questions

39. "Life of Prior" (*Works*, VIII, 20).
40. *Essay*, IV, xiv, 3.

of propriety in cases where there is insufficient evidence for completely rational decision. Moreover, there is always some element of uncertainty in the operations of judgment because, as Imlac remarks in *Rasselas,* "All judgment is comparative." Only reason deals with the realm of indisputable fact and absolute truth. This explains why "human judgment, though it be gradually gaining upon certainty, never becomes infallible," [41] and also why, in Johnson's view, even the soundest reasoning may go astray for want of proper materials on which to operate. It is judgment—fallible as it is—"which selects from life or nature what the present purpose requires." [42] Plainly, if that selection is liable to error—as in Johnson's opinion it always is—then the inferences and conclusions based upon facts or propositions so selected are equally liable to go astray.

Reason is thus inseparably linked with judgment and dependent upon it for its own proper functioning, just as, in turn, both "judgment and ratiocination suppose something already known, and draw their decisions only from experience." Both reason and judgment, therefore, depend upon the intermediary offices of memory and, ultimately, upon the senses, which supply information from the external world. As Hagstrum observes, "The most fundamental characteristic of Johnsonian reason" is "that it is a faculty of mind which is helpless without materials provided by sense and reflection, that is, by the experience and contemplation of objective life and nature." [43]

Reason itself is defined by Johnson as "The power by which man deduces one proposition from another, or proceeds from premises to consequences; the rational faculty; discursive power." He illustrates his second definition of *to deduce* ("To form a regular chain of consequential propositions") by Locke's statement that "reason is nothing but the faculty of deducing unknown truths from principles already known." The key term here is *truths,* for Johnson surely

41. "Preface to Shakespeare" (*Works,* V, 105).
42. "Life of Pope" (*Works,* VIII, 343).
43. *Samuel Johnson's Literary Criticism,* p. 14.

agreed with Locke's assertion that the primary function of reason is the discovery of indisputable truth. As Hagstrum has shown, Johnson evidently assumed that reason may perform as many as five more or less distinct services in going about its primary task: it may "watch, divide, combine, moderate, or generalize." [44] But the supreme task of reason, and the one usually uppermost in Johnson's thought, is that of providing (by any of the five means available to it) the individual with those truths which should (ideally) serve to guide his conduct. Johnson's definition of reason is illustrated by a quotation taken from Hooker: "Reason is the director of man's will, discovering in action what is good; for the laws of well doing are the dictates of right reason." There can be little doubt that Johnson wholeheartedly agreed with Hooker in viewing right reason as above all else the proper director of man's will.

He defined *will* in the *Dictionary* as "That power by which we desire, and purpose. . . . Choice; arbitrary determination." These definitions are illustrated by Locke's statement that "will is the power, which the mind has to order the consideration of any idea, or the forebearing to consider it, or to prefer the motion of any part of the body to its rest, and vice versa." [45] Johnson defined the verb *to will* as meaning "To desire that any thing should be, or be done; or not be, or not be done." This definition is illustrated by two relevant quotations, the first from South: "Whoever wills the doing of a thing, if the doing of it be in his power, he will certainly do it; and whoever does not do that thing, which he has in his power to do, does not properly will it." This statement provides a pragmatic interpretation of will that differentiates it from mere desire or longing: only action producing some definite effect can be said to give evidence of having willed; if there is no such action we can only be said to have desired. This distinction is also suggested by the second illustration, taken from Locke's *Essay:* "A man that sits still, is said to be at liberty,

44. *Ibid.*, p. 16.
45. *Essay*, II, xxi, 5.

because he can walk if he wills it." [46] This statement also implies that the measure of will is action.

Thus Johnson viewed the will as an inner agency immediately responsible for actually carrying out some desire. He defined *freewill* as "The power of directing our own actions without constraint by necessity or fate." In his definition, so-called freedom of the will is explained as freedom to direct "our own *actions.*" The wording of this statement, together with its accompanying illustrative quotation from Locke, suggests that Johnson had not only read, but accepted, Locke's explanation of free will and the Lockean conception of the will.

That explanation is found in the twenty-first chapter of the second book of Locke's *Essay Concerning Human Understanding*—a chapter from which Johnson drew at least twenty-one quotations to illustrate the meaning of various words in his *Dictionary.*[47] Locke denies that, strictly speaking, there can be any such thing as freedom of the *will.* After elaborating various arguments to substantiate that denial, he concludes in paragraph 24, "That *a man is not at liberty to will, or not to will, anything in his power that he once considers of:* liberty consisting in a power to act or to forbear acting, and in that only." Johnson's use of Locke's next sentence ("A man that sits still, is said to be at liberty, because he can walk if he wills it") as the second illustration of *to will,* as well as the twenty other citations from the same chapter of the *Essay,* shows that he had carefully examined Locke's argument. Johnson's use of the term *actions*—rather than *thoughts, de-*

46. *Ibid.,* par. 24.

47. The words illustrated by a quotation from Book II, Chap. xxi of Locke's *Essay* and the paragraphs in that chapter from which each word is illustrated, are the following: *passion* (par. 4); *will* (par. 5); *faculty* (par. 6); *liberty* (par. 8); *liberty* (par. 12); *forbearance* (par. 15); *to need* (par. 16); *to will* (par. 24); *motive* (par. 29); *misery* (par. 43); *to determine* (par. 44); *determination* (par. 45); *freewill* (par. 48); *superiour* (par. 50); *to act* (par. 51); *to suspend* (par. 53); *suspense* (par. 53); *happiness* (par. 55); *answer* (par. 55); *to suspend* (par. 57); and *to determine* (par. 57).

sires, or *will*—in his definition of *freewill* as "The power of directing our own actions without constraint by necessity or fate" suggests that he had probably accepted that argument.

Moreover, this probability is further strengthened by the fact that Johnson chose to illustrate his definition of *freewill* with a sentence that concisely summarizes Locke's position: "We have a power to suspend the prosecution of this or that desire: this seems to me the source of all liberty; in this seems to consist that which is improperly called *freewill*." Thus in Locke's view—and, I think, in Johnson's as well—freedom of the will, so-called, actually consists of the power to refrain from action long enough to weigh rationally the issues involved, in order to decide whether or not to allow the will to proceed with the prosecution of its intent. The entire paragraph in Locke's *Essay* from which Johnson drew his illustration of *freewill* makes this conception quite clear:

There being in us a great many uneasinesses, always soliciting and ready to determine the will, it is natural, as I have said, that the greatest and most pressing should determine the will to the next action; and so it does for the most part, but not always. For, the mind having in most cases, as is evident in experience, a power to *suspend* the execution and satisfaction of any of its desires; and so all, one after another; is at liberty to consider the objects of them, examine them on all sides, and weigh them with others. In this lies the liberty man has; and from the not using of it right comes all that variety of mistakes, errors, and faults which we run into in the conduct of our lives, and our endeavours after happiness; whilst we precipitate the determination of our wills, and engage too soon, before due examination. To prevent this, we have a power to suspend the prosecution of this or that desire; as every one daily may experiment in himself. This seems to me the source of all liberty; in this seems to consist that which is (as I think improperly) called *free-will*. For, during this suspension of any desire, before the will be determined to action, and the action (which follows that determination) done, we have opportunity to examine, view, and judge of the good or evil of what we are going to do; and when, upon due examination, we have judged, we have done our duty, all that we can, or ought to do, in pursuit of our happiness; and it is not a fault, but a perfection of our nature, to desire, will, and act according to the last result of a fair examination.[48]

In Locke's opinion our ability to suspend action allows us to examine the various factors bearing upon any decision and then to judge whether to permit our desire to be translated into action by the will. Thus, in his view, as in Hooker's, reason and judgment are seen as the proper directors of man's will.

In an earlier paragraph, Locke asserts that "the will being nothing but a power in the mind to direct the operative faculties of a man to motion or rest, as far as they depend on such direction; to the question, What is it determines the will? the true and proper answer is, The mind." [49] Locke goes on to explain (in a sentence cited by Johnson to illustrate the meaning of *motive*) that "what moves the mind, in every particular instance, to determine its general power of directing, to this or that particular motion or rest" is really apperception of pleasure or pain. "The motive for continuing in the same state or action, is only the present satisfaction in it; the motive to change is always some uneasiness: nothing setting us upon the change of state, or upon any new action, but some uneasiness." [50] Thus, in Locke's opinion, there can be no such thing as free *will*—the will itself is always determined and, moreover, reason and judgment are not what determine it. Rather, it is pleasure ("present satisfaction") and pain ("some uneasiness") which inevitably sway the will towards "motion or rest." Reason and judgment, however—as Locke makes abundantly clear in the paragraph from which Johnson drew his illustration of *freewill*—may direct the will to proceed with the action it has been determined upon, or to refrain from that course.

Such direction is the mechanism by which the intellectual faculties—providing, of course, that they are operating properly and are not imbalanced in some way—assume their responsibility for con-

48. *Essay*, II, xxi, 48.
49. *Ibid.*, par. 29.
50. *Ibid.*

trolling our conduct. If reason and judgment lose, from whatever cause, their power to enforce such direction, the individual inevitably loses his freedom of agency. In Locke's view, the intellectual faculties—especially reason and judgment—hold the key to what is loosely called freedom of the will but is, more accurately, freedom of agency.

Johnson evidently agreed with, and adopted, Locke's viewpoint when he defined *freewill*. I do not know of any place outside the *Dictionary* where Johnson provides an extensive—or even fragmentary—explanation of just what it is that the will does. He avoids any generalization upon the precise mechanism of its operation, as though he considered this problem either insoluble or—what is more likely—irrelevant, even to a thorough consideration of the moral discipline of the mind. But it is significant that he does consider very extensively the factors which *limit* our exercise of free will.

Indeed, throughout Johnson's moral essays there is a striking amount of attention devoted to considering the situations which prevent the exercise of free will—which constrain, in other words, our freedom of agency. That consideration most often takes the form of detailed examinations of the conditions responsible for what Imlac calls "disorders of intellect." To cure such disorders, in Johnson's view, is to restore freedom of agency. The method of effecting such cures is first to understand and then to remove the conditions that prevent reason and judgment from exercising their proper role as the directors of our conduct. I believe that Johnson approaches the moral discipline of the mind in this way and avoids treating the will, even for the purposes of analysis, as an autonomous faculty, because he agreed with, and shared, Locke's opinion that the will, properly speaking, is not and can never be free, although our actions certainly can, provided the faculties that direct them are operating correctly.

Even though in his opinion motives are determined by pleasure and pain, Johnson emphatically insisted that so far as we can avoid "disorders of intellect"—but no farther—we can always maintain our freedom of agency, that is, our *freewill:* "The power of directing our actions without constraint by necessity." This is why Johnson was at pains in the *Rambler*, No. 8, to remind us "that all action has its origin in the mind, and that therefore to suffer the thoughts to be vitiated, is to poison the fountains of morality." To allow our thoughts to be vitiated, in Johnson's opinion, is to relinquish freedom of agency. He believed that because this happens so frequently it is absurd to assert that the majority of men have any significant degree of free will at all: "Most minds are the slaves of external circumstances, and conform to any hand that undertakes to mold them, roll down any torrent of custom in which they happen to be caught, or bend to any importunity that bears hard against them." [51] But he also believed that such mental slavery is the most dangerous bondage. Therefore, Johnson took up his pen as a moral essayist, largely in order to waken what he regarded as the almost universally dormant capacity for exercising our most important freedom.

51. *Rambler*, No. 70.

◦ Chapter III ◦

Locke and Johnson

WHEN HIS *Dictionary* was at last ready for publication Johnson confessed in the Preface that he had "sometimes, though rarely, yielded to the temptation of exhibiting a genealogy of sentiments, by showing how one authour copied the thoughts and diction of another." In defense of this self-indulgence he added that "such quotations are indeed little more than repetitions, which might justly be censured, did they not gratify the mind, by affording a kind of intellectual history." While Johnson's interest in this particular gratification is one measure of his keen historical sense, it is also a reminder that we may properly ask where he himself stood with respect to the opinions of any author whose works he carefully read while writing his *Dictionary*. By answering this question we can advance towards a fuller understanding of how the moral essays and *Rasselas* are related to at least some important aspects of their intellectual milieu. The immense task of relating Johnson's views to those of all the authors cited in the *Dictionary* is, however, far beyond the scope of any one study. And many different works could equally well serve as jumping-off points. But the observations which I have made in Chapter II will be most usefully amplified by defining the extent of Johnson's agreement with Locke's observations on the imagination, in order to show exactly how far Johnson, as a prescriptive moralist, incorporated in his works the essentially descriptive outlook of the tradition exemplified by the *Essay Concerning Human Understanding*.

It is especially important to do this because the nature of Johnson's relationship to Locke and the scientific outlook which he represents is still misunderstood. In the only full-dress study to date of Johnson's moral views, for example, Robert Voitle remarks, after usefully showing how Johnson accepts the Lockean concept of reason:

We could hardly expect him to sympathize wholly with the men who evolved this new notion of reason, for when we grant that he and Locke share a strong faith in the importance of the hard facts of experience, we reach the end of the essential similarity between the two men. Locke, his predecessors, and many of his successors look at the mind in a scientific rather than a moral spirit. Johnson's outlook on the mind, indeed, on the sum of human experience, is not naturalistic; it is profoundly moral.[1]

To assume that the naturalistic and moral viewpoints are mutually exclusive, however, is to set up a false disjunction which makes it difficult to appreciate the real nature of Johnson's achievement as a moralist. For one of the distinctive qualities of his moral essays is their harmonious acceptance of Lockean descriptive psychology within a broader framework of ethical concern. Far from rigidly

1. *Samuel Johnson the Moralist* (Cambridge, Mass., 1961), p. 24.

opposing his prescriptive morality to the scientific aims of Locke, Johnson was able to remain, as he asserted we all are, perpetually a moralist, while at the same time enlisting the naturalistic theories of Locke in the service of an endeavor to teach the moral discipline of the mind. That impressive achievement may be illustrated by tracing several extremely close but hitherto neglected parallels between the views of both men on the dangers of the imagination.

First, however, it would be well to recall the amply documented fact that Johnson was profoundly interested in Locke's philosophy. The 1,674 quotations from Locke's works in Volume I alone of Johnson's *Dictionary* eloquently attest to his interest.[2] That interest has been further illustrated by several studies which have pointed out how closely Johnson's epistemological views match Lockean doctrines which, if they were not the source of Johnson's parallel views, must at least have provided the strongest confirmation of his own thinking.[3]

2. W. K. Wimsatt, Jr., *Philosophic Words: A Study of Style and Meaning in the "Rambler" and "Dictionary" of Samuel Johnson* (New Haven, 1948), p. 34, n. 17. See also Lewis Freed, "The Sources of Johnson's Dictionary" (diss., Cornell University, 1939).

3. Wimsatt, for example, points out that "the work of Locke alone would have been enough to insure a thorough immersion of Johnson's mind in empirical epistemology. Johnson excluded Hobbes from the *Dictionary*, no doubt because of his impiety. Berkeley he quoted only eight times, five times from a letter to Pope and three from Berkeley's religious writings. . . . Locke was evidently the British philosopher chosen to represent his kind in the *Dictionary*. He is pre-eminently the philosopher of the *Dictionary*, one of its most important prose sources. There is also Isaac Watts, whose *Logic* and *Improvement of the Mind* are *Dictionary* sources from which Johnson chose epistemological passages and whom Johnson in his *Life of Watts* correctly considers as both critic and disciple of Locke. A recent study has pointed out Johnson's interest, expressed at various times, in such current epistemological themes of a Lockean cast as the distinction of colors by touch, simple ideas, and undefinable names, the innate equality of minds, the limitations of human knowledge, and the uncertainty of history. Locke is the philosopher of Johnson's conversation and of his prose writings, of *Rasselas*, for example, where the fine philosophic passage in chapter XLVIII shows Johnson (or Imlac among the Egyptian tombs) at grips with the Lockean heresy that God might if He pleased 'superadd to matter a faculty of thinking.' In the *Rambler*

Moreover, the two men were in complete agreement on some extremely fundamental issues apart from epistemological matters. Locke, for example, after arguing on the basis of his theory of knowledge that our minds are "not fitted to penetrate into the internal fabric and real essenses of bodies," was led to suspect that we can never make natural philosophy an exact science, and consequently he found it "rational to conclude, that our proper employment lies in those inquiries, and in that sort of knowledge which is most suited to our natural capacities, and carries in it our greatest interest, i.e., the condition of our eternal estate. Hence I think I may conclude, that *morality* is the *proper science and business of mankind in general.*" [4] Thus Locke's naturalistic exploration of the mind, far from leading him to ignore or minimize the importance of morality, actually resulted in the strongest possible affirmation of its overriding significance for those who accepted his empiricist epistemology.

Whatever the later divergences between psychology and morality may have been, it remains true that Locke's naturalistic outlook carried him towards rather than away from ethical considerations. In the introduction to his *Essay* Locke remarks that "if we can find out those measures, whereby a rational creature, put in that state in which man is in this world, may and ought to govern his opinions, and

---

Johnson alludes to Locke by name five times, and in a passage where he refers to a blind man who identified the color scarlet with the 'clangour of a trumpet,' he is indebted, probably at firsthand, to the *Essay Concerning Human Understanding*" (*Philosophic Words*, pp. 95–96).

The study referred to by Wimsatt is Kenneth MacLean's *John Locke and English Literature of the Eighteenth Century* (New Haven, 1936). However, the usefulness of MacLean's study is limited because most of his observations on Johnson refer to statements recorded by Boswell.

For further discussion of Locke's influence on Johnson see Chap. 1 of Jean H. Hagstrum, *Samuel Johnson's Literary Criticism* (Minneapolis, 1952) and Donald J. Greene, *The Politics of Samuel Johnson* (New Haven, 1960), pp. 76–80, 244–46.

4. John Locke, *An Essay Concerning Human Understanding*, ed. A. C. Fraser (2 vols.; New York, 1959), II, 351. (Subsequent references to Locke's text will cite book, chapter, and paragraph of Locke's *Essay*.)

actions depending thereon, we need not be troubled that some other things escape our knowledge. This was that which gave the first rise to this *Essay* concerning the understanding." Johnson's career as a moralist was given impetus by a very similar concern with the problem of how men might better govern their opinions and the actions which depend upon them: "My purpose," he announced in the *Rambler*, No. 8, is "to consider the moral discipline of the mind, and to promote the increase of virtue rather than of learning."[5] In thus turning his gaze inward upon the operations of the mind, Johnson was clearly reaffirming a Lockean (though not exclusively Lockean) view. Both men affirmed the primary importance of morality. Both were concerned with explaining the necessity and defending the propriety of an attempt to arrive at a sound method of regulating the mind. Furthermore, both men vigorously reaffirmed the Christian doctrine that men *can* know all they need to know in order properly to regulate their opinions and conduct, just as they both affirmed the importance of the *consensus gentium* and asserted that the human mind is naturally attracted by truth and repelled by falsehood. Because both men rejected the doctrine of innate ideas, they took pains to stress the extreme importance of social environment in molding men's opinions and conduct.[6] It is against the backdrop of these broad

5. *The Works of Samuel Johnson, LL.D.* (9 vols.; Oxford, 1825), II, 36. (Cited hereafter as *Works.*)

6. Locke remarks, for example, that even "though the comprehension of our understandings comes exceeding short of the vast extent of things . . . men have reason to be well satisfied with what God hath thought fit for them, since he hath given them (as St. Peter says) whatsoever is necessary for the conveniences of life and information of virtue; and has put within the reach of their discovery, the comfortable provision for this life, and the way that leads to a better" (*Essay*, Introduction, par. 5; also I, iii, 12). In the *Rambler*, No. 81, Johnson alleges a proof of "that tenderness for mankind which providence has, I think, universally displayed, by making attainments easy in proportion as they are necessary." In the *Idler*, No. 41, he observes that "we know little of the state of departed souls, because such knowledge is not necessary to a good life." For the remarks of Johnson and Locke on the *consensus gentium*, cf. *Essay*, IV, xvi, 6, the *Rambler*, No. 52, and the *Idler*,

areas of fundamental accord that we should view their agreement on the peculiar dangers of the imagination and their equally objective interest in the operations of this faculty.

❧ 2 ❧

Throughout his works Johnson consistently uses the terms *fancy* and *imagination* interchangeably, while calling attention with equal consistency to the difference between rational and merely imaginative opinions. He very frequently makes this distinction in order to point out the dangers of irrational thinking, as in Chapter XLIV of *Rasselas*, for example, where Imlac discourses on "the dangerous prevalence of imagination":

Disorders of intellect . . . happen much more often than superficial observers will easily believe. Perhaps, if we speak with rigorous exactness, no human mind is in its right state. There is no man, whose imagination does not, sometimes, predominate over his reason, who

---

No. 52. Though Locke believed that absolute certainty was possible in such matters as knowledge of one's own existence, the existence of others, and the existence of God, he argued that we can only attain probable knowledge of many facts and asserted that the *"highest degree of probability,* is, when the general consent of all men, in all ages, as far as it can be known, concurs with a man's constant and never-failing experience in like cases, to confirm the truth of any particular matter of fact attested by fair witnesses." Similarly, Johnson, who was always inclined to trust the "common voice of the multitude," asserts that "when an opinion to which there is no temptation of interest spreads wide and continues long, it may be reasonably presumed to have been infused by nature or dictated by reason." For the views of both men on how the mind (unless it is in some way corrupted) is attracted by truth and repelled by falsehood, cf. the *Essay*, IV, iii, 20, and Johnson's assertion in the "Life of Pope" that "the heart naturally loves truth" (*Works*, VIII, 334). See also the *Rambler*, No. 20, in which Johnson mentions the likelihood that "every man hates falsehood, from the natural congruity of truth to his faculties of reason." Locke remarks that nothing is "so beautiful to the eye as truth is to the mind; nothing so deformed and irreconcilable to the understanding as a lie. For though many a man can with satisfaction enough own a no very handsome wife in his bosom; yet who is bold enough openly to avow that he has espoused a falsehood, and received into his breast so ugly a thing as a lie?"

can regulate his attention wholly by his will, and whose ideas will come and go at his command. No man will be found, in whose mind airy notions do not, sometimes, tyrannise, and force him to hope or fear beyond the limits of sober probability. All power of fancy over reason, is a degree of insanity; but while this power is such as we can control and repress, it is not visible to others, nor considered as any depravation of the mental faculties: it is not pronounced madness but when it becomes ungovernable, and apparently influences speech or action.

To indulge the power of fiction, and send imagination out upon the wing, is often the sport of those who delight too much in silent speculation. When we are alone we are not always busy; the labour of excogitation is too violent to last long; the ardour of enquiry will, sometimes, give way to idleness or satiety. He who has nothing external that can divert him, must find pleasure in his own thoughts, and must conceive himself what he is not; for who is pleased with what he is? He then expatiates in boundless futurity, and culls, from all imaginable conditions, that which for the present moment, he should most desire; amuses his desires with impossible enjoyments, and confers upon his pride unattainable dominion. The mind dances from scene to scene, unites all pleasures in all combinations, and riots in delights which nature and fortune, with all their bounty, cannot bestow.

In time some particular train of ideas fixes the attention; all other intellectual gratifications are rejected; the mind, in weariness or leisure, recurs constantly to the favourite conception, and feasts on the luscious falsehood, whenever she is offended with the bitterness of truth. By degrees, the reign of fancy is confirmed; she grows first imperious, and in time despotick. Then fictions begin to operate as realities, false opinions fasten upon the mind, and life passes in dreams of rapture or of anguish.

Imlac's observations may be summarized in part as follows: (1) intellectual disorders are frequent; (2) no one is entirely free from such disorders; (3) no one can entirely govern his own thoughts; (4) any abrogation of rational control over fancy is "a degree of insanity"; (5) no one who can keep his insane tendencies sufficiently under control to escape notice and comment is labeled a madman; (6) solitude, self-dissatisfaction, and idleness lead men to indulge their fancies; (7) in time "some particular train of ideas" recurs continually;

and (8) when that happens, and the train of ideas is a delusion ("luscious falsehood"), the individual loses sight of the fact that his ideas are falsehoods and mistakes them for realities. Imlac's analysis is intended to explain the peculiar obsession of the astronomer who believed that he "had possessed for five years the regulation of the weather and the distribution of the seasons." Except for this particular delusion, the astronomer is quite rational and considered sane: Imlac's revelation of his obsession astonishes Rasselas, Nekayah, and Pekuah.

Locke was as concerned as Johnson was, though for partly different reasons, with the dangers of relying too heavily on imagination as a guide to conduct. Arguing against religious "enthusiasm," Locke asks, "What readier way can there be to run ourselves into the most extravagant errors and miscarriages, than . . . to set up fancy for our supreme and sole guide, and to believe any proposition to be true, any action to be right, only because we believe it to be so?" (*Essay*, IV, xix, 11) A similar concern with the dangers of fancy is also expressed in a context which is much closer to that of Imlac's cautions against the dangerous prevalence of imagination: in Book II, Chapter xi, paragraph 13 of the *Essay*, Locke discusses the difference between idiots and madmen, observing that madmen

do not appear to me to have lost the faculty of reasoning, but having joined together some ideas very wrongly, they mistake them for truths; and they err as men do that argue right from wrong principles. *For, by the violence of their imaginations, having taken their fancies for realities, they make right deductions from them.* Thus you shall find a distracted man fancying himself a king, with a right inference require suitable attendance, respect, and obedience: others who have thought themselves made of glass, have used the caution necessary to preserve such brittle bodies. *Hence it comes to pass that a man who is very sober, and of a right understanding in all other things, may in one particular be as frantic as any in Bedlam;* if either by any sudden very strong impression, or *long fixing his fancy upon one sort of thoughts*, incoherent ideas have been cemented together so powerfully, as to remain united. But there are degrees of madness, as of folly; the disorderly jumbling ideas together is in some more, and some less. In short, herein seems to lie the difference between idiots and madmen: that madmen put wrong ideas together, and so make wrong propositions, but argue and reason right from them; but idiots make very few or no propositions, and reason scarce at all [italics added].

This interesting passage—from which Johnson drew his illustrations in the *Dictionary* of the words *madness* and *distracted*—might well provide the speculative rationale for the portrayal of a man whose intellect is disordered in just the way that the astronomer's intellect is: for he is perfectly calm, rational, and unexceptionable in everything save what touches upon his delusive belief that he controls the weather. He could well be described as "a man who is very sober, and of a right understanding" save for the fact that "in one particular" he is as "frantic as any in Bedlam." Moreover, even in the one area of his thought in which "the reign of fancy is confirmed" and his "fictions begin to operate as realities (or, using Locke's terms, the area in which he has "taken . . . fancies for realities"), the astronomer could well be described as making "right deductions" from his fanciful assumptions. He realizes that his remarkable power over the weather is something which he "cannot prove . . . by any external evidence"; he knows "too well the laws of demonstration to think that" his "conviction ought to influence another." Therefore, he wastes no time attempting to prove his power to Imlac; he endeavors to exercise his power justly; and, realizing that he is getting on in years, he is concerned to find a worthy successor to take over his important responsibility. If his initial assumption that he does control the weather is taken for granted, none of his conclusions therefrom, his methods of attempting to exercise his powers, or his efforts to find a successor can be criticized as illogical or unreasonable. He can certainly "argue and reason right" from his "wrong propositions." If anyone had challenged the plausibility of this characterization of the mad astronomer, Johnson might have pointed to Locke's passage and cited it as ample theoretical justification for just such a portrait.

Imlac expresses Johnson's rationale for that portrait when he

discourses on "the dangerous prevalence of imagination." His analysis
is strikingly reminiscent of Locke's views in several respects. By remarking that "all power of fancy over reason is a *degree* of insanity,"
Imlac clearly implies what Locke asserts: that "there are degrees of
madness." Johnson and Locke evidently agreed in their conception of
what comprises madness, for neither drew an entirely qualitative
distinction between the sane and the insane. Both clearly agreed that a
man "may in one particular be as frantic as any in Bedlam," while
nevertheless retaining a legitimate claim to being treated and regarded as sane. The difference between sanity and madness is in their
view a difference primarily of degree, not of kind. One holding this
view would ask not merely whether there were any obsessions (or
even necessarily what kind) but, in addition, how many there were
which had gone out of control and become evident to others.

Not that many writers did hold this view. As Kathleen M. Grange
points out, Imlac's "speech no less than the delineation of the astronomer himself marked an important advance in eighteenth-century
understanding of insanity, an advance recognized at the time but completely ignored by twentieth-century historians of either literature or
psychiatry." [7] Doing justice at last to "Johnson's penetrating insight,"
Dr. Grange adds that "it was probably not until our own day that the
concept of a close relationship between normal and abnormal states of
mind was as emphatically restated." She even affirms that "Johnson's
statement is probably more explicit and certainly more expressive
than Freud's exposition of the identical concept." There is no need to
go further in staking out the rival claims of Lichfield and Vienna.
Nor does it detract from Johnson's achievement to add that his
insight had been anticipated by Locke. What is remarkable, and much
to Johnson's credit, is that the Christian moralist is no less forward-
looking than the scientific philosopher.

In his famous chapter "Of the Association of Ideas," Locke is
primarily concerned with elaborating upon his discussion of the

---

7. "Dr. Samuel Johnson's Account of a Schizophrenic Illness in *Rasselas*,"
Medical History, VI (1962), 162–68.

"difference between idiots and madmen" for the purpose of explaining in greater detail how fancy can lead men into mistaken opinions that can only be described as mad. Though important to note, this concern is too often overlooked by those who write on the Lockean concept of association. I wish, therefore, to emphasize the fact that Locke's analysis of association was prompted by a specific concern with the relationship between imagination and observable "degrees of madness." He begins the chapter, in fact, by noting that "there is scarce any one that does not observe something that seems odd to him, and is in itself really extravagant, in the opinions, reasonings, and actions of other men" (*Essay*, II, xxxiii, 1). Thus, at the outset he addresses himself to the problem of why there is "something unreasonable in most men." A. C. Fraser has remarked that "it is curious that Locke, midway chronologically between Hobbes and Hartley, introduces 'association' not, as they did, to explain human knowledge, but with the opposite intent of accounting for human errors." [8] The curious bent of Locke's concern may account in large part for whatever interest Johnson took in this particular aspect of the *Essay*.

After his initial remark, Locke proceeds towards his discussion of association by observing that the unreasonable actions which everyone notices in his neighbor's conduct (though never in his own) do not proceed wholly from self-love, education, or prejudice, although these latter two are often involved. He urges those "to look a little further, who would trace this sort of madness to the root it springs from, and so explain it, as to show whence this flaw has its original in very sober and rational minds, and wherein it consists." Then he remarks:

I shall be pardoned for calling it by so harsh a name as madness, when it is considered that opposition to reason deserves that name, and is really madness; and there is scarce a man so free from it, but that if he should always, on all occasions, argue or do as in some cases he constantly does, would not be thought fitter for Bedlam than civil conversation. I do not here mean when he is under the power of an

---

8. *Essay*, I, 527, n. 1.

unruly passion, but in the steady calm course of his life. That which
will yet more apologize for this harsh name, and ungrateful imputa-
tion on the greatest part of mankind, is, that inquiring a little by the
bye into the nature of madness (b. ii, ch. xi, 13) I found it to spring
from the very same root, and to depend on the very same cause [that
is, on "having joined together some ideas very wrongly" and mistaking them for truths] we are here speaking of. This consideration of
the thing itself, at a time when I thought not the least on the subject
which I am now treating of, suggested it to me. And if this be a
weakness to which all men are so liable, if this be a taint which so
universally infects mankind, the greater care should be taken to lay it
open under its due name, thereby to excite the greater care in its
prevention and cure (*Essay*, II, xxxiii, 4).

If this passage is compared with Imlac's discourse on "the dangerous prevalence of imagination," several parallels will be observed.
Both stress the frequency of intellectual disorders. Both insist that
any surrender of rational control is madness and should be recognized
and described as such: Locke states that "opposition to reason deserves
that name and is really madness," while Imlac asserts that "all power
of fancy over reason is a degree of insanity." Finally, both passages
make a similar assertion but qualify it with a similar reservation by
maintaining that practically no one is free from such disorders: Locke
observes that "there is scarce a man so free from it, but that if he
should always, on all occasions, argue or do as in some cases he
constantly does, would not be thought fitter for Bedlam than civil
conversation," while Imlac asserts that "perhaps, if we speak with
rigorous exactness, no human mind is in its right state." Moreover,
Locke concludes his paragraph by suggesting that "greater care
should be taken to lay it open under its due name, thereby to excite
the greater care in its prevention and cure." He thus urges his
readers, in effect, to join in an effort to publicize the fact that madness
is by no means confined to the inmates of Bedlam; he implies that we
must recognize the more common forms of madness if we hope to
prevent or cure them; and he clearly implies that such recognition is
in fact a major step towards their cure.

In calling attention to "the dangerous prevalence of imagination,"

Johnson was certainly carrying out Locke's suggestion, although it is of course impossible to say whether Johnson was thinking of Locke when he sat down to write Chapter XLIV of *Rasselas*. The chances are that he was not consciously putting Locke's advice into effect. In any case it is quite clear that he was doing what Locke hoped more people would do. Moreover, the entire strategy of Johnson's career as a moral essayist reflects a similar Lockean concern with pointing out and emphasizing the frequency of what Imlac refers to as "maladies of the mind." Johnson was no less interested than Locke in calling attention to "disorders of intellect" which are not sufficiently recognized as such, for the purpose of stimulating people to greater care in preventing and curing them. There is in fact surprisingly little overt prescription in the *Rambler,* the *Adventurer,* and the *Idler* as compared with such works as Taylor's *Holy Living,* Law's *Serious Call to a Devout and Holy Life,* or even, for that matter, the *Spectator:* Johnson was evidently more interested in analyzing the causes and calling attention to the corrupting effects of various maladies of the mind. He seems to have assumed that a good deal would be accomplished if he could simply reveal precisely what goes wrong and why men fall into error or "wander in the wrong way." This assumption, which underlies Johnson's method as a moralist, is a very important aspect of his sympathy with the temper, as well as with the specific doctrines, of Locke's philosophy. This marked similarity of temper makes it misleading to oppose Locke's naturalism to Johnson's moralistic outlook on the mind, for on the issue of calling attention to the prevalence and causes of intellectual maladies, the method of Johnson's moral instruction is really naturalistic analysis designed to compel assent to the need for precisely that "greater care in [their] prevention and cure" which Locke had argued for.

After pointing out the prevalence of madness, Locke proceeds with his explanation of how "a wrong connexion of ideas" frequently creates unreasonable behavior:

Some of our ideas have a *natural* correspondence and connexion one with another: it is the office and excellency of our reason to trace these, and hold them together in that union and correspondence which is founded in their peculiar beings. Besides this, there is another connexion of ideas wholly owing to *chance* or *custom*. Ideas that in themselves are not all of kin, come to be so united in some men's minds, that it is very hard to separate them; they always keep in company, and the one no sooner at any time comes into the understanding, but its associate appears with it; and if they are more than two which are thus united, the whole gang, always inseparable, show themselves together.

This strong combination of ideas, not allied by nature, the mind makes in itself either voluntarily or by chance; and hence it comes in different men to be very different, according to their different inclinations, education, interest, &c. *Custom* settles habits of thinking in the understanding, as well as of determining in the will, and of motions in the body: all which seems to be but trains of motions in the animal spirits, which, once set a going, continue in the same steps they have been used to; which, by often treading, are worn into a smooth path, and the motion in it becomes easy, and as it were natural. As far as we can comprehend thinking, thus ideas seem to be produced in our minds; or, if they are not, this may serve to explain their following one another in an habitual train, when once they are put into their track, as well as it does to explain such motions of the body (*Essay*, II, xxxiii, 5–6).

When this explanation is compared with Imlac's discourse, one notices that both refer to trains of ideas, although Imlac does not discuss the chance association of ideas that later become inseparably united. He does, however, in part explain the tyranny of fancy by suggesting that when some delusive "particular train of ideas fixes the attention" it becomes habitual, its recurrence is easy "and in time despotick" so that eventually the mind is no longer at liberty to consider anything but the habitual (and delusive) train of ideas. In Lockean terms, this would seem to be a description of the displacement of natural (that is, rational) associations by a train of "ideas wholly owing to . . . custom." [9]

9. For an amusing citation from Locke's chapter "Of the Association of Ideas," see Johnson's *Dictionary* under *trunk* and compare with the *Essay*, II, xxxiii, 16.

Such displacement is always possible and therefore a constant threat, Imlac implies, because "there is no man whose imagination does not sometimes predominate over his reason, who can regulate his attention wholly by his will, and whose ideas will come and go at his command." This remark is reminiscent of Locke's observation in his essay *Of the Conduct of the Understanding* that

men forwardly conclude, and frequently say, nothing is so free as thought, and it were well it were so; but the contrary will be found true in several instances; and there are many cases wherein there is nothing more resty and ungovernable than our thoughts: they will not be directed what objects to pursue, nor be taken off from those they have once fixed on, but run away with a man in pursuit of those ideas they have in view, let him do what he can.[10]

After pointing to the fact that we cannot always control our thoughts, Imlac proceeds to suggest how, as a consequence, we may in certain circumstances lose all ability to direct our thoughts: "By degrees the reign of fancy is confirmed; she grows first imperious, and in time despotick." Similarly, Locke goes on to observe:

Matters that are recommended to our thoughts by any of our passions take possession of our minds with a kind of authority, and will not be kept out or dislodged, but, as if the passion that rules were for the time the sheriff of the place, and came with all the posse, the understanding is seized and taken with the object it introduces, as if it had a legal right to be alone considered there. There is scarce any body, I think, of so calm a temper who hath not sometime found this tyranny on his understanding, and suffered under the inconvenience of it.[11]

Although Imlac is discussing the usurpation of the mind by imagination and Locke proceeds to note the possibility of its usurpation by passions, they both proceed from the same observation to a similar conclusion: the possibility of losing even what control we usually have over our thoughts. Both use the same strong term to describe the situation: Locke refers to "this tyranny on his understanding," while

10. *Locke's Conduct of the Understanding*, ed. Thomas Fowler (5th ed.; Oxford, 1901), p. 97. See also *Essay*, II, xxi, 12.

11. *Locke's Conduct of the Understanding*, p. 97.

Imlac asserts that "no man will be found in whose mind airy notions do not sometimes tyrannise." These parallels do not by any means suggest that Locke's passage was consciously imitated or echoed by Johnson, but they do provide another illustration of a noteworthy similarity in theme and method.

Thus Johnson's entire conception of the nature, frequency, causes, prevention, and cure of "the dangerous prevalence of imagination" is strikingly similar to Locke's view, with one major exception: Johnson, unlike Locke, emphasizes the danger of solitude acting in conjunction with self-dissatisfaction to bring about delusions and stresses the curative influence of society. But this emphasis merely supplements the Lockean analysis of madness. Locke is interested in tracing the machinery of the individual mind, while Johnson, accepting Locke's view of mental mechanisms and their disorders, looks abroad to note the part played by the individual's commerce with his fellows.

❧ 3 ☙

This broader view is in many ways reminiscent of Burton's reiterated warnings against solitude and idleness; and since Johnson's respect for *The Anatomy of Melancholy* is very well known, it is useful to ask, as a means of gaining perspective on the Lockean parallels which I have pointed out, how closely Johnson's views on the dangers of the imagination match those of Burton.[12] An examina-

---

12. Boswell records Johnson's observation that *The Anatomy of Melancholy* "was the only book that ever took him out of bed two hours sooner than he wished to rise" and his judgment that it "is a valuable work. It is, perhaps, overloaded with quotation. But there is great spirit and great power in what Burton says, when he writes from his own mind." In a letter to Boswell dated October 27, 1779, Johnson wrote that "the great direction which Burton has left to men disordered like you, is this, *Be not solitary; be not idle:* which I would thus modify;—if you are idle, be not solitary; if you are solitary, be not idle" (James Boswell, *The Life of Samuel Johnson*, ed. G. B. Hill, rev. L. F. Powell [Oxford, 1934–50], II, 121, 440; III, 415).

Despite his evident regard for *The Anatomy of Melancholy*, however, there are, according to Lewis Freed, only twenty citations from Burton in Vol. I of

tion of his work reveals that Burton, like Johnson and Locke, stresses the hazards of indulging too frequently in the imaginary delights of building "castles in the air" and otherwise indulging in "phantastical meditations" from which, after a while, it becomes impossible to break away in order to go about our "more necessary business." [13] If anything, Burton speaks out even more strongly than either Locke or Johnson on the dangerous consequences of unchecked imagination. For this reason *The Anatomy of Melancholy* must certainly be assigned an important place in the intellectual tradition which led to and must in some measure have accounted for the bent of Johnson's moral instruction.

But the very force of Burton's cautions against the dangers of imagination is a measure of an important difference between his discussions of the subject and those of Locke and Johnson. Burton, grounding his theories on a more rigid conception of the difference between madness and sanity, was inclined to point out how "phantastical imaginations" lead not to the kind of partial and mostly concealed insanity from which the astronomer suffers but rather to the most violent forms of total derangement. Thus, in a passage which is the closest parallel in *The Anatomy of Melancholy* to Imlac's discourse in Chapter XLIV of *Rasselas*, Burton begins, like Imlac, by pointing out that solitude may lead to indulgence in "a thousand phantastical imaginations" which, while pleasant at first, become habitual and then inescapable, after which "fear and sorrow supplant those pleasing thoughts, suspicion, discontent, and perpetual anxiety succeed in their places." Imlac, however, carries his analysis only to the point of explaining that eventually "fictions begin to operate as realities, false opinions fasten upon the mind, and life passes in dreams of rapture or

---

Johnson's *Dictionary*, whereas there are 1,674 from the works of Locke. No doubt this disparity is primarily an index of Johnson's evaluation of Burton's lexicographical utility, but it may also reveal a higher regard for Locke's general philosophical value.

13. Robert Burton, *The Anatomy of Melancholy*, ed. Floyd Dell and Paul Jordan-Smith (New York, 1955), p. 214.

of anguish." He leaves open the possibility that, even though life may pass away in dreams, those dreams will be pleasant, whereas Burton emphasizes that "melancholy, this feral fiend," is the inevitable outcome of unchecked imagination. Moreover, Burton points to some physiological effects by noting that in time the dreamers' "bodies are lean and dried up, withered, ugly, their looks harsh, very dull, and their souls tormented, as they are more or less intangled." [14] Then Burton proceeds, as Imlac does not, to point out (following "Rhasis the Arabian") the three degrees of derangement which succeed one another as the victim succumbs to the disease he has brought upon himself: "The first is false conceits and idle thoughts: to misconstrue and amplify, aggravating every thing they conceive or fear; the second is to talk to themselves, or to use inarticulate, incondite voices. . . . The third is to put in practice that which they think or speak." [15]

The ultimate and evidently inevitable outcome of indulging in "phantastical imaginations," according to Burton, is that those "that have been so affected . . . go smiling to themselves at first, at length they laugh out; at first solitary, at last they can endure no company: or, if they do, they are now dizzards, past sense and shame, quite moped, they care not what they say or do, *all their actions, words, gestures, are furious or ridiculous*" [italics added]. [16] This statement, unlike Locke's differentiation between idiots and madmen, cannot

14. *Ibid.*, p. 346.

15. *Ibid.*, pp. 346–47.

16. *Ibid.*, p. 347. Burton goes on to amplify his general statement and make it more graphic by explaining that "at first his mind is troubled, he doth not attend what is said, if you tell him a tale, he cries at last, what said you? but in the end he mutters to himself, as old women do many times, or old men when they sit alone, upon a sudden they laugh, whoop, halloo, or run away, and swear they see or hear Players, Devils, Hobgoblins, Ghosts, strike, or strut, &c. grow humorous in the end: like him in the Poet, he often keeps two hundred slaves, often only ten, he will dress himself, and undress, careless at last, grows insensible, stupid, or mad. He howls like a wolf, barks like a dog, and raves like Ajax and Orestes, hears Musick and outcries which no man else hears."

serve as a rationale for Johnson's portrait of the astronomer because, as I have pointed out, he is, though suffering from "a degree of insanity," perfectly willing to see people. "He admits a few friends once a month to hear his deductions. . . . To his closest retreat, at his most busy moment all are admitted that want his assistance"; at the same time he is thoroughly sensible in everything save what touches on his one great delusion and even aware that he must be very cautious about broaching that subject. He is hardly "past sense and shame."

Johnson is referring to the commonly accepted notion of insanity when he makes Imlac remark that "all power of fancy over reason" is, though a "degree of insanity," not in fact "*pronounced* madness but when it becomes ungovernable, and apparently influences speech or action." This observation may be compared with Burton's conventional observation that

Madness is therefore defined to be a vehement *dotage,* or raving without a fever, far more violent than *melancholy,* full of anger and clamour, horrible looks, actions, gestures, troubling the patients with far greater vehemency both of body and mind, without all fear and sorrow, with such impetuous force & boldness, that sometimes three or four men cannot hold them. Differing only in this from *phrenzy,* that it is without a fever, and their memory is most part better.[17]

This definition, unlike Locke's explanation of insanity, sets up a very rigid distinction between it and normalcy, whereas Johnson, like Locke, is vigorously calling attention to the fact that certain delusions brought about in part by overindulged imagination must be regarded as "a degree of insanity" even though they do not result in totally deranged behavior. Whether Burton meant to suggest that solitary dreaming must inevitably lead to total madness, or whether he meant to leave open the possibility that one could stop at either the first or second step in the progress he outlines, the fact remains that in that discussion, as in his entire section "Of the Force of Imagination," he points out much more explicitly than either Locke or Johnson the

17. *Ibid.,* p. 122.

physical and mental extremes toward which unchecked imagination can lead.[18] Johnson, like Locke, is more concerned with pointing out less violent and hitherto insufficiently remarked forms of madness, labeling them as such, and relating them to the "power of fancy" and the association of ideas. Neither Johnson nor Locke is opposed to the conventional views represented in *The Anatomy of Melancholy*, but each man is interested in refining upon those views for strikingly similar didactic purposes of encouraging "greater care in . . . prevention and cure."

❧ 4 ☙

Another vantage point from which the parallels between Locke and Johnson can be placed in perspective is that of the religious literature which we know Johnson read. For this purpose it is illuminating to see what Jeremy Taylor and Robert South have to say about the dangers of imagination. Both discuss this issue, and, though their discussions are not identical, each illustrates an important aspect of the Anglican homiletic background out of which, partly in agreement and partly in opposition or at least divergence, Johnson's moral essays grew.

In *The Rule and Exercises of Holy Living*, Taylor provides two

18. Among the "wonderful effects and power of" imagination which Burton discusses in his section "Of the Force of Imagination" are "ecstasies" which cause people to "lie whole days together in a trance," vices such as "anger, revenge, lust, ambition, covetousness, which prefers falsehood before that which is right and good, deluding the soul with false shows and suppositions," imaginative visions of "bugbears, Devils, Witches, Goblins," and a variety of physiological effects. Imagination, Burton explains, "works not in sick and melancholy men only, but even most forcibly sometimes in such as are sound: it makes them suddenly sick, and alters their temperature, in an instant. And sometimes a strong conceit or apprehension, as Valesius proves, will take away diseases: in both kinds it will produce real effects. . . . Sometimes death itself is caused by force of phantasy" (*ibid.*, pp. 220–22). For other references to the power of imagination, see pp. 219, 458–59, 469.

warnings against indulging in what he calls "imaginative pleasure." The first occurs as the twelfth of nineteen rules designed to guide us in "Acts or Offices of Humility." It advises us to

Entertain no fancies of vanity and private whispers of this devil of pride: such as was that of Nebuchadnezzar: "Is not this great Babylon, which I have built for the honour of my name, and the might of my majesty, and the power of my kingdom?" Some fantastic spirits will walk alone, and dream waking of greatnesses, of palaces, of excellent orations, full theaters, loud applauses, sudden advancement, great fortunes, and so will spend an hour with imaginative pleasure; all their employment being nothing but fumes of pride and secret indefinite desires and significations of what their heart wishes. In this, although there is nothing of its own nature directly vicious, yet it is either an ill mother or an ill daughter, an ill sign or an ill effect; and therefore at no hand consisting with the safety and interests of humility.[19]

Thus Taylor, unlike Burton, Locke, and Johnson, sees nothing inherently dangerous about "imaginative pleasure" ("there is nothing of its own nature directly vicious") but nevertheless condemns it on the purely religious grounds that it encourages the sin of pride. Similarly, when he comes to discuss "helps to increase our Love to God, as a habit," Taylor advises us to "lay fetters and restraints upon the imaginative and fantastic part; because our fancy, being an imperfect and higher faculty, is usually pleased with the entertainment of shadows and gauds: and because the things of the world fill it with such beauties and fantastic imagery, the fancy presents such objects as are amiable to the affections and elective powers."[20] This condemnation

19. Jeremy Taylor, *Holy Living and Dying: Together With Prayers Containing the Whole Duty of a Christian and the Parts of Devotion Fitted to All Occasions, and Furnished for All Necessities* (London, 1867), p. 76. There are, according to Freed's count, 138 citations from *Holy Living* in Vol. 1 of Johnson's *Dictionary*.

20. *Ibid.*, pp. 178–79. Taylor goes on to complete his paragraph by remarking that "persons of fancy, such as are women and children, have always the most violent loves; but, therefore, if we be careful with what representments

of unchecked fancy is made on the equally religious ground that
it hinders essential otherworldly attitudes by making us too fond of
the beauties of this earth. Although Johnson approved sufficiently of
the passage to draw upon it for illustrations of *imaginative* and *imagery* in his *Dictionary*, he nevertheless in his own moral essays and
in *Rasselas* turned away from the kind of religious warnings provided
by Taylor in order to emphasize the purely secular and psychological
dangers of the imagination that had been pointed out by Burton and
Locke.

In one respect, however, Johnson's concern with the dangers of the
imagination does parallel the kind of warning which is found in such
Anglican sermons as those of Robert South. Johnson explains (in the
Rambler, No. 8) how by imagining certain future pleasures we may
be led to immoral actions.[21] Similarly, in the first of seven "Discourses
Concerning Temptation," South observes that the second degree of
temptation to evil is "when a Man does not only think upon a sinful
Object, or Proposal, but also suffers his Thoughts to dwell, and (as it
were) to *brood* upon it with *Delight;* pleasing his Imagination by
frequent Reflections upon it, and representing it to himself under its
most advantageous Colours and Circumstances, while he thus turns
and rolls it about in his Fancy." [22] Later, in "The Seventh Discourse
concerning Temptation," South remarks even more emphatically that

---

we fill our fancy, we may the sooner rectify our love. To this purpose it is
good that we transplant the instruments of fancy into religion; and for this
reason music was brought into churches, and ornaments, and perfumes, and
comely garments, and solemnities, and decent ceremonies, that the busy and
less discerning fancy, being bribed with its proper objects, may be instrumental
to a more celestial and spiritual love."

21. South's sermons are cited more frequently in Johnson's *Dictionary* than
those of any other seventeenth-century preacher. In Vol. I alone there are,
according to Freed's count, 1,092 quotations taken from South, and this fact is
sufficient evidence of Johnson's interest and general approval. See also my
article "Robert South, William Law, and Samuel Johnson," *SEL*, VI (Summer, 1966), 499–528.

22. Robert South, *Sermons and Discourses on Several Subjects and Occasions* (6 vols.; London, 1715, 1717), VI, 168.

the first and generally the most fatal Way, by which the Tempter accosts a Man, is by the Suggestion of evil Thoughts; for when the Temptation is once lodged in the *Imagination,* he knows it is in the next neighbourhood to the *Affections,* and from the *Affections* that it is usually no long Step to the *Actions,* and that when it once reaches them, he is pretty sure, that his Work is then done.[23]

Johnson does not refer to Satan, nor does he emphasize the moral dangers of the imagination as frequently as he emphasizes the more purely psychological dangers, but it is nevertheless important to recognize that there is a significant tradition of religious concern with the dangerous prevalence of imagination. This tradition is partially reflected in, and must in some ways have given impetus to, Johnson's own treatment of that theme.

These brief remarks have hardly exhausted the religious backgrounds of Johnson's warnings against the "power of fancy." For example, More, Glanvill, Rust, and Hallywell, members of the group recently described as "Anglican rationalists," provided a physiological explanation of those melancholy imaginings which lead, in their opinion, to the dangerous excesses of religious enthusiasm, and their warning against such pernicious religious consequences of unchecked imagination is another noteworthy aspect of the Anglican homiletic tradition which must be taken into account when considering the backgrounds of Johnson's moral essays.[24] But since my subject

23. *Ibid.,* p. 397.
24. For an account of the Anglican rationalists, see Phillip Harth, *Swift and Anglican Rationalism* (Chicago, 1961), especially Chap. IV ("Reason and Imagination"), pp. 101–53. After pointing out that in their anti-Puritan polemics the Anglican rationalists frequently indulged in hyperbolic description of their antagonists as "mad," or "fit for Bedlam," Harth observes that "when they come to a clinical discussion of enthusiasm as the effect of a redundancy of vapors they tend to become more accurate and to distinguish the melancholy of enthusiasm from true madness" (p. 112). In making this distinction, as Harth also points out, the Anglican rationalists were accepting the conventional definition of madness explained in such works as Burton's *Anatomy of Melancholy.* In this respect then, as well as in their warning that unchecked imagination may usurp the function of reason and thus lead to the

in this chapter is the relationship between Johnson and Locke, I hope that what I have said about Taylor and South has been sufficient to suggest both the multiplicity of influences that may have shaped Johnson's statements and the equally significant fact that in many ways Johnson, as a moralist, is closer to the secular and naturalistic tradition represented by Burton and Locke than to the religious and homiletic tradition represented by the Anglican divines. Certainly the parallels in doctrine and method between Locke and Johnson should make us hesitate to rule out the possibility of direct causal influence, and the number and nature of these parallels must surely make us give over any attempt to characterize the moral essays and *Rasselas* in terms of oppositions between science and morality. We must, instead, note the remarkable ways in which Johnson was able to transcend this distinction in his consideration of the moral discipline of the mind.

---

religious error of enthusiasm, the Anglican rationalists differ from Johnson, who accepted Locke's more novel definition of insanity and did not provide warnings against the dangerous prevalence of imagination primarily to discourage religious enthusiasm. It should also be noted that, as Harth observes, the Anglican rationalists "were 'rationalists' indeed, in the philosophical sense; for as supporters of a theory that reason is a separate source of knowledge, superior to and independent of the senses and the imagination, they were altogether distinct from those contemporary empiricists—the physico-theologians—who also emphasized the importance of reason in religion, but on quite different grounds" (p. 146). Johnson, however, was anything but a rationalist in the epistemology he accepted, and his empiricism is another important difference between his views and those of the Anglican rationalists. This difference may help to account for the fact that although Locke is cited 1,674 times in Vol. I of Johnson's *Dictionary*, Henry More is only cited 54 times.

Chapter IV

Freedom and

Voluntary Delusion

In *Rasselas,* Imlac remarks to Nekayah, Pekuah, and the Prince that "disorders of the intellect . . . happen much more often than superficial observers will easily believe." Then Johnson, who had painful knowledge of his own disorders as well as firsthand experience of the derangements which plagued such Grub Street acquaintances as Savage and Smart, and who was very far indeed from being a superficial observer of human nature, makes Imlac continue his observations with the reflection that "perhaps, if we speak with rigorous exactness, no human mind is in its right state." This perceptive conviction, so rare in the eighteenth century, goes far to explain the approach taken by Johnson throughout his moral essays. If he had not been convinced that some degree of mental imbalance is almost inevitable, he never would have been as concerned with the application of "mental anatomy" to the problems of moral discipline. Instead, he might have spent more time merely telling people how they *ought* to behave, without considering the various states of mind which help or hinder efforts to live up to such ideal standards. But in fact he extensively considers those mental dispositions or indispositions which lead to moral or immoral actions: and that consideration of what he called the "fountains of morality" is almost certainly Johnson's most enduring contribution as a moralist.

The permanent value of Johnson's moral essays may also be explained in part by his assumption that mere knowledge of the right pathway through the wilderness of this world—or even, paradoxically, theoretical knowledge of how to stay on that pathway—will in practice insure neither virtuous conduct nor freedom from disorders of intellect. He clearly recognized that "there will always be a wide interval between practical and ideal excellence; and, therefore, if we allow not ourselves to be satisfied while we can perceive any errour or defect, we must refer our hopes of ease to some other period of existence." [1] He also observed:

It sometimes happens that too close an attention to minute exactness, or a too rigorous habit of examining every thing by the standard of perfection, vitiates the temper, rather than improves the understanding, and teaches the mind to discern faults with unhappy penetration. . . . Knowledge and genius are often enemies to quiet, by suggesting ideas of excellence, which men and the performances of men cannot attain. [2]

Because Johnson did believe that overly scrupulous concern with "the standard of perfection" would vitiate the temper rather than improve the understanding, his moral essays avoid setting unattainable goals

1. *Rambler*, No. 112.
2. *Rambler*, No. 74.

and are largely confined to the consideration of how we can bring ourselves as close as is practically possible—and desirable—to our theoretically "right state."

He seldom forgot that men are hedged round with obstacles which obstruct their progress towards perfection. In Johnson's view, such obstructions are made still more troublesome by various "disorders of intellect" which make it doubly hard to surmount outward difficulties. But the effect of these disorders can be minimized even though, as Imlac goes on to explain, "There is no man, whose imagination does not, sometimes, predominate over his reason, who can regulate his attention wholly by his will, and whose ideas will come and go at his command." [3] Hence, no one can ever completely achieve what Johnson refers to in the *Rambler*, No. 7, as "that conquest of the world and ourselves, which has been always considered as the perfection of human nature." Much can be accomplished, however, if one knows where to start. Therefore, Johnson frequently calls attention to the external influences and inner states which limit the role played by reason in our mental life and thereby circumscribe our freedom.

He remarks in the "Life of Collins," for example, that "in a long continuance of poverty, and long habits of dissipation, it cannot be expected that any character should be exactly uniform. There is a degree of want, by which the freedom of agency is almost destroyed; and long association with fortuitous companions will, at last, relax the strictness of truth, and abate the fervour of sincerity." [4] Similarly, in the *Life of Savage* Johnson observes that "an irregular and dissipated manner of life had made [Savage] the slave of every passion that happened to be excited by the presence of its object, and that slavery to his passions reciprocally produced a life irregular and dissipated. He was not master of his own motions." [5] Both of these remarks illustrate Johnson's profound realization that external circumstances

3. *Rasselas* (*The Works of Samuel Johnson* [9 vols.; Oxford, 1825], I, 293). (Cited hereafter as *Works*.)
4. *Works*, VIII, 402.
5. *Works*, VIII, 188–89.

may not only circumscribe but may practically destroy all freedom of agency, if no steps are—or can be—taken in time to prevent this destruction. Such awareness is more usual now than it was in the eighteenth century. Moreover, Johnson realized that his outlook was somewhat novel, because he wrote in the *Rambler*, No. 184, that "it is not commonly observed, how much, even of actions, considered as particularly subject to choice, is to be attributed to accident, or some cause out of our own power, by whatever name it be distinguished." [6] The significance of this statement becomes even more striking when it is recalled that in his *Dictionary* Johnson's second definition of *will* is "Choice." Thus he is calling attention to the numerous situations in which freedom of agency is severely limited: to the large number "even of actions considered as particularly subject to choice"—that is, to *will*—which in fact are actions set in motion by "some cause out of our own power." The extent to which Johnson recognized, if never complete social or psychological determinism, at least severe restrictions on free will has not been sufficiently appreciated, although it plays an important part in setting the tone of his moral essays and literary criticism.

Though he certainly holds the individual morally accountable for his conduct, Johnson's sympathetic awareness of the social pressures that are in many instances "out of our power" ultimately prevents his moral essays from degenerating into coldly doctrinaire prescriptions.

6. Although Johnson maintains that a large part of our conduct is "out of our power" he nevertheless denies that we are governed by mere chance and concludes that it is God's will which really determines this portion of our conduct: "In this state of universal uncertainty, where a thousand dangers hover about us, and none can tell whether the good that he pursues is not evil in disguise, or whether the next step will lead him to safety or destruction, nothing can afford any rational tranquillity, but the conviction that, however we amuse ourselves with unideal sounds, nothing in reality is governed by chance, but that the universe is under the perpetual superintendence of Him who created it; that our being is in the hands of Omnipotent Goodness, by whom what appears casual to us, is directed for ends ultimately kind and merciful; and that nothing can finally hurt him who debars not himself from the divine favour."

He explains what is ethically desirable but also suggests how difficult it often is, even with the best intentions, to follow "the standard of perfection." Moreover, his keen realization that beyond a certain point the individual is powerless to shape his own destiny lends a peculiar urgency to the prescriptions that Johnson does venture to put forward. Tough-minded advice confined to what is possible is bound to have more enduring value than facile explanations of what *ought* to be done in every situation. Continued interest in the content of Johnson's moral essays is unquestionably due in large measure to the fact that he never blandly assumed that where there is a will there is a way.

In Johnson's literary criticism, the extent to which he recognized severe restrictions on free will had two consequences. First, it strengthened his acceptance of the historical and biographical approach to literature by making him alert to the fact that an author's literary performances will be just as subject as the rest of his conduct to influences "out of his power" and that such external circumstances must therefore be taken into account in order to arrive at an accurate evaluation of what a writer is himself responsible for and what, on the other hand, he cannot help doing. Thus Johnson's awareness of how sharply external circumstances may reduce freedom of agency partly accounts for his declaration that

Every man's performances, to be rightly estimated, must be compared with the state of the age in which he lived, and with his own particular opportunities; and though to the reader a book be not worse or better for the circumstances of the author, yet, as there is always a silent reference of human works to human abilities, and as the inquiry, how far man may extend his designs, or how high he may rate his native force, is of far greater dignity than in what rank we shall place any particular performance, curiosity is always busy to discover the instruments, as well as to survey the workmanship, to know how much is to be ascribed to original powers, and how much to casual and adventitious help.[7]

7. "Preface to Shakespeare" (*Works*, V, 124).

The second notable effect on Johnson's literary criticism of his awareness that unlimited free will does not exist appears in his immediate
response to the rise of the novel. The impact of *Pamela, Joseph
Andrews, Clarissa,* and *Tom Jones* was not lost on Johnson, for he
was among those who immediately realized that the new genre was
unlike any species of romance that had been known before and was
likely to be vastly more influential than most other forms of literature. In 1750—only one year after the appearance of *Tom Jones,*
whose hero is presented as worthy of imitation despite some notable
frailties of the flesh—Johnson observed:

> In the romances formerly written, every transaction and sentiment
> was so remote from all that passes among men, that the reader was in
> very little danger of making any applications to himself; the virtues
> and crimes were equally beyond his sphere of activity; and he amused
> himself with heroes and with traitors, deliverers and persecutors, as
> with beings of another species, whose actions were regulated upon
> motives of their own, and who had neither faults nor excellencies in
> common with himself.
> But when an adventurer is levelled with the rest of the world, and
> acts in such scenes of the universal drama, as may be the lot of any
> other man; young spectators fix their eyes upon him with closer
> attention, and hope, by observing his behaviour and success, to regu-
> late their own practices, when they shall be engaged in the like
> part.
> For this reason these familiar histories may, perhaps, be made of
> greater use than the solemnities of professed morality, and convey the
> knowledge of vice and virtue with more efficacy than axioms and
> definitions. But *if the power of example is so great as to take posses-
> sion of the memory by a kind of violence, and produce effects almost
> without the intervention of the will,* care ought to be taken, that,
> when the choice is unrestrained, the best examples only should be
> exhibited; and that which is likely to operate so strongly, should not
> be mischievous or uncertain in its effects [italics added].[8]

The implication of the passage I have italicized is clear: Johnson
saw, with some alarm, that "familiar histories" must be numbered

8. *Rambler,* No. 4.

among the influences which can severely limit freedom of agency by producing "effects almost without the intervention of the will."

Consequently, he asserted that "the fear of not being approved as just copiers of human manners, is not the most important concern that an author of this sort ought to have before him." [9] Johnson believed that the *novelist's* most important concern should be to refrain from abusing his immense power by limiting himself to the selective portrayal of conduct that is either worthy of imitation or else clearly contemptible:

In narratives, where historical veracity has no place, I cannot discover why there should not be exhibited the most perfect idea of virtue; of virtue not angelical, nor above probability (for what we cannot credit, we shall never imitate), but the highest and purest that humanity can reach, which, exercised in such trials as the various revolutions of things shall bring upon it, may, by conquering some calamities, and enduring others, teach us what we may hope, and what we can perform. Vice, for vice is necessary to be shown, should always disgust; nor should the graces of gaiety, or the dignity of courage, be so united with it, as to reconcile it to the mind. Wherever it appears, it should raise hatred by the malignity of its practices, and contempt by the meanness of its stratagems: for while it is supported by either parts or spirit, it will be seldom heartily abhorred. The Roman tyrant was content to be hated, if he was but feared; and there are thousands of the readers of romances willing to be thought wicked, if they may be allowed to be wits.[10]

Thus, in Johnson's view, the novel must be judged above all by the criterion of its moral effects, because of the special nature of its influence.

So far as I am aware, Johnson always maintained this opinion, although he did not consider it necessary to apply the same measure quite so rigorously to either drama or poetry. He does reproach Shakespeare's lack of moral purpose, but he also asserts in the "Life of Addison" that

9. *Ibid.*
10. *Ibid.*

whatever pleasure there may be in seeing crimes punished and virtue rewarded, yet, since wickedness often prospers in real life, the poet is certainly at liberty to give it prosperity on the stage. For if poetry is an imitation of reality, how are its laws broken by exhibiting the world in its true form? The stage may sometimes gratify our wishes; but, if it be truly the "mirror of life," it ought to show us sometimes what we are to expect.[11]

He remarked of *The Beggar's Opera* that

the play, like many others, was plainly written only to divert, without any moral purpose, and is, therefore, not likely to do good; nor can it be conceived, without more speculation than life requires or admits, to be productive of much evil. Highwaymen and housebreakers seldom frequent the play-house, or mingle in any elegant diversion; nor is it possible for any one to imagine that he may rob with safety, because he sees Macheath reprieved upon the stage.[12]

Johnson did not believe that either drama or poetry could short-circuit the higher faculties as prose fiction may: only a novel can produce "effects almost without the intervention of will." Therefore, it is most important to prevent that particular genre from becoming pernicious. It is significant that Johnson qualifies his statement: a novel cannot *totally* subvert the will. But it is equally noteworthy that, in his opinion, it can *almost* do so. This is one of the many illustrations of Johnson's conviction that "most minds are the slaves of external circumstances."

The primary source of such slavery, however, is not the powerfully coercive action of external influences but the intellectual disorders which predispose an individual to fall under the sway of external circumstances. In Johnson's view, no one is ever wholly free from such disorders or at liberty to govern his thoughts entirely as he would choose.[13] Yet Johnson never allowed these limitations upon the

---

11. *Works*, VII, 458.

12. "Life of Gay" (*Works*, VIII, 68).

13. In the *Rambler*, No. 8, Johnson gives some advice on how to bring under control certain trains of thought which, if not checked, could lead a person into immoral conduct. But he also remarks that "our thoughts on present things being determined by the objects before us, fall not under those

exercise of free will to excuse abject submission to immoral impulses or corrupting influences. "Though the boast of absolute independence is ridiculous and vain," he wrote in the *Rambler*, No. 6, "yet a mean flexibility to every impulse, and a patient submission to the tyranny of casual troubles, is below the dignity of that mind, which, however depraved or weakened, boasts its derivation from a celestial original, and hopes for an union with infinite goodness, and unvariable felicity." It is thus up to every individual to resist "a mean flexibility to impulse." As I have pointed out, Johnson always insisted that we are morally accountable for our actions. Although quick to appreciate the force of mitigating circumstances as well as the very real limitations

---

indulgences, or excursions, which I am now considering. But I cannot forbear, under this head, to caution pious and tender minds, that are disturbed by the irruptions of wicked imaginations, against too great dejection, and too anxious alarms; for thoughts are only criminal, when they are first chosen, and then voluntarily continued." This remark implicitly demonstrates Johnson's conviction that we are not at liberty to choose all our thoughts.

Johnson's statement may be compared with Locke's expression (in Book II, Chap. xxi, par. 12 of *An Essay Concerning Human Understanding*) of what is essentially the same opinion. "As it is in the motions of the body," Locke observes (in a sentence which Johnson chose to illustrate the third meaning of *liberty* in his *Dictionary*), "so it is in the thoughts of our minds: where any one is such, that we have power to take it up or lay it by, according to the preference of the mind, there we are at liberty. A waking man, being under the necessity of having some ideas constantly in his mind, is not at liberty to think or not to think; no more than he is at liberty, whether his body shall touch any other or no: but whether he will remove his contemplation from one idea to another is many times in his choice; and then he is, in respect of his ideas, as much at liberty as he is in respect of bodies he rests on; he can at pleasure remove himself from one to another. But yet some ideas to the mind, like some motions to the body, are such as in certain circumstances it cannot avoid, nor obtain their absence by the utmost effort it can use. A man on the rack is not at liberty to lay by the idea of pain, and divert himself with other contemplations: and sometimes a boisterous passion hurries our thoughts, as a hurricane does our bodies, without leaving us the liberty of thinking on other things, which we would rather choose. But as soon as the mind regains the power to stop or continue, begin or forbear, any of these motions of the body without, or thoughts within, according as it thinks fit to prefer either to the other, we then consider the man as a *free agent* again."

upon freedom of agency, he was nevertheless strongly opposed to all doctrines which affirm complete social or psychological determinism.

He was equally opposed to people who, like "the deep-read Misothea," endeavor "to demonstrate the folly of attributing choice and self-direction to any human being," for Johnson feared that a widespread acceptance of determinism would tear apart the fabric of society by weakening the bonds of mutual responsibility which bind individuals together in stable cooperation.[14] Even if Revelation had not taught that deterministic doctrines are morally pernicious, Johnson would have asserted men's capacity for free will, just as he affirmed the importance of telling the truth and forgiving injuries, by explaining that, unless such principles are upheld, the edifice of civilized society will collapse in ruins, and every man will then be forced to "disunite himself from others, inhabit his own cave, and seek prey only for himself." [15]

But, as I have suggested, Johnson firmly believed that man's capacity for free will and his actual exercise of that capacity are two very different matters. Because Johnson did not look upon free will as a static feature of our mental anatomy but regarded it instead as an emergent power dependent upon the properly harmonious cooperation of the intellectual faculties, and all too easily stifled if they are disordered, he devoted a major portion of his attention throughout the moral essays to considering those conditions under which—and

14. *Rambler*, No. 113.

15. *Idler*, No. 20. In the *Rambler*, No. 185, Johnson observes that "scarcely any law of our Redeemer is more openly transgressed, or more industriously evaded, than that by which he commands his followers to forgive injuries, and prohibits, under the sanction of eternal misery, the gratification of the desire which every man feels to return pain upon him that inflicts it. Many who could have conquered their anger, are unable to combat pride, and pursue offences to extremity of vengeance, lest they should be insulted by the triumph of an enemy. But certainly no precept could better become him, at whose birth *peace* was proclaimed *to the earth*. For, what would so soon destroy all the order of society, and deform life with violence and ravage, as a permission to every one to judge his own cause, and to apportion his own recompense for imagined injuries?"

only under which—man can exercise his capacity for freedom. In *The Vision of Theodore* he allegorically asserts that religion must ultimately come to the aid of reason in order to insure freedom from domination by habits, appetites, and passions. This suggests, in a general way, that faith is the indispensable requisite for insuring freedom of agency. The moral essays themselves, however, are primarily confined to consideration of what can be accomplished by a rational approach to the problem.

In them, Johnson for the most part leaves faith, along with the problem of how best to achieve it, to the theologians. He restricts his discussions to explanations of how various obstacles may be overcome by the proper application of reason to dispel ignorance. "Every errour in human conduct," he asserts emphatically in the *Rambler*, No. 24, "must arise from ignorance in ourselves, either perpetual or temporary; and happen either because we do not know what is best and fittest, or because our knowledge is at the time of action not present to the mind." To achieve the greatest possible freedom of agency, the most important form of knowledge, in Johnson's view, is undoubtedly self-knowledge. But it is also the hardest to obtain, because of the proliferation of what Johnson refers to in the *Rambler*, No. 8, as "the artifices of self-deceit." Consequently, the ways of recognizing and avoiding self-deception are among the most persistently recurring and brilliantly explored topics of the Johnsonian canon.

❧ 2 ❧

Johnson's earliest extensive discussion of what he later called "the arts of voluntary delusion" [16] is found in the *Life of Savage*, where he observes that Savage "was always able to live at peace with himself" by refusing to admit the part played by his own faults in bringing about many of the misfortunes that overwhelmed him. Savage was "always applauding his past conduct, or, at least, forgetting it to

16. *Rambler*, No. 146.

amuse himself with phantoms of happiness, which were dancing before him; and willingly turned his eyes from the light of reason,
when it would have discovered the illusion, and shown him, what he
never wished to see, his real state." After describing some of the ways
in which Savage managed to avoid admitting—even to himself—what
he was really like, Johnson observes that "arts like these" are in fact
"arts which every man practises in some degree, and to which too
much of the little tranquillity of life is to be ascribed." [17] It is certainly
true, as W. B. C. Watkins has pointed out, that Johnson "recognized
as clearly as Swift the complex defenses of the human mind and the
role of deception." [18] The moral essays surely surpass Swift's satire
(which has other goals) in providing a thoroughly objective exploration and enumeration of the various forms, causes, cures, and consequences of self-deception.

It is characteristic of Johnson that his earliest extended discussion of
self-deception not only sets forth the dangerous consequences of "the
artifices of self-deceit" but also points out the advantages gained by
practicing such deceptions and even suggests when it is proper—or at
least harmless—to do so. Johnson observes of Savage that had he

indeed only made use of these expedients to alleviate the loss or want
of fortune or reputation, or any other advantages, which it is not in
man's power to bestow upon himself, they might have been justly
mentioned as instances of a philosophical mind, and very properly
proposed to the imitation of multitudes, who, for want of diverting
their imaginations with the same dexterity, languish under afflictions
which might be easily removed.[19]

Thus Johnson did not see any great harm in those minor self-
deceptions which enable a man to bear up more cheerfully than he
otherwise might under misfortunes that are beyond his control and
which no amount of fretting, or unclouded insight, will alleviate.

---

17. *Works*, VIII, 143–44.
18. *Perilous Balance: the Tragic Genius of Swift, Johnson, and Sterne*
(Cambridge, 1960), p. 42.
19. *Life of Savage* (*Works*, VIII, 143).

Johnson never insisted upon unnecessary acts of fortitude: he realized how little point there often is in dwelling upon unpleasant facts. That is why he also observes, in the *Rambler*, No. 98, that "unnecessarily to obtrude unpleasing ideas, is a species of oppression. . . . It is little more criminal to deprive another of some real advantage, than to interrupt that forgetfulness of its absence which is the next happiness to actual possession." Johnson regarded tranquillity as sufficiently rare to be more than welcome even at the cost of some slight distortion or avoidance of truth.

In the *Life of Savage*, he goes on to observe:

It were, doubtless, to be wished, that truth and reason were universally prevalent; that every thing were esteemed according to its real value; and that men would secure themselves from being disappointed in their endeavours after happiness, by placing it only in virtue, which is always to be obtained; but, if adventitious and foreign pleasures must be pursued, it would be, perhaps, of some benefit, since that pursuit must frequently be fruitless, if the practice of Savage could be taught, that folly might be an antidote to folly, and one fallacy be obviated by another.[20]

This observation should give pause to those who accuse Johnson's moral stance of being as inflexible and outmoded as a suit of armor. On certain issues, as a Christian, he was adamant. On several points of conduct—such as the relative culpability of sexual lapses in men and women—he notoriously shared the prevailing social values of eighteenth-century England.[21] But he was never opposed to all compromise with the standard of perfection. "He, that does much good, may be allowed to do sometimes a little harm," Johnson observes in the *Idler*, No. 14, an essay as typical of his outlook as any of the more dogmatic statements which Boswell has assiduously recorded.

Johnson was able to see that limited advantages may legitimately be derived from practices that, in principle, are to be avoided whenever

20. *Ibid.*
21. See, for example, James Boswell, *The Life of Samuel Johnson*, ed. G. B. Hill, rev. L. F. Powell (Oxford, 1934–50), III, 406.

possible. One beneficial consequence of self-deception, for example (in addition to its role of providing tranquillity when nothing can be done to alter an unpleasant situation), is noted in the *Rambler*, No. 2. "There would . . . be few enterprises of great labour or hazard undertaken," Johnson asserts, "if we had not the power of magnifying the advantages which we persuade ourselves to expect from them." Since most of the world's progress has involved "great labour or hazard," self-delusion is, ironically, one of the great causes of progress, in Johnson's view. He also believed, however, that even those delusive expectations which do not result in any particular benefits are necessary forms of self-deception because, as he observes in the *Idler*, No. 58, "It is necessary to hope, tho' hope should always be deluded, for hope itself is happiness, and its frustrations, however frequent, are yet less dreadful than its extinction." [22]

Other consequences of self-deception, however, Johnson regarded as thoroughly harmful. He warns in the *Life of Savage* that "the danger of this pleasing intoxication must not be concealed," and then goes on to remark that Savage, "by imputing none of his miseries to himself . . . continued to act upon the same principles, and to follow the same path; was never made wiser by his sufferings, nor preserved by one misfortune from falling into another." [23] Thus the first dangerous consequence of self-delusion is moral: excessive indulgence in "this pleasing intoxication" leads to various failures in moral conduct, of which the most serious is the failure to grow either better or wiser. The second dangerous consequence of self-delusion is psychological as well as moral: habitual self-deception may prevent proper employ-

22. In the *Rambler*, No. 2, Johnson observes that "the natural flights of the human mind are not from pleasure to pleasure, but from hope to hope." He also observes in the *Rambler*, No. 203, that the surest hope is of eternal happiness and "on this therefore every mind ought finally to rest. Hope is the chief blessing of man, and that hope only is rational, of which we are certain that it cannot deceive us." Again in the *Rambler*, No. 67, he asserts that "hope is neessary in every condition."

23. *Works*, VIII, 143–44.

ment of our intellectual faculties and thereby lead to wickedness. Johnson observes in the *Rambler*, No. 31,

Men who cannot deceive others are very often successful in deceiving themselves; they weave their sophistry till their own reason is entangled, and repeat their positions till they are credited by themselves; by often contending, they grow sincere in the cause; and by long wishing for demonstrative arguments, they at last bring themselves to fancy that they have found them. They are then at the uttermost verge of wickedness, and may die without having that light rekindled in their minds, which their own pride and contumacy have extinguished.

In Johnson's view the moral and psychological consequences of self-deception are completely interwoven. Any willfully induced reduction of mental capacity, such as that brought about by "the arts of voluntary delusion," is criminal as well as socially and psychologically detrimental to the individual, because it prevents him from acting as rationally—and therefore as morally—as he would otherwise be able to. Consequently, willful extinction of the light of reason leads to "the uttermost verge of wickedness" and not merely to some handicap on the order of feeble-mindedness, which is to be pitied but not reproached. This opinion helps to explain why, as a moralist, Johnson was so profoundly concerned with the problem of self-deception.

He usually considered the cause together with each form of self-delusion in order to emphasize the relationship between particular delusions and the underlying "maladies of the mind" (as he calls them in *Rasselas*) which are responsible for all such disturbances. But he realized that there is not always a one-to-one relationship: several forms of self-deception may be traced to one cause or, conversely, several different causes may produce the same, or a similar, effect. Therefore, to appreciate Johnson's accomplishment I believe it is useful to discuss separately the forms of self-delusion described by him before proceeding to consider his explanations of their underlying causes and his remedial suggestions. It is thus possible to show that even though Johnson avoided anything that smacked of a systematic treatise, his practical suggestions on moral discipline flow from extensive, orderly groupings of distinct observations, on the one hand, and coherent theories explaining such observations, on the other.

❧ 3 ❧

In the *Life of Savage, Rasselas,* the biographical portions of the *Lives of the Poets,* and above all, in the great moral essays of the fifties, Johnson describes two major kinds of self-deception which are related, although decidedly different in their modes of operation. They are both referred to when he observes, in the *Rambler,* No. 104, that "we always think ourselves better than we are, and are generally desirous that others should think us still better than we think ourselves." The first large class of self-deceptions consists of devices for increasing or maintaining self-esteem. Usually Johnson regards these as causing us to refrain, as Savage too often did, from corrective or other necessary action. For so long as we are not prompted by some painful sense of dissatisfaction with ourselves, we are likely to remain (since, in Johnson's view, pleasure and pain determine our motivations), like Savage, treading "the same steps on the same circle." The second large class of self-deceptions, on the other hand, is composed of those which do goad us into activity but invariably lead to the wrong kind of action. Johnson usually regards this second major kind of self-deception as responsible for conduct designed to make others "think us still better than we think ourselves" and thus insure an income of praise that has not really been earned.

The first major class operates to increase self-esteem in two important ways, one of which, at least, may often be relatively harmless. First, and least dangerous in Johnson's view, this kind of self-delusion works to blunt judgment of what might be termed secular accomplishments—of, in other words, those literary, artistic, and other efforts that are not immediately related to morality. "The mind," as

Johnson remarks in the "Life of Pope," "is always enamoured of its own productions." Consequently, everyone persuades himself that his accomplishments are really admirable no matter what others may say. In the *Rambler*, No. 21, Johnson suggests why even "that judgment which appears so penetrating, when it is employed upon the works of others, very often fails" when it turns to evaluate its own efforts, "where interest or passion can exert their power":

We are blinded in examining our own labours by innumerable prejudices. Our juvenile compositions please us, because they bring to our minds the remembrance of youth; our later performances we are ready to esteem, because we are unwilling to think that we have made no improvement; what flows easily from the pen charms us, because we read with pleasure that which flatters our opinion of our own powers; what was composed with great struggles of the mind we do not easily reject, because we cannot bear that so much labour should be fruitless.

This explanation is not limited to literary composition but applies with equal force to most other human activities as well, because, as Johnson observes in the *Idler*, No. 70, "Vanity inclines us to find faults any where rather than in ourselves." In Johnson's view, our inclination to indulge in self-deceptions of this kind is almost impossible to eliminate. But it is comparatively harmless. The world will quickly enough pass its sentence upon the value of a man's accomplishments. If, in the meantime, he manages to cheer himself by resolutely maintaining a high opinion of his own endeavours, no great damage is done. Johnson, after all, had not suffered from having gone up to London under the illusion that the first draft of *Irene* was worth completing and producing.

The second way in which the first major kind of self-delusion operates is far more serious, because it blunts our judgments of those actions which are always immediately related to morality. A man can write a poor (though not a licentious) poem or paint a barely recognizable likeness without endangering his soul. Little harm is done if, in such matters, "every man willingly gives value to the praise which he receives, and considers the sentence passed in his favour as the sentence of discernment." [24] But there is greater danger in deceiving ourselves while taking stock of moral worth. Yet, as Johnson observes in the *Rambler,* No. 28, "We shall find almost all with whom we converse so nearly as to judge of their sentiments, indulging more favourable conceptions of their own virtue than they have been able to impress upon others, and congratulating themselves upon degrees of excellence, which their fondest admirers cannot allow them to have attained." This area of self-deception is widespread, even in the face of accurate criticism, because, as Johnson remarks in the *Rambler,* No. 76, "It is easy for every man, whatever be his character with others, to find reasons for esteeming himself, and therefore censure, contempt, or conviction of crimes, seldom deprive him of his own favour."

The great danger of maintaining such unwarranted self-esteem is evident, for without dissatisfaction there will be no moral reformation: men will continue, like Savage, "to tread the same steps on the same circle." Savage's *Life,* in fact, provides a classical illustration of the chief form taken by this kind of moral self-deception. "There are men," Johnson observes in the *Rambler,* No. 28, "who always confound the praise of goodness with the practice, and who believe themselves mild and moderate, charitable and faithful, because they have exerted their eloquence in commendation of mildness, fidelity, and other virtues." Johnson probably had Savage in mind when he made this statement, for six years earlier he had written of his friend that "the reigning errour of his life was, that he mistook the love for the practice of virtue, and was, indeed, not so much a good man as the friend of goodness." [25] Although commendable, it is never sufficient, for Johnson, to be the mere friend of goodness: virtue must be active—the more active the better, for, as Imlac remarks, "He that lives well in the world is better than he that lives well in a monastery." Therefore, all forms of self-delusion that paralyze or inhibit

24. "Life of Halifax" (*Works,* VII, 396).
25. *Life of Savage* (*Works,* VIII, 144).

impulses towards necessary activity and improvement are thoroughly destructive.

So, according to Johnson, are those self-deceptions which impel men towards any activity that is morally wrong. Delusions of this kind make up the second large class of self-deceptions which he describes. "There are," for example, "many ways of telling a secret, by which a man exempts himself from the reproaches of his conscience, and gratifies his pride, without suffering himself to believe that he impairs his virtue." [26] All the self-deceptions which prompt us to speak when we should be silent are just as destructive, although opposite in their effect, as those which make us passively hold our tongue or stay our hand when we should be active. Equally harmful are the closely related delusions which set in motion unwarranted psychological responses such as resentment of just criticism. Johnson observes in the *Rambler*, No. 155,

Self-love is often rather arrogant than blind; it does not hide our faults from ourselves, but persuades us that they escape the notice of others, and disposes us to resent censures lest we should confess them to be just. We are secretly conscious of defects and vices, which we hope to conceal from the publick eye, and please ourselves with innumerable impostures, by which, in reality, nobody is deceived.

This assertion suggests that, in Johnson's opinion, men often recognize their own faults while nevertheless reacting as though they did not exist, by overtly or covertly resenting perfectly accurate criticism on the deluded assumption that such faults somehow "escape the notice of others." This kind of wishful thinking may result in an angry refusal to admit even the most evident errors. It certainly results in "innumerable impostures."

Thus the same kind of wishful thinking responsible for unwillingness to accept criticism also causes a good deal of *affectation* ("An artificial shew; an elaborate appearance; a false pretense") and *hypocrisy* ("Dissimulation with regard to the moral or religious

26. *Rambler*, No. 13.

character").[27] In Johnson's view it is therefore self-deception cooperating with an immoderate degree of self-esteem which explains why some people persist in many deliberately affected or hypocritical attitudes that fool no one. Such people, who know their own shortcomings and are "secretly conscious of defects and vices," differ greatly from those who rely upon various self-delusions to conceal their faults from themselves and who are often unjustly accused of hypocrisy. "The truth is," Johnson observes in the *Idler*, No. 27, "that there is very little hypocrisy in the world; we do not so often endeavour or wish to impose on others as on ourselves." In the *Rambler*, No. 28, he remarks that "representations of imaginary virtue are generally considered as arts of hypocrisy, and as snares laid for confidence and praise. But I believe the suspicion often unjust; those who thus propagate their own reputation, only extend the fraud by which they have been themselves deceived."

A less serious, though similar, form of self-deception leads to the kind of literary affectation which is, I suppose, sufficiently familiar. "The ambition of superior sensibility and superior eloquence," Johnson observes in the *Idler*, No. 50, "disposes the lovers of arts to receive rapture at one time, and communicate it at another; and each labours first to impose upon himself, then to propagate the impos-

27. Johnson's *Dictionary*. In the *Rambler*, No. 20, Johnson carefully distinguishes between affectation and hypocrisy, observing that "affectation is to be always distinguished from hypocrisy, as being the art of counterfeiting those qualities which we might, with innocence and safety, be known to want. Thus the man who, to carry on any fraud, or to conceal any crime, pretends to rigours of devotion, and exactness of life, is guilty of hypocrisy; and his guilt is greater, as the end, for which he puts on false appearance, is more pernicious. But he that, with an awkward address, and unpleasing countenance, boasts of the conquests made by him among the ladies, and counts over the thousands which he might have possessed if he would have submitted to the yoke of matrimony, is chargeable only with affectation. Hypocrisy is the necessary burden of villany, affectation part of the chosen trappings of folly; the one completes a villain, the other only finishes a fop. Contempt is the proper punishment of affectation, and detestation the just consequence of hypocrisy."

ture." But Johnson did not strongly condemn this kind of self-delusion, because he was never inclined to rule out any source of innocent happiness in a world where "the utmost felicity which we can ever attain will be little better than alleviation of misery, and [where] we shall always feel more pain from our wants than pleasure from our enjoyments." [28] Johnson does severely reproach any one who "darkens the prospect of futurity, and multiplies the pains of our condition by useless terror." But he concedes that "those who magnify their delights are less criminal deceivers," even though "they raise hopes which are sure to be disappointed." Despite this concession, however, Johnson's final conclusion is that "it would be undoubtedly best, if we could see and hear every thing as it is, that nothing might be too anxiously dreaded, or too ardently pursued." [29]

There was certainly not a trace of doubt in Johnson's mind, however, on the subject of self-deceptions in the political arena. Although he was willing to tolerate a certain amount of muddled enthusiasm among critics, Johnson had no patience with most other forms of fuzzy thinking. In the political sphere, as in the moral, he strongly emphasized the supreme importance of seeing "every thing as it is." In his opinion, too much is at stake in these areas to allow any scope for even well-intentioned mistakes. Moreover, some political opinions serve to encourage immoral attitudes by throwing a misleading cloak of respectability over them. Therefore, it is especially necessary to be on guard against falling prey to such deceptions. Thus Johnson reproaches Akenside because

he certainly retained an unnecessary and outrageous zeal for what he called, and thought, liberty; a zeal which sometimes disguises from the world, and not rarely from the mind which it possesses, an envious desire of plundering wealth or degrading greatness; and of

28. *Rambler*, No. 165.
29. *Idler*, No. 50. In the *Idler*, No. 18, Johnson explains why "pleasure is . . . seldom such as it appears to others, nor often such as we represent it to ourselves."

which the immediate tendency is innovation and anarchy, an impetuous eagerness to subvert and confound, with very little care what
shall be established.[30]

This reproof goes far to explain Johnson's notorious distrust of all
those who spoke up in favor of political democracy or social leveling,
because it reveals his belief that any form of egalitarianism poses a
twofold danger. Socially and politically, egalitarianism results in destructive enthusiasm for tearing down the existing fabric of society
without giving any constructive attention to the important problem of
"what shall be established" when the old order is gone; and secondly,
egalitarianism undermines individual morality because it often serves
to encourage greed or envious spite, while at the same time disguising
these criminal attitudes—even "from the mind which it possesses"—as
a praiseworthy zeal for improving the world. This example clearly
shows why Johnson strongly emphasizes the necessity of avoiding
self-deceptive political thinking, for in his view the strongest, most
selfish, and therefore most potentially criminal, motives are called
into being to guide political conduct. Moreover, the issues at stake are
far more vital to those concerned than questions of artistic propriety
or pleasure.

It is striking that one major form of self-delusion remains almost
entirely neglected by Johnson. His assertion that we always think
ourselves better than we are leaves no room for those dejected moments in which we think ourselves worse than we really are. Johnson
himself was certainly no stranger to such depressions, and yet, so far
as I am aware, he never deals explicitly with the problem of unwarranted self-depreciation. In the *Rambler*, No. 189, he observes that
"we are almost all naturally modest and timorous." But he does not
explore the forms of excessive modesty. His extensive discussions of
self-deception all revolve around an assumption that we invariably err
in our own favor by endeavoring to delude ourselves (or others) with
the conviction that we are better than we really are. Johnson observes

---

30. "Life of Akenside" (*Works*, VIII, 469).

in the *Idler*, No. 31, for example, that "many moralists have re-marked, that pride has of all human vices the widest dominion, appears in the greatest multiplicity of forms, and lies hid under the greatest variety of disguises; of disguises, which, like the moon's 'veil of brightness,' are both its 'lustre and its shade,' and betray it to others, tho' they hide it from ourselves." Thus pride serves, in Johnson's opinion, to create or maintain some measure of self-deception, while, conversely, practically every kind of self-delusion operates to stave off what he refers to in the *Idler*, No. 18, as "the natural discontent of inferiority." In other words, the vast majority of self-deceptions ultimately serve only one purpose: they sustain that variety of felt superiority known as pride and defined by Johnson as "inordinate and unreasonable self-esteem."

Johnson clearly recognized that "power and superiority are so flattering and delightful, that, fraught with temptation and exposed to danger as they are, scarcely any virtue is so cautious, or any prudence so timorous, as to decline them." [31] This recognition of the widespread longing for superiority permeates Johnson's view of self-deception, although it is noteworthy that his moral essays do not explicitly recognize the relationship between obsessive feelings of inferiority and the various methods of compensating for such felt inadequacies by endeavoring to become—or feel—superior to others. Johnson never explains that it is often exaggerated feelings of inferiority which first mobilize diverse methods of compensating for real or imaginary inadequacies. He does deal at length, however, with the various self-deceptions by which men persuade themselves they are not inferior to anyone.

Johnson's own temperament makes it all the more puzzling that he never directly warns against the dangers of exaggerating our

---

31. *Rambler*, No. 114. In the *Rambler*, No. 2, Johnson observes that "censure is willingly indulged, because it always implies some superiority; men please themselves with imagining that they have made a deeper search, or wider survey, than others, and detected faults and follies, which escape vulgar observation."

shortcomings. His continual private self-depreciation is as well-known
as his refusal to tolerate any public criticism that might threaten his
position of intellectual superiority. Throughout his life he felt a sense
of moral unworthiness apparently out of all proportion to his actual
sins. But this religious self-depreciation is only reflected obliquely in
his assertion that "we always think ourselves better than we are." The
reason, however, is surely that, as a Christian, Johnson regarded any
feeling of religious unworthiness—even if exaggerated—as a useful
corrective against the dangers of moral complacency. Thus he affirms
in one of the sermons which he wrote for Taylor that "nothing is
more dangerous than spiritual pride. The man that esteems himself a
saint will be in danger of relaxing his circumspection, of stopping in
his progress of virtue, and, if once he stops, of falling back into those
infirmities from which his imaginary exemption made him presumptuous and supine." [32] In another sermon such spiritual pride is described
to illustrate how "deceitful are our own hearts." [33] In a sermon
on fear of God and hardness of heart, moreover, Johnson explains that Christianity "implicitly condemns all self-confidence, all
presumptuous security; and enjoins a constant state of vigilance and
caution, a perpetual distrust of our own hearts . . ." He adds that "of
that religion which has been taught from God, *the basis is humility;* a
holy fear which attends good men, through the whole course of their
lives; and keeps them . . . always unsatisfied with their progress in
holiness" [italics added]. [34] Similarly, Johnson observes in the *Rambler*, No. 155, that "no corruption is great but by long negligence,
which can scarcely prevail in a mind regularly and frequently awakened by periodical remorse." If in matters not immediately related to

32. Sermon XVI (*Works*, IX, 436).
33. Sermon VI (*Works*, IX 348–49).
34. Sermon III, (*Works*, IX, 311). In Sermon VIII Johnson asserts that
"it will soon be discovered, how much evil is avoided by repressing that
opinion of ourselves, which vanity suggests; and that confidence, which is
gained only by measuring ourselves by ourselves, dwelling on our own excellence, and flattering ourselves with secret panegyricks" (*ibid.*, p. 362).

the moral character Johnson unblushingly displayed a truly Miltonic sense of his own talents ("Slow rises worth," he complained at the outset of his career), he was inclined when writing moral essays to concentrate attention upon the dangerous mental habits which maintain pride rather than upon those which lead to an unwarranted sense of inferiority, because he was trying to make his works, as he said he had made the *Rambler*, "exactly conformable to the precepts of Christianity."

✤ 4 ✤

In the *Lives of the Poets*, Johnson observes that John Hughes "showed his knowledge of human nature by an essay on the Pleasure of being deceived." [35] This playful observation suggests what Johnson considered to be the most general cause of self-deceptions: they are pleasant. But they are pleasing largely because they provide an alternative to truth, which is usually painful. "Truth is, indeed," Johnson remarks in the *Rambler*, No. 96, "not often welcome for its own sake; it is generally unpleasing, because contrary to our wishes and opposite to our practices." It follows that self-deceptions are likely to please because they will fall in line with our wishes and, what is even more delightful, because they will help us avoid painful efforts to reform our conduct. By retreating from knowledge of our real state, we may continue, like Savage, treading "the same steps on the same circle." It is easy to avoid self-knowledge because, "as our attention naturally follows our interest, we hear unwillingly what we are afraid to know, and soon forget what we have no inclination to impress upon our memories." [36] This convenient disposition to attend only to what is pleasing while suppressing everything which makes us uncomfortable, is, in Johnson's opinion, the immediate cause of an immense variety of self-deceptions.

Thus, if "it is, indeed, the faculty of remembrance, which may be

35. "Life of Hughes" (*Works*, VII, 474).
36. *Rambler*, No. 96.

said to place us in the class of moral agents," it is simple forgetfulness which can most easily induce immoral conduct.[37] "We frequently fall into errour and folly," Johnson points out in the *Rambler*, No. 175, "not because the true principles of action are not known, but because, for a time, they are not remembered." The habit of remembering selectively only what pleases allows us to conceal important truths that we could otherwise be aware of. When this happens such knowledge ceases to exist, for all practical purposes, because "between falsehood and useless truth there is little difference. As gold which he cannot spend will make no man rich, so knowledge which he cannot apply will make no man wise."[38]

Johnson was convinced that deliberate avoidance of unpleasant truths is a major cause of self-delusion. Men seldom look very deeply into their own character because, as he points out in the "Life of Pope," "very few can boast of hearts which they dare lay open to themselves, and of which, by whatever accident exposed, they do not shun a distinct and continued view."[39] Consequently, "as very few can search deep into their own minds without meeting what they wish to hide from themselves, scarce any man persists in cultivating such disagreeable acquaintance, but draws the veil again between his eyes and his heart, leaves his passions and appetites, as he found them, and advises others to look into themselves."[40] The circle is completely vicious: if men were more nearly perfect, self-examination would be not only less painful but less necessary as well, for it is chiefly undertaken as a means of moral discipline. Yet, since men are generally so imperfect, they shy away from closely examining their own character. In Johnson's view, this willful avoidance of self-knowledge is grotesque, because "we all know our own state if we could be induced to consider it."[41] Nothing stands in the way of useful self-

---

37. *Rambler*, No. 41.
38. *Idler*, No. 84.
39. *Works*, VIII, 314.
40. *Idler*, No. 27.
41. *Rambler*, No. 155.

knowledge but shortsighted desire to avoid facing up to painful facts—yet reason is insufficient to overcome this desire in most men. They would rather die than face the surgeon's knife.

Johnson's deep respect for human reason is matched only by his profound conviction that most men are almost hopelessly irrational. Throughout the moral essays he exposes an incredible variety of illogical conduct to substantiate his conviction. The recurring theme of self-delusion alone provides a lucid illustration of just how far into the murky depths of irrationality man can sink, and perhaps the nadir of that process is reached in the employment of those perverted reasonings by which we endeavor to minimize the importance of unpleasant facts that we have not been able either to avoid or to forget. "Those faults which we cannot conceal from our own notice," Johnson observes in the *Rambler*, No. 28, "are considered, however frequent, not as habitual corruptions, or settled practices, but as casual failures, and single lapses." Thus, when it comes to listing moral failures, men persuade themselves that a large number must really be interpreted as small. When it comes to listing virtues, however, this strange arithmetic is altered so that small numbers are regarded as impressive. "One sophism by which men persuade themselves that they have those virtues which they really want," Johnson notes, "is formed by the substitution of single acts for habits. A miser who once relieved a friend from the danger of a prison, suffers his imagination to dwell for ever upon his own heroic generosity." [42] Johnson was painfully aware that men have an amazing capacity for twisting logic when it suits their purposes.

Moreover, despite his firm assertion that "there is no crime more infamous than the violation of truth," Johnson also knew that few crimes are more tempting, or easier, because "men are willing to

42. *Rambler*, No. 28. In the *Rambler*, No. 155, Johnson observes that "no weakness of the human mind has more frequently incurred animadversion, than the negligence with which men overlook their own faults, however flagrant, and the easiness with which they pardon them, however frequently repeated."

credit what they wish, and encourage rather those who gratify them with pleasure, than those that instruct them with fidelity." [43] (In the last number of the *Rambler*, he noted ruefully that his own instruction had "never been much a favourite of the public.") Unwillingness to believe what they do not wish to hear even causes men to find excuses for remaining unperturbed by accusations that they really know to be true. Johnson observes, for example, that "the charge of an enemy is often totally false, and commonly so mingled with falsehood, that the mind takes advantage from the failure of one part to discredit the rest, and never suffers any disturbance afterward from such partial reports." [44] Thus, when an unpleasant aspect of our own character is brought to our attention, we may easily minimize the importance of the charge by pointing to its association with obviously inaccurate statements and then may dismiss it because of the company it keeps, rather than because it is itself false.

In similar fashion, when an unpleasant fact is inescapably brought to our attention and when we cannot deny its truth, it is often possible to minimize its importance by thinking of extenuating circumstances which create an aura of inevitability around the unpleasantness, thereby making it easier to live with. Why be disturbed, after all, by something which cannot be helped? Above all, why bother to do anything about such situations? In the *Rambler*, No. 146, for example, Johnson drolly outlines the typical response of a writer upon discovering the melancholy fact that his book is universally unread.

Many are the consolations with which the unhappy author endeavours to allay his vexation, and fortify his patience. He has written with too little indulgence to the understanding of common readers; he has fallen upon an age in which solid knowledge, and delicate refinement, have given way to a low merriment, and idle buffoonery, and therefore no writer can hope for distinction, who has any higher purpose than to raise laughter. He finds that his enemies, such as superiority will always raise, have been industrious, while his per-

43. *Idler*, No. 20.
44. *Rambler*, No. 28.

formance was in the press, to vilify and blast it; and that the book-seller, whom he had resolved to enrich, has rivals that obstruct the circulation of the copies. He at last reposes upon the consideration, that the noblest works of learning and genius have always made their way slowly against ignorance and prejudice; and that reputation, which is never to be lost, must be gradually obtained, as animals of longest life are observed not soon to attain their full stature and strength.

All such rationalizations serve the purpose of laying the blame for failures, like the notorious baby, at someone else's doorstep.

Moreover, we not only succeed by this means in concealing our own culpability from ourselves and in minimizing the seriousness of our failures, but we also manage at the same time to hide our insignificance. "By such arts of voluntary delusion," Johnson goes on, "does every man endeavour to conceal his own unimportance from himself. It is long before we are convinced of the small proportion which every individual bears to the collective body of mankind; or learn how few can be interested in the fortune of any single man." Here too, Johnson implies that many voluntary delusions are motivated by what he refers to elsewhere as "the natural discontent of inferiority." The universal longing for some kind of superiority makes it especially galling to admit any failing that brings home what a small part we actually play in the course of human events. All men, in Johnson's opinion, struggle against the uncomfortable feeling of being lost in the herd. Almost anything is preferable to that, including a delusive conviction that we are being actively persecuted by "enemies, such as superiority will always raise."

The self-deceptions that result from our impulse to avoid unpleasant truths or minimize their importance usually involve some element of deliberate complicity. "Few that wander in the wrong way," Johnson remarks, "mistake it for the right, they only find it more smooth and flowery, and indulge their own choice rather than approve it." [45]

45. *Rambler*, No. 155.

The sin is one of omission because "we all know our own state if we could be induced to consider it." [46]

Another cause of self-deception, however, Johnson regarded as involving little if any active cooperation on the part of the victim. "We are sometimes not ourselves conscious of the original motives of our action," Johnson observes in the *Rambler,* No. 87. Later, in the pamphlet on Falkland's Islands, he remarks that "obstinacy and flexibility, malignity and kindness, give place, alternately, to each other; and the reason of these vicissitudes, however important may be the consequences, often escapes the mind in which the change is made." [47] Whenever we remain unaware of our real reason for adopting a particular attitude, we expose ourselves to all the dangerous consequences attendant upon other causes of self-deception. In recognizing the existence of unconscious motivation as well as in pointing out the importance of our disposition to forget whatever makes us uncomfortable, Johnson anticipates two major concerns of Freudian psychology, although he does not stress, as the Freudians do, the great difficulty of sitting down alone and unmasking our own deepest motives. Johnson's assumption that "we all know our own state if we could be induced to consider it" underlies his entire discussion of moral discipline.

Freudians, of course, also assume that it is possible to uncover the unconscious motivation that governs much of our behavior. But the psychoanalytical tradition is grounded upon a conviction that almost every individual needs the assistance of a trained observer in order to do so. Johnson, on the other hand, assumes that everyone can achieve adequate knowledge of his own mind by himself. After accepting, as he emphatically did, the doctrine that each man is morally accountable for his conduct, Johnson could hardly have denied the possibility of achieving sufficient self-knowledge to recognize and eliminate those mental dispositions which "poison the fountains of morality." Yet he

46. *Ibid.*
47. *Works,* VI, 195. In the "Life of Dryden" Johnson observes that "we do not always know our own motives" (*Works,* VII, 340).

never minimized the extreme difficulty of this achievement. "If it be reasonable to estimate the difficulty of any enterprise by frequent miscarriages," he states in the *Rambler*, No. 28, "it may justly be concluded that it is not easy for a man to know himself." Later in the same essay Johnson notes that

to lay open all the sources from which errour flows in upon him who contemplates his own character, would require more exact knowledge of the human heart, than, perhaps, the most acute and laborious observers have acquired. And since falsehood may be diversified without end, it is not unlikely that every man admits an imposture in some respect peculiar to himself, as his views have been accidently directed, or his ideas particularly combined.

Despite this realistic appraisal of the difficulties involved, however, Johnson does suggest several ways to free ourselves from the more common self-delusions.

5

In the *Idler*, No. 80, Johnson caustically observes that "however we may labour for our own deception, truth, though unwelcome, will sometimes intrude upon the mind." But these intrusions are infrequent. It is necessary to encourage the process. The errors of omission—failing to recollect what is displeasing and unawareness of our own motives—must be reduced to a minimum, while the errors of commission—avoiding truth or denying the importance of unpleasant facts—must be eliminated. The first step towards the accomplishment of these necessary tasks appears simple. After noting that each of us is likely to harbor a unique form of self-delusion that will remain unnoticed by even "the most acute and laborious observers," Johnson goes on in the *Rambler*, No. 28, to remark that there are "some fallacies . . . more frequently insidious, which it may, perhaps, not be useless to detect; because, though they are gross, they may be fatal, and because nothing but attention is necessary to defeat them." Johnson thus assumes that many delusions persist merely because they

remain unnoticed, although once attention is called to their existence—and their menace—it is not hard to eliminate them. This assumption is somewhat at variance with Johnson's equally emphatic
conviction that we cling most illogically to delusions and regard their
elimination as an almost unbearable threat to our tranquillity. It is
nevertheless clear that he based the rhetorical strategy of his moral
essays upon the assumption that a vast number of intellectual maladies such as self-deception remain unchecked largely because they pass
unremarked or, what is equally deplorable, because they are regarded
as quite normal and acceptable. Throughout the *Rambler* and the
Idler Johnson usually confines himself to the task of first describing
the mental anatomy in its healthy state and then pointing out the
form taken by unbalanced (and therefore potentially immoral) responses. Sometimes Johnson tries to show, by an apt illustration or
characterization, how foolish certain kinds of imbalance are; at other
times he shows why they are extremely dangerous as well as absurd in
a reasonable creature. He frequently discusses their causes. But he less
often supplies prescriptive advice on specific methods of correcting
each kind of disturbance. Though there is a good deal of direction in
the moral essays, his prescriptions most frequently appear obliquely in
the form of an unstated injunction to avoid those responses whose
absurdity or danger is described and whose causes are explained.
Thus, even though simply recognizing the causes, forms, and consequences of self-deception is the first step towards their elimination, it
is a crucial one and not nearly as easy as it may seem.

Therefore, Johnson emphasized the extreme importance of regular
self-examination. "It might perhaps be useful to the conquest of all
these ensnarers of the mind," he remarks in the *Rambler*, No. 155,
"if, at certain stated days, life was reviewed." In the *Rambler*, No.
28, he is even more positive in affirming the necessity of each individual's "assigning proper portions of his life to the examination of the
rest." After recalling how Pontanus urged the importance of self-
knowledge by having his tombstone carved with an inscription enjoin-
ing passers-by, who cannot know him, to know themselves, Johnson

adds his hope that "every reader of this paper will consider himself engaged to the observation of a precept, which the wisdom and virtue of all ages have concurred to enforce: a precept, dictated by philosophers, inculcated by poets, and ratified by saints." [48] Frequent self-examination is especially important because it is the only method of detecting the appearance of new forms of self-delusion while there is still time to eradicate them. After they—or any other vices—have become habitual, it is in Johnson's opinion too late to remove them. "The disproportions of absurdity," he notes in the *Rambler*, No. 95, "grow less and less visible as we are reconciled, by degrees, to the deformity of a mistress; and falsehood, by long use, is assimilated to the mind, as poison to the body."

It would be useful, Johnson admits, if someone were on hand to help this process along by pointing out failings that escape our own notice. He remarks in the *Rambler*, No. 40, that friendship without sincerity "is of very little value, since the great use of so close an intimacy is, that our virtues may be guarded and encouraged, and our vices repressed in their first appearance by timely detection and salutary remonstrances." But for several reasons such assistance is normally out of the question. In the first place, it is often very difficult for others to discern even some aspects of ourselves that we are aware of, much less perceive the hidden springs of conduct. For example, after noting that "we are sometimes not ourselves conscious of the original motives of our actions," Johnson adds that

when we know them, our first care is to hide them from the sight of others, and often from those most diligently, whose superiority either of power or understanding may entitle them to inspect our lives; it is therefore very probable, that he who endeavours the cure of our intellectual maladies, mistakes their cause; and that his prescriptions avail nothing, because he knows not which of the passions or desires is vitiated. [49]

48. The *Rambler*, No. 7, is another statement of the importance of self-examination.
49. *Rambler*, No. 87.

Even when we remain unaware of our shortcomings, our companions are likely to have the same blind spots because "friends are often chosen for similitude of manners, and therefore each palliates the other's failings, because they are his own." [50] This palliation usually takes the form of flattery which encourages us to minimize the importance of failings that we are really aware of when we trouble to be honest with ourselves. The self-deceptions arising from our avoidance of this kind of honesty are evidently, in Johnson's opinion, the most common forms of self-delusion:

Many of the follies which provoke general censure, are the effects of such vanity as, however it might have wantoned in the imagination, would scarcely have dared the publick eye, had it not been animated and emboldened by flattery. Whatever difficulty there may be in the knowledge of ourselves, scarcely any one fails to suspect his own imperfections, till he is elevated by others to confidence. [51]

This assertion reveals Johnson's underlying assumption that most self-deceptions would never occur if they did not receive a measure of social approval. He also implies that when such approval is continued, we gradually forget our initial intimations of the truth. This is how self-delusions are most often "assimilated to the mind, as poisons to the body." We are encouraged by outward approval of our conduct habitually to minimize the importance of our failings, to push knowledge of them out of mind, and to avoid searching our memory for the truth, until eventually we act as though we had not the slightest suspicion of our greatest follies.

But, in Johnson's view, self-deceptions seldom, if ever, deceive completely. No matter how they may vitiate conduct, there will always remain some small corner of the mind that knows better, even if such knowledge remains dormant and therefore useless on those occasions when it might retrieve men from their greatest follies. It is, in fact, worse than useless when we have sunk to this state, because,

50. *Rambler*, No. 28.
51. *Rambler*, No. 189.

oddly enough, it does not always remain dormant then but rather has a way of springing to life for the sole purpose of allowing us to resent sound advice. Johnson asserts in the *Rambler*, No. 155, that

advice is offensive, not because it lays us open to unexpected regret, or convicts us of any fault which had escaped our notice, but because it shows us that we are known to others as well as to ourselves; and the officious monitor is persecuted with hatred, not because his accusation is false, but because he assumes that superiority which we are not willing to grant him, and has dared to detect what we desired to conceal. For this reason advice is commonly ineffectual.[52]

Aversion to any admission of inferiority makes us unwilling to accept the assistance of anyone who has enough perception to recognize, and call our attention to, those aspects of our conduct that seem to be grounded upon self-delusion. It is one of the perversities of human nature that allows us to act as though we were blind to our failings until they are pointed out to us and then—but only then—to summon our neglected knowledge so that we can feel superior because we are not being caught in unbecoming ignorance; we reply, in effect, that we know our shortcomings perfectly well, thank you. Because Johnson assumed that every man is cursed with a streak of satanic pride, if for no other reason, he reluctantly concluded that, however desirable outside assistance might be in theory, it is well-nigh useless in practice. Therefore, in his opinion the only workable method of eliminating our delusions is systematic self-examination.

There is, however, a theoretical advantage of telling people their shortcomings no matter how unreceptive they may seem. Johnson observes—after realistically conceding that "advice is commonly ineffectual"—that "the benefit of advice arises commonly not from any new light imparted to the mind, but from the discovery which it

---

52. Johnson goes on to observe that "if those who follow the call of their desires, without inquiry whither they are going, had deviated ignorantly from the paths of wisdom, and were rushing upon dangers unforeseen, they would readily listen to information that recalls them from their errours, and catch the first alarm by which destruction or infamy is denounced."

affords of the publick suffrages. He that could withstand conscience is
frighted at infamy, and shame prevails when reason is defeated." [53]
Thus, in principle—and occasionally in practice—the coercive social
pressure exerted by informing an individual that his faults are known
may have the desired effect of making him recall, and act upon,
knowledge which he has pushed into the back of his mind. Public
disapproval may jar an individual out of his self-deluded conduct
because the prospect of infamy is painful. On the other hand, as
Johnson remarks in the "Life of Swift": "He that is much flattered,
soon learns to flatter himself: we are commonly taught our duty by
fear or shame, and how can they act upon the man who hears nothing
but his own praises?" [54] On this question, as on others, Johnson dis-
plays his assumption that desire of pleasure and fear of pain are "the
two great movers of the human mind." One of the most efficient
methods of inducing people to abandon their delusions, in Johnson's
opinion, would certainly be the exertion of sufficient social pressure to
make everyone afraid of exposure—so thoroughly afraid that such
fear would outweigh all the pleasures that attract us to the "arts of
voluntary delusion." But this would require a nation of moralists
ruled by a philosopher-king.

Therefore, Johnson relies upon another method. He notes in the
Rambler, No. 7:

That conquest of the world and of ourselves, which has been always
considered as the perfection of human nature . . . is only to be
obtained by fervent prayer, steady resolutions, and frequent retire-
ment from folly and vanity, from the cares of avarice, and the joys of
intemperance, from the lulling sounds of deceitful flattery, and the
tempting sight of prosperous wickedness.

If we cannot make vice and deceit—including self-deceit—universally
dreaded, we can at least remove ourselves from surroundings which
make them seem infinitely attractive. Prayer and high resolve are

53. *Rambler*, No. 155.
54. *Works*, VIII, 217.

important, but by retreating from "the lulling sounds of deceitful flattery," we eliminate the chief external inducement to go on deceiving ourselves and thus provide an essential condition for reviewing our own conduct and maintaining an adequate degree of self-knowledge. Johnson, however, goes far beyond merely suggesting the ideal conditions for self-examination. His essays provide a rich fund of specific advice on how we are to regulate our inner life for the purpose of insuring virtuous conduct.

Chapter V

Moral Discipline

AFTER REMARKING IN THE *Rambler*, No 8, that his purpose is "to consider the moral discipline of the mind, and to promote the increase of virtue rather than of learning," Johnson goes on "to show what thoughts are to be rejected or improved, as they regard the past, present, or future; in hopes that some may be awakened to caution and vigilance, who, perhaps, indulge themselves in dangerous dreams, so much the more dangerous, because, being yet only dreams, they are concluded innocent." Johnson's discussion is limited to the specific problem of "the snares . . . by which the imagination is entangled"; Johnson's prescriptions are addressed to the difficult though necessary business of controlling the dangerous "pleasures of fancy, and the emotions of desire." But, as he so frequently does throughout the individual essays, Johnson here generalizes his specific topic by relating his advice to the larger ethical concern which forms a unifying theme of all his moral essays. "He, therefore, that would govern his actions by the laws of virtue," Johnson concludes, "must regulate his thoughts by those of reason." This general advice is given substance throughout the *Rambler,* the *Idler,* and the *Adventurer* by a wide variety of concrete suggestions, just as it is in the *Rambler,* No. 8. One of the problems confronting all students of Johnson is that of reducing to order the rich abundance of specific counsel which is scattered throughout the moral essays, for if we do not perceive the underlying patterns of his effort as a moral disciplinarian it is difficult to estimate his achievement.

One useful method of reducing to order Johnson's suggestions on the moral discipline of the mind is to generalize the straightforward, though fundamental, proposal advanced in the *Rambler,* No. 8, for dealing with the particular problem of bringing under control the "dangerous dreams" of fancy. All of Johnson's specific proposals for the right conduct of mental processes may be viewed as efforts "to show what thoughts are to be rejected or improved, as they regard the past, present, or future." If his suggestions are grouped under these three heads, they will not seem so random, nor will the scope of Johnson's total effort as a moralist be so likely to elude observation. To be sure, every item of Johnson's "dictatorial instruction" cannot be ranged neatly under any one of these three categories: there is significant overlap, even though the majority of his suggestions for governing the mind concern themselves primarily with either the past, the present, or the future. The threefold classification remains useful, however, because it is sufficiently valid to provide points of reference with respect to which individual suggestions can be ranged. Those falling entirely under each head can be enumerated to provide a means of characterizing the direction and nature of Johnson's concerns as moral disciplinarian, while those suggestions which deal with more than one segment of time and which therefore cannot be conveniently lumped under only one of the headings will provide some measure of the complexity of Johnson's advice.

A further distinction, within each of the three larger headings provided by Johnson's observation in the *Rambler*, No. 8, is suggested by his statement in the final number of the *Rambler* that it has been his "principal design to inculcate wisdom or piety." In his *Dictionary* Johnson defines *piety* as "1. Discharge of duty to God; 2. Duty to parents or those in superior relation." *Wisdom*, in turn, is defined as "1. Sapience; the power of judging rightly; 2. Prudence; skill in affairs; judicious conduct." The first meaning of *wisdom* is illustrated by Temple's assertion that "wisdom is that which makes men judge what are the best ends, and what the best means to attain them, and gives a man advantage of counsel and direction." These definitions make clear the fact of Johnson's twofold concern: on the one hand, with directing us to the proper discharge of the duties and obligations imposed upon us from above, and, on the other hand, with advising us on how best to conduct our own affairs. He believes that wise conduct of our own affairs is part of our duty, for, as he observes in the *Idler*, No. 88, "Every man is obliged by the supreme master of the universe to improve all the opportunities of good which are afforded him, and to keep in continual activity such abilities as are bestowed upon him." [1] Implicit in this injunction to activity is the further injunction to judicious activity. But even though the wisest use of our faculties serves the ultimate end of conforming to duty, it also helps us achieve the personal goal of temporal as well as eternal happiness, and this personal goal was certainly taken into account in Johnson's attempts to inculcate wisdom. "The fountain of content," he observes in the *Rambler*, No. 6, "must spring up in the mind; and

---

1. In the *Idler*, No. 43, Johnson states that man is "a being, placed here only for a short time, whose task is to advance himself to a higher and happier state of existence, by unremitted vigilance of caution, and activity of virtue."

. . . he who has so little knowledge of human nature, as to seek happiness by changing any thing but his own dispositions, will waste his life in fruitless efforts, and multiply the griefs which he purposes to remove." Johnson's advice was as often directed toward the attainment of happiness as it was toward the discharge of duties. Therefore, it is useful to distinguish between his suggestions for the judicious use of our faculties to achieve happiness or contentment and his suggestions for the pious use of our faculties to achieve virtuous conduct. Conversely, we can distinguish between misdirections of our thoughts that are merely foolish and wasteful (*follies* is the usual term applied by Johnson), because they make us inefficient or miserable, and misdirections of our thoughts that are sinful (*crimes* is the usual term applied by Johnson), because they make us omit some duty imposed by God.

Before turning to a classification of Johnson's suggestions regarding the moral discipline of the mind, it may be well to recall his most explicit affirmation of the premise that our thoughts can indeed be directed. In the *Rambler*, No. 78, he observes:

The manner in which external force acts upon the body is very little subject to the regulation of the will. . . . But our ideas are more subjected to choice; we can call them before us, and command their stay, we can facilitate and promote their recurrence, we can either repress their intrusion, or hasten their retreat. It is, therefore, the business of wisdom and virtue, to select among numberless objects striving for our notice, such as may enable us to exalt our reason, extend our views, and secure our happiness.[2]

As I have pointed out earlier, Johnson recognized important limitations on our power to control the direction of thoughts, but it is nevertheless true that he always assumed the possibility of achieving a significant measure of control over our ideas if we know how—and when—to bridle them for the purpose of living judiciously and virtuously. It is upon the foundation of this assumption that Johnson

2. See also the concluding paragraphs of the *Idler*, No. 72, and Chapter IV, p. 116, n. 13, above.

builds an elaborate framework of suggestions for directing our
thoughts "as they regard the past, present, or future."

❧ 2 ☙

Although most of his suggestions deal with thoughts regarding the
present and the future, Johnson provides explicit advice for dealing
with time past. Some of that advice concerns the judicious regulation
of memories for the more secular purpose of avoiding unnecessary
misery because, as Johnson observes in the *Idler*, No. 44, "Whether it
be that life has more vexations than comforts, or, what is in the event
just the same, that evil makes deeper impression than good, it is
certain that few can review the time past without heaviness of heart."
Johnson concludes this *Idler* by pointing out that "all shrink from
recollection, and all wish for an art of forgetfulness." In the *Idler*,
No. 72, he returns to this theme:

> It would add much to human happiness, if an art could be taught
> of forgetting all of which the remembrance is at once useless and
> afflictive, if that pain which never can end in pleasure could be driven
> totally away, that the mind might perform its functions without
> incumbrance, and the past might no longer encroach upon the
> present.

The emphasis in this paper is primarily upon the wisdom of driving
out of mind recollections that are wasteful because they make one
needlessly unhappy. Johnson concedes that "to forget or remember at
pleasure, are equally beyond the power of man," but he goes on to
affirm that "the power of forgetting is capable of improvement" and
concludes by suggesting that we can most successfully drive away
unpleasant memories by forcing ourselves to find some employment
that will turn our thoughts to the present moment: "Employment is
the great instrument of intellectual dominion. The mind cannot retire
from its enemy into total vacancy, or turn aside from one object but
by passing to another. . . . We must be busy about good or evil, and

he to whom the present offers nothing will often be looking backward on the past." [3] These suggestions concerning an art of forgetfulness, as well as the advice in the *Idler*, No. 74, on the best methods of remembering what we have read [4] comprise Johnson's most important advice on the judicious regulation of thoughts regarding the past for the purpose of avoiding needless unhappiness.

The majority of Johnson's suggestions for the regulation of memories are concerned with the importance and methods of avoiding sinful preoccupation with the past. In the *Rambler*, No. 8, he advises that if a man is

dwelling with delight upon a stratagem of successful fraud, a night of licentious riot, or an intrigue of guilty pleasure, let him summon off his imagination as from an unlawful pursuit, expel those passages from his remembrance, of which, though he cannot seriously approve them, the pleasure overpowers the guilt, and refer them to a future hour when they may be considered with greater safety.

The key word here is *unlawful*. Johnson advises us to shun the recollection of earlier sins not because such recollections will necessarily make us unhappy (we may dwell upon them "with delight") but rather because such pleasure is in itself criminal. Conversely, he remarks in the *Rambler*, No. 203, that "there are few higher gratifications, than that of reflection on surmounted evils, when they were not incurred nor protracted by our fault, and neither reproach us with cowardice nor guilt." Thus Johnson stamps his seal of approval upon the pleasures of recollecting virtuous endeavors and successes. It is only the memory of criminal pleasures that is itself unlawful and is to be avoided for that reason.

Another kind of thought directed toward time past is sorrow or grief for some loss, and Johnson asserts in the *Rambler*, No. 47, that

3. See also the *Rambler*, No. 52.
4. "What is read twice is commonly better remembered than what is transcribed. . . . The true art of memory is the art of attention. . . . If the mind is employed on the past or future, the book will be held before the eyes in vain."

grief "deserves the particular attention of those who have assumed
the arduous province of preserving the balance of the mental constitution." He concedes the inevitability of expressing grief but goes on to
advise that "all beyond the bursts of passion, or the forms of solemnity, is not only useless, but culpable; for we have no right to sacrifice,
to the vain longings of affection, that time which providence allows us
for the task of our station." [5] Here undue preoccupation with "vain
longing" for those who now exist only in our memories is condemned
not primarily because it makes us unhappy but rather because it is a
"culpable" violation of the obligation, imposed upon us by God, to
carry out our share of the tasks of this world. Just as Johnson rejected
the monastic ideal because it is one form of retreat from our obligation to help carry on the business of the world, so did he counsel
against an inward retreat from the responsibilities of the present
moment to the shelter of "vain longings" for a vanished past.

Regretful dwelling upon past failings, however, was, with one
essential reservation, encouraged by Johnson. "Regret is indeed useful and virtuous, and not only allowable but necessary," he observes
in the *Idler*, No. 72, "when it tends to the amendment of life, or to
admonition of error which we may be again in danger of commit-
ting." Both virtue and utility are here invoked as standards by which
we may decide to encourage or repress remorse. If any particular
regret will serve to make conduct either more virtuous or more
judicious, it is permissible to persist in that regret, but if not, it is our
duty, as well as our interest, to suppress it. Johnson thus encourages
remorse on both secular and religious grounds.

Throughout the moral essays, however, he emphasizes most frequently the religious uses of remorse. In the *Rambler*, No. 110, for
example, Johnson defines repentance as "the relinquishment of any
practice, from the conviction that it has offended God" and observes
that "sorrow and fear, and anxiety, are properly not parts, but ad-
juncts of repentance; yet they are too closely connected with it to be

---

5. For methods of dealing with grief, see the *Rambler*, No. 52.

easily separated; for they not only mark its sincerity, but promote its efficacy." Later in the same paper Johnson firmly asserts that "sorrow and terrour must naturally precede reformation; for what other cause can produce it? He, therefore, that feels himself alarmed by his conscience, anxious for the attainment of a better state, and afflicted by the memory of his past faults, may justly conclude, that the great work of repentance is begun . . ."

These remarks provide ample sanction for encouraging thoughts of past lapses from virtue, provided that such memories are accompanied by remorse and not pleasure. In the *Rambler*, No. 155, Johnson states categorically that "no corruption is great but by long negligence, which can scarcely prevail in a mind regularly and frequently awakened by periodical remorse."

Thus, even though Johnson clearly discerned the dangers of injudicious or impious concern with time past, he nevertheless took pains to explain how we can turn our thoughts back to the past in ways that are not only useful in preserving us from folly but essential to the task of delivering ourselves from evil. "The serious and impartial retrospect of our conduct," he observes in the *Rambler*, No. 8, "is indisputably necessary to the confirmation or recovery of virtue, and is, therefore, recommended under the name of self-examination, by divines, as the first act previous to repentance." Here, as throughout his moral essays, Johnson's primary concern with the past is religious: his advice for rejecting or improving thoughts "as they regard the past" is sometimes designed to inculcate wisdom, but it most often serves to inculcate virtue. It is in this primarily religious context that we must interpret Johnson's most general statement that "the recollection of the past is only useful by way of provision for the future." [6]

❧ 3 ❧

The most fundamental misuse of the present moment, in Johnson's view, is simply the failure to use it at all. "We must snatch the

6. *Rambler*, No. 8.

present moment, and employ it well, without too much sollicitude for the future," he counsels in the *Idler*, No. 4, adding: "He that waits for an opportunity to do much at once, may breathe out his life in idle wishes, and regret, in the last hour, his useless intentions, and barren zeal." The primary outward violation of the present in our conduct is idleness, which Johnson condemns on both secular and religious grounds. His preoccupation with this theme is one of the best-known aspects of his thought, just as it is one of the most notorious struggles of his personal life. The inward violation of the present takes various forms, but the two most elementary—and crippling—are indecision and procrastination. Johnson's condemnation of indecision in the *Rambler*, No. 178, reveals the twofold danger he found in this particular misuse of thoughts regarding the present:

Providence has fixed the limits of human enjoyment by immoveable boundaries, and has set different gratifications at such a distance from each other, that no art or power can bring them together. This great law it is the business of every rational being to understand, that life may not pass away in an attempt to make contradictions consistent, to combine opposite qualities, and to unite things which the nature of their being must always keep asunder.

Of two objects tempting at a distance on contrary sides, it is impossible to approach one but by receding from the other; by long deliberation and dilatory projects, they may be both lost, but can never be both gained. It is, therefore, necessary to compare them, and, when we have determined the preference, to withdraw our eyes and our thoughts at once from that which reason directs us to reject. This is more necessary, if that which we are forsaking has the power of delighting the senses, or firing the fancy. He that once turns aside to the allurements of unlawful pleasure, can have no security that he shall ever regain the paths of virtue.[7]

7. See also Chap. XXIX of *Rasselas*, in which Nekayah concludes the debate on marriage with the following observation: "Every hour . . . confirms my prejudice in favour of the position so often uttered by the mouth of Imlac, 'That nature sets her gifts on the right hand and on the left.' These conditions, which flatter hope and attract desire, are so constituted, that, as we approach one, we recede from another. . . . Flatter not yourself with contrarieties of pleasure. Of the blessings set before you make your choice, and be

The discussion in these two paragraphs moves from "human enjoyment" to "the paths of virtue." Johnson first points out that it is injudicious to suspend thoughts in indecision, because in so doing we run the risk of missing all possibilities of pleasure. He then observes that if we postpone the act of rational choice we run the risk of choosing irrationally and hence immorally. Thus Johnson condemns indecision by appealing to our sense of religious obligation as well as to our desire for temporal happiness.

A similar twofold appeal is included in Johnson's warnings against procrastination. In the *Rambler*, No. 134, for example, he suggests that "when evils cannot be avoided, it is wise to contract the interval of expectation; to meet the mischiefs which will overtake us if we fly; and suffer only their real malignity, without the conflicts of doubt, and anguish of anticipation." Here the emphasis is upon the injudicious aspect of procrastination: the "anguish of anticipation" is what we are warned to avoid by dealing with unavoidable evils at once rather than unwisely wasting the present moment in unhappy expectation.

In the *Rambler*, No. 71, Johnson's warning against procrastination is placed in a more explicitly religious context. After describing Prospero's plan of planting trees on his estate at the age of fifty-five, Johnson remarks:

Thus is life trifled away in preparations to do what never can be done, if it be left unattempted till all the requisites which imagination can suggest are gathered together. Where our design terminates only in our own satisfaction, the mistake is of no great importance . . . but when many others are interested in an undertaking, when any design is formed, in which the improvement or security of mankind is involved, nothing is more unworthy either of wisdom or benevolence, than to delay it from time to time. . . .

Divines have, with great strength and ardour, shown the absurdity of delaying reformation and repentance; a degree of folly, indeed, which sets eternity to hazard. It is the same weakness, in proportion

---

content" (*The Works of Samuel Johnson, LL.D.* [9 vols.; Oxford, 1825], I, 263). (Cited hereafter as *Works*.)

to the importance of the neglect, to transfer any care, which now claims our attention, to a future time.

Procrastination in matters which relate only to our own or other people's temporal happiness is thus affirmed to be similar in kind ("the same weakness") to procrastination in matters relating to our obligation to repentance. This explicit association lends force to Johnson's warning against delaying what should be done to further individual or social happiness in this world. But it is only "when many others are interested in an undertaking" that procrastination is condemned as supremely injudicious. Even though Johnson strongly implies a religious obligation to refrain from every kind of procrastination, he nevertheless views thoughts that wander away from present secular concerns as primarily unwise rather than sinful.

Perpetual dissatisfaction with the present, on the other hand, is condemned by Johnson for reasons that are primarily religious. His classic example of such dissatisfaction is Tetrica, who "finds in every place something to grate her mind, and disturb her quiet. If she takes the air, she is offended with the heat or cold, the glare of the sun, or the gloom of the clouds; if she makes a visit, the room in which she is to be received, is too light, or too dark, or furnished with something which she cannot see without aversion." No aspect of what she experiences pleases Tetrica while she is experiencing it, and the dangers of this disposition are pointed out when Johnson observes:

No disease of the mind can more fatally disable it from benevolence, the chief duty of social beings, than ill-humour or peevishness. . . .
Peevishness, when it has been so far indulged, as to outrun the motions of the will, and discover itself without premeditation, is a species of depravity in the highest degree disgusting and offensive.[8]

Ill-natured and irrational dissatisfaction with the present moment is condemned because it is "a species of depravity" which prevents us

8. *Rambler*, No. 74.

from carrying out our responsibilities to our fellows. In his *Diction-ary*, Johnson defines *depravity* as "Corruption," and *corruption* as "Wickedness." Clearly, peevishness was in his view sinful and crimi-nal rather than merely injudicious.

Johnson never argues that we ought always to be enchanted with whatever we are experiencing. In the *Idler*, No. 100, he specifically condemns such unremitting optimism by showing that Tim Warner's wife (a "good sort of woman") is morally deficient in part because, although she is "an enemy to nothing but ill nature and pride," she woefully misunderstands the true symptoms of both vices:

all who are not equally pleased with the good and bad, with the elegant and gross, with the witty and the dull, all who distinguish excellence from defect she considers as ill-natured; and she condemns as proud all who repress impertinence or quell presumption, or expect respect from any other eminence than that of fortune, to which she is always willing to pay homage.

In Johnson's view certain kinds of dissatisfaction, far from being criminal, are not only judicious but essential to a proper moral out-look: unhappiness with what is gross, dull, inelegant, or defective is the better part of wisdom, while dislike of what is evil is of course essential to piety. Peevishness, as he is at pains to point out, is simply misdirected and irrational discontent. It is, he observes in the *Ram-bler*, No. 112, "generally the vice of narrow minds, and, except when it is the effect of anguish and disease, by which the resolution is broken, and the mind made too feeble to bear the lightest addition to its miseries, proceeds from an unreasonable persuasion of the impor-tance of trifles." Here again Johnson explicitly labels ill nature as both irrational and vicious. These are the grounds on which peevish-ness is condemned, and it is for these primarily religious reasons that we are warned to avoid it, first in our own thinking and then also in our conduct.

Johnson's suggestions for combatting ill-natured discontentments, however, appeal primarily to our sense of how injudicious the vice of

peevishness is. "The proper remedy against it," he remarks in the
Rambler, No. 112, "is to consider the dignity of human nature, and
the folly of suffering perturbation and uneasiness from causes unworthy of our notice." Even though we are to avoid peevishness because
it is a religious duty to do so, just as it is our duty to avoid all vices,
the *method* of avoiding it is distinctly secular: we are to think of how
foolishly injudicious and undignified it is to be irritated at trifles
rather than of how wicked we are being and of the punishments that
await the sinful.

Similarly, Johnson urges good humor [9] by inviting us to consider
how irrational it is not to be good-humored. "Surely nothing can be
more unreasonable," he remarks in the *Rambler*, No. 72, "than to
lose the will to please, when we are conscious of the power, or show
more cruelty than to choose any kind of influence before that of
kindness." Cruelty is, to be sure, more explicitly wicked than irrationality, but the total emphasis in this essay is upon the injudicious rather
than upon the sinful aspect of failing to be good-humored. Johnson
also remarks, for example, that "without good-humour, virtue may
awe by its dignity, and amaze by its brightness; but must always be
viewed at a distance, and will scarcely gain a friend or attract an
imitator." This remark clearly implies that it is possible to be virtuous
even though not good-humored and suggests that one of the great
recommendations of good humor is its power of making us happy by
attracting friends. Johnson here appeals primarily to our sense of
what is most judicious rather than to dread of what is forbidden
because it is sinful. Indeed, in the *Rambler*, No. 99, Johnson remarks
that "to love all men is our duty, so far as it includes a general habit
of benevolence, and readiness of occasional kindness; but to love all
equally is impossible." In Johnson's view the Christian obligation of
universal love extends no farther than an obligation to constant *be-*

9. "A habit of being pleased; a constant and perennial softness of manner,
easiness of approach, and suavity of disposition . . . a state between gaiety and
unconcern; the act of emanation of a mind at leisure to regard the gratification
of another" (*Rambler*, No. 72).

nevolence ("Disposition to do good; kindness; charity; good will") but does not entail loving everybody as part of Christian duty. Therefore, good humor, which is merely "a habit of being pleased" together with a willingness to make our virtues—including benevolent acts—attractive as well as admirable, is not, however judicious it may be, any crucial part of the duties which have been imposed by God. Indirectly as well as explicitly, then, Johnson describes good humor as a necessary part of wisdom, though hardly an indispensable adjunct of virtue and piety.

It may seem inconsistent that Johnson condemns "ill-humour or peevishness" as a violation of religious obligations, while merely recommending "good-humour" as a desirable though not obligatory trait. This seeming inconsistency diminishes, however, when we recognize that, despite the terms he uses, "good-humour" is really not quite the converse of "ill-humor." Johnson's discussion of peevishness in the *Rambler*, No. 74, makes it clear that in his view ill-humor is perennial dissatisfaction with whatever we are experiencing in the present moment; his definition of "good-humour" in the *Rambler*, No. 72, makes it clear that in his view good humor is perennial willingness to be pleased by other people, and to please them. As Johnson uses them, the terms thus overlap to some extent because thoroughgoing peevishness would evidently make it impossible to be good-humored, while persistent good humor would inevitably make us less disposed to peevish discontentment and complaints than we might otherwise be. Despite this overlap, however, Johnson seems to draw a line between the vice he condemns as peevishness or ill-humor and the folly which he advises us to avoid by adopting the attitude of good humor as we think about—and speak with—other people.

Johnson unquestionably draws a sharper line between irrationally peevish discontentment over trifles and unwillingness to be pleased with other people, on the one hand, and impatient discontentment in the face of real calamity, on the other hand. In the *Rambler*, No. 150, Johnson characteristically chides the excessive optimism of the "panegyrists of calamity," but then goes on to concede:

The antidotes with which philosophy has medicated the cup of life, though they cannot give it salubrity and sweetness, have at least allayed its bitterness, and contempered its malignity. . . . By suffering willingly what we cannot avoid, we secure ourselves from vain and immoderate disquiet; we preserve for better purposes that strength which would be unprofitably wasted in wild efforts of desperation, and maintain that circumspection which may enable us to seize every support, and improve every alleviation. This calmness will be more easily obtained, as the attention is more powerfully withdrawn from the contemplation of unmingled, unabated evil, and diverted to those accidental benefits which prudence may confer on every state.

This counsel of patience when confronted with unavoidable unpleasantness is secular in its appeal, because it suggests how foolish it is to be impatient when impatience merely aggravates suffering by dissipating our strength and distracting attention from thoughts which might afford some measure of consolation. In the *Rambler,* No. 32, Johnson uses similar arguments to dissuade us from impatience, but these arguments are subordinated to religious considerations. "With regard to futurity," he observes, impatience "is yet less to be justified, since, without lessening the pain, it cuts off the hope of that reward which he, by whom it is inflicted, will confer upon them that bear it well." This reminder is reiterated and reinforced in Johnson's concluding suggestion:

The chief security against the fruitless anguish of impatience, must arise from frequent reflection on the wisdom and goodness of the God of nature, in whose hands are riches and poverty, honour and disgrace, pleasure and pain, and life and death. A settled conviction of the tendency of every thing to our good, and of the possibility of turning miseries into happiness, by receiving them rightly, will incline us to *bless the name of the* LORD, *whether he gives or takes away.*

Thus impatience in the face of real calamity, like ill-humored peevishness over trifles, is condemned as sinful, though Johnson follows classical Christian tradition in making his condemnation of impatience far more severe by explicitly linking this sin with deprivation of heaven. In proposing repeated meditation upon God's wisdom together with faith in "the tendency of every thing to our good" as a remedy for impatience, Johnson's advice on the moral discipline of the mind also takes a more decidedly religious turn.

His warning against excessive distrust of others is similarly grounded on recognition of religious obligations. "Suspicion is not less an enemy to virtue than to happiness," Johnson observes in the *Rambler*, No. 79, adding that "he that is already corrupt is naturally suspicious, and he that becomes suspicious will quickly be corrupt. . . . It is our duty not to suppress tenderness by suspicion; it is better to suffer wrong than to do it, and happier to be sometimes cheated than not to trust." In this passage Johnson balances the unhappiness of occasionally being wronged against what he suggests is the greater unhappiness of always clouding thoughts with suspicions; but the force of this hedonistic appeal, though certainly present, is overshadowed by his assertion that repressing suspicion *is our duty* and by his corollary statement that it is *better*, even when not happier, to comply with our duty. Even though the wisdom of trusting others and thereby avoiding unnecessary unhappiness is suggested, Johnson's emphasis is upon a religious obligation to repress undue suspicion.

The traditionally deadly sin of envy, however, is most often discussed by Johnson in a secular context. In the *Rambler*, No. 58, for example, after observing that "there is no topick more copiously treated by the ancient moralists than the folly of devoting the heart to the accumulation of riches," Johnson goes on to remark:

Since far the greatest part of mankind must be confined to conditions comparatively mean and placed in situations from which they naturally look up with envy to the eminences before them, those writers cannot be thought ill employed that have administered remedies to discontent almost universal, by showing, that what we cannot reach may very well be forborne; that the inequality of distribution, at which we murmur, is, for the most part, less than it seems, and that the greatness, which we admire at a distance, has much fewer advantages, and much less splendour, when we are suffered to approach it.

It is the business of moralists to detect the frauds of fortune, and to show that she imposes upon the careless eye, by a quick succession of shadows, which will shrink to nothing in the gripe; that she disguises life in extrinsick ornaments, which serve only for show, and are laid aside in the hours of solitude, and of pleasure; and that when greatness aspires either to felicity or to wisdom, it shakes off those distinctions which dazzle the gazer, and awe the supplicant.

This passage is remarkable not only because it is one of the rare places where Johnson explicitly defines some part of "the business of moralists" but also because it clearly puts envy among those discontentments which make us unhappy rather than among those sins which deprive us of heaven. Similarly, Johnson suggests in the *Rambler*, No. 128, that whoever "finds himself inclined to envy another, should remember that he knows not the real condition which he desires to obtain, but is certain that by indulging a vitious passion, he must lessen that happiness which he thinks already too sparingly bestowed." This suggestion is also noteworthy for its failure to condemn envy as a sin which it is our religious duty to avoid, on pain of damnation. To be sure, *vitious* is defined in Johnson's *Dictionary* as "Corrupt; wicked; opposite to virtuous." It is a variant of *victious*, which is defined as "Devoted to vice; not addicted to virtue." But even though his application of the adjective *vitious* identifies the passion of envy as sinful, Johnson here points most explicitly at the folly of allowing ourselves to suffer a passion that must inevitably lessen our happiness in this world. His chief remedy for such unhappiness is simply a suggestion that we consider how little likelihood there is that we would in fact be happier if we could change places with those whom we mistakenly envy. This same suggestion is found in the *Rambler*, No. 38, while in the *Idler*, No. 32, Johnson first remarks emphatically that "all envy would be extinguished, if it were universally known that there are none to be envied." He then goes on to argue that in fact no one has ever been enviably happy. In the *Rambler*, No. 52, however, he refers briefly to "the vice of envy." In the *Rambler*, No. 17, he defines it as "that vice which is, above most others, tormenting to ourselves, hateful to the world, and productive of mean artifices and sordid projects." He then goes on to argue that if we contemplate mortality, we will realize that no one can count on enjoying his advantages for a sufficiently long time to be envied his brief possession of them. Thus envy is treated as an attitude which, though sinful, is above all eminently injudicious. Johnson proposes that we cure this intellectual malady by the secular method of learning to make more accurate comparisons between our own state and that of others, in order to perceive the truth that all men are prey to similar causes of unhappiness no matter what temporary or superficial advantages may seem to separate them.

Johnson advances an alternative suggestion, however, in the *Rambler*, No. 186: "One of the great arts of escaping superfluous uneasiness, is to free our minds from the habit of comparing our condition with that of others on whom the blessings of life are more bountifully bestowed, or with imaginary states of delight and security, perhaps unattainable by mortals." Thus, instead of making the difficult effort to notice the inevitable discomforts attached to those states that superficially seem more enviable than our own, we may simply turn our thoughts away to some other aspect of the present. More rewarding objects are not far to seek, for, as Johnson goes on to point out, "Few are placed in a situation so gloomy and distressful, as not to see every day beings yet more forlorn and miserable, from whom they may learn to rejoice in their own lot." [10] This alternative method of freeing ourselves from the "superfluous uneasiness" of envy is as secular as Johnson's first, and more frequently reiterated, proposal.

Johnson's advice on how to rid ourselves of boredom, another form of injudicious discontentment with our present state, is also primarily

10. In the *Rambler*, No. 2, Johnson observes that "it is the sage advice of Epictetus, that a man should accustom himself often to think of what is most shocking and terrible, that by such reflections he may be preserved from too ardent wishes for seeming good, and from too much dejection in real evil." See also the *Rambler*, No. 52.

secular. Considering, in the *Rambler*, No. 5, those who "are burdensome to themselves merely because they want subjects for reflection,"
Johnson asserts:

It ought to be the endeavour of every man to derive his reflections
from the objects about him; for it is to no purpose that he alters his
position, if his attention continues fixed to the same point. The mind
should be kept open to the access of every new idea, and so far
disengaged from the predominance of particular thoughts, as easily to
accommodate itself to occasional entertainment.

This general advice is primarily designed to increase happiness rather
than virtue by making our situation more acceptable in our own
estimation. It is unfortunate, but hardly sinful, to be burdensome to
ourselves. Johnson does, however, go on to point out:

A man that has formed this habit of turning every new object to his
entertainment, finds in the productions of nature an inexhaustible
stock of materials upon which he can employ himself, without any
temptations to envy or malevolence; faults, perhaps, seldom totally
avoided by those, whose judgement is much exercised upon the works
of art. He has always a certain prospect of discovering new reasons for
adoring the sovereign author of the universe, and probable hopes of
making some discovery of benefit to others, or of profit to himself.

Thus Johnson turns from his more general advice to suggest the
particular benefits of entertaining ourselves by contemplating nature
rather than the contrivances of man, thereby encouraging adoration
of God while at the same time removing ourselves from temptations
to become envious or malevolent. But despite the inclusion of these
religious advantages in his prescription for avoiding boredom, his
emphasis in the *Rambler*, No. 5, is clearly upon the secular advantages of turning to nature for entertainment. "He that enlarges his
curiosity after the works of nature," Johnson notes in his concluding
paragraph, "demonstrably multiplies the inlets to happiness."

His major suggestions for curing the disorders induced by unchecked imagination are also predominantly secular, even though (as
I have pointed out in Chapter II) Johnson enforces the importance of

his suggestions by calling attention to the fact that "the luxury of a vain imagination" may very well undermine virtue and hence threaten salvation. He usually stresses the unhappiness as much as the sinfulness caused by "the tyranny of fancy" and recommends redirection of our thoughts outside ourselves to the realities of the present moment as a means of inducing the kinds of secular activities that will rescue us from the dangerous dreams induced by idleness. In the *Rambler*, No. 89, for example, Johnson remarks:

This captivity [by the imagination], however, it is necessary for every man to break, who has any desire to be wise or useful, to pass his life with the esteem of others, or look back with satisfaction from his old age upon his earlier years. In order to regain liberty, he must find the means of flying from himself; he must, in opposition to the Stoick precept, teach his desires to fix upon external things; he must adopt the joys and the pains of others, and excite in his mind the want of social pleasures and amicable communication.

Here emphasis is placed on the wisdom of bridling fancy by the secular means of looking abroad for "social pleasures" that will increase present happiness. Johnson goes on to recommend (with reservations) some new study, but especially "active employment or public pleasure":

The great resolution to be formed, when happiness and virtue are thus formidably invaded, is, that no part of life be spent in a state of neutrality or indifference; but that some pleasure be found for every moment that is not devoted to labour; and that, whenever the necessary business of life grows irksome or disgusting, an immediate transition be made to diversion and gaiety.

Unchecked imagination is seen as a threat to virtue as well as to happiness, but Johnson emphasizes the importance of finding pleasures that are more judicious as well as less threatening to our moral state. He does not dwell upon the sinfulness of imaginary delights in quite the way that he spells out the damnation awaiting those who are wickedly impatient.

Indeed, among the major intellectual misuses of the present

moment, only impatience and suspicion are discussed by Johnson in a thoroughly religious context. Both are viewed as primarily sinful rather than merely injudicious, and both are to be cured by considerations that are primarily religious. Suspicion may be overcome by reflecting upon our duty, Johnson suggests, while impatience may be repressed by meditating upon God's wisdom and beneficence. Indecision, ill-humor, envy, and "the luxury of a vain imagination" are condemned as sinful in themselves or conducive to sin, but all four are to be cured, in Johnson's opinion, by methods that are primarily secular: indecision may be overcome by reflecting upon the natural law which makes it impossible to enjoy two mutually exclusive pleasures; ill-humor may be repressed by considering how undignified it is to be annoyed over trifles; the discomforts of envy may be overcome either by making more accurate and therefore less disturbing comparisons between our own situation and that of others who seem happier, or by making more immediately pleasant comparisons between our situation and that of others who are in worse shape; and we may free ourselves from "the tyranny of fancy" by learning to look abroad for "social pleasures." Finally, the importance of good humor and the means of overcoming boredom are both discussed by Johnson in a thoroughly secular context. We may, in his opinion, make ourselves more good-humored by reflecting upon how desirable it is to be loved as well as esteemed for our virtues; and we may escape boredom by learning to derive entertainment from those thoughts which are stimulated by our present surroundings.

Thus, even though Johnson takes into account the religious aspect of our thoughts "as they regard the present," his specific recommendations on the moral discipline of these thoughts are, with the exception of his remedies for impatience and suspicion, predominantly secular. He emphasizes the judicious discipline of the mind for the purpose of showing us how to be as happy as possible in our responses to the present moment. The religious obligations enforcing such discipline, though not ignored, are not placed in the foreground of Johnson's recommendations, which are most frequently designed to inculcate wisdom rather than piety, although, from the broadest perspective, the two designs are ultimately synonymous. It is in this primarily secular context that we must read Johnson's most general statement that

the great consideration which ought to influence us in the use of the present moment, is to arise from the effect which, as well or ill applied, it must have upon the time to come; for though its actual existence be inconceivably short, yet its effects are unlimited; and there is not the smallest point of time but may extend its consequences, either to our hurt or our advantage, through all eternity, and give us reason to remember it for ever, with anguish or exultation.[11]

4

Johnson's suggestions for directing thoughts "as they regard the future" are primarily religious, although he by no means neglects the secular aspects of our concern with what lies in store for us in this world. "It seems to be the fate of man to seek all his consolations in futurity," Johnson observes in the *Rambler*, No. 203, adding that "the time present is seldom able to fill desire or imagination with immediate enjoyment, and we are forced to supply its deficiencies by recollection or anticipation." In the *Dictionary* he defines *futurity* as "1. Time to come; 2. Event to come; 3. The state of being to be; futurition." Thus, in remarking that we seek all our "consolations in futurity," Johnson is pointing not to the primary fact that we look for happiness in an afterlife but rather to the more general fact that, dissatisfied with our thoughts about the present, we look for consolation by anticipating what is to befall us here in this world as well as in the hereafter. Throughout the moral essays he is concerned with both kinds of anticipation and offers suggestions for regulating them in order to live judiciously as well as piously.

In the *Rambler*, No. 73, for example, Johnson uses the device of a

11. *Rambler*, No. 41.

letter from Cupidus, a legacy hunter, to show the most fundamentally injudicious regulation of our thoughts as they regard the future.

Being accustomed [Cupidus complains] to give the future full power over my mind, and to start away from the scene before me to some expected enjoyment, I deliver up myself to the tyranny of every desire which fancy suggests, and long for a thousand things which I am unable to procure . . . and the rest of my life must pass in craving solicitude, unless you can find some remedy for a mind, corrupted with an inveterate disease of wishing, and unable to think on any thing but wants, which reason tells me will never be supplied.

This complaint suggests how irrational, and hence injudicious, it is to devote all thoughts to future pleasures and thus, by dwelling on anticipated happiness, contract "an inveterate disease of wishing." Johnson's emphasis here is not upon the sinfulness of refusing to think about the present but rather upon the supreme absurdity of making ourselves miserable by such misdirection of our thoughts.

Dreaming of future happiness to the exclusion of all thought about the present is only one form of undue preoccupation with the future. The other alternative is morbid anticipation of disasters that may never occur. "All useless misery is certainly folly," Johnson remarks in the *Idler*, No. 72, adding that "he that feels evils before they come may be deservedly censured." He concedes that "to dread the future is more reasonable than to lament the past," but this concession does not weaken his condemnation of exaggerated fears. "False hopes and false terrors are equally to be avoided," he observes in the *Rambler*, No. 25, while nevertheless arguing that of the two, unreasonable fears are often the more crippling in our secular endeavors. One effect of exaggerated fears, for example, is excessive prudence, as Johnson shows in the *Idler*, No. 57, by portraying the character of Sophron, who "creeps along, neither loved nor hated, neither favoured nor opposed: he has never attempted to grow rich for fear of growing poor, and has raised no friends, for fear of making enemies." The folly of Sophron's paralyzing fears is evident for, as Johnson also points out in the *Idler*, No. 57, "Prudence keeps life safe, but does not often make it happy." The main trouble with allowing worries about the future to dominate responses to the present is that mere safety rather than positive happiness then becomes our chief pleasure in this world.

Despite Johnson's pessimism about the possibility of finding enduring earthly happiness, he was at pains to insist that snatches of real happiness are within our grasp and that it is foolish not to seize them when we can.[12] Thus, in the *Rambler*, No. 47, he remarks that "many who have laid down rules of intellectual health, think preservatives easier than remedies, and teach us not to trust ourselves with favourite enjoyments, not to indulge the luxury of fondness, but to keep our minds always suspended in such indifference, that we may change the objects about us without emotion." This stoic recommendation is dictated by fear that what we allow ourselves to enjoy may be taken away from us, just as Sophron's excessive prudence is dictated by fear that definite actions may have unpleasant consequences. Johnson is equally firm in rejecting stoic indifference:

An exact compliance with this rule might, perhaps, contribute to tranquillity, but surely it would never produce happiness. . . . An attempt to preserve life in a state of neutrality and indifference, is unreasonable and vain. If by excluding joy we could shut out grief, the scheme would deserve our serious attention; but since, however we may debar ourselves from happiness, misery will find its way at many inlets . . . we may surely endeavour to raise life above the middle point of apathy at one time, since it will necessarily sink below it at another.

12. In *Rasselas*, Imlac observes (at the end of Chap. XXI) that "Human life is every where a state, in which much is to be endured, and little to be enjoyed" (*Works*, I, 226). By writing "little" rather than "nothing" Johnson meliorates the pessimism of Imlac's remark by suggesting that there are some things to be enjoyed in life. This suggestion is variously reiterated throughout *Rasselas*. For an excellent discussion of the artistry with which the pessimism of *Rasselas* is qualified, see Sheldon Sacks, *Fiction and the Shape of Belief* (Berkeley and Los Angeles, 1964), pp. 52–55.

Johnson's emphasis in this rejection of stoicism is upon the irrational folly rather than upon the sinfulness of allowing fears to make us indifferent when we might well be happy. In the *Rambler*, No. 32, Johnson considers from a religious viewpoint the stoic suggestion that we remain indifferent to earthly pleasures:

This counsel, when we consider the enjoyment of any terrestrial advantage, as opposite to a constant and habitual solicitude for future felicity, is undoubtedly just, and delivered by that authority which cannot be disputed; but in any other sense, is it not like advice, not to walk lest we should stumble, or not to see lest our eyes should light upon deformity? It seems to be reasonable to enjoy blessings with confidence, as well as to resign them with submission; and to hope for the continuance of good which we possess, without insolence or voluptuousness, as for the restitution of that which we lose without despondency or murmurs.

However, despite this warning Johnson is here primarily reassuring us that we have no obligation to refrain from those innocent enjoyments which providence allots us. He is more concerned with removing a possible scruple than with calling attention to a positive duty imposed upon us by God. Thus many of Johnson's important warnings against morbid concern with possibilities of disaster, like his equally vigorous warnings against excessive anticipation of future pleasures, emphasize the folly rather than the impiety of giving the future a disproportionate amount of our attention.

Johnson is careful, moreover, to suggest the judicious secular uses of both fears and hopes by showing how, when properly encouraged, they may increase happiness in this world. In the *Rambler*, No. 43, for example, he suggests that "whoever would complete any arduous and intricate enterprise, should, as soon as his imagination can cool after the first blaze of hope, place before his own eyes every possible embarrassment that may retard or defeat him." The wisdom of thus thinking about all possible hindrances to our plans is evident because "if we alarm ourselves beforehand with more difficulties than we really find, we shall be animated by unexpected facility with double spirit; and if we find our cautions and fears justified by the consequence, there will, however, happen nothing against which provision has not been made, no sudden shock will be received, nor will the main scheme be disconcerted." Johnson always approves of such useful fears, just as he notes the practical advantages of even mildly delusory—and hence irrational—expectations. In the *Rambler*, No. 2, for example, he notes that there would "be few enterprises of great labour or hazard undertaken, if we had not the power of magnifying the advantages which we persuade ourselves to expect from them." Indeed, he goes so far as to assert, in the *Idler*, No. 58, that "it is necessary to hope, tho' hope should always be deluded, for hope itself is happiness, and its frustrations, however frequent, are yet less dreadful than its extinction." There is thus in the moral essays no lack of perfectly secular advice on the uses and abuses of hope and fear.

But despite his careful inclusion of such advice, Johnson emphasizes most strongly the religious role of both passions. The *Rambler*, No. 29, which is devoted to "the folly of anticipating misfortunes," argues that "if the breast be once laid open to the dread of mere possibilities of misery, life must be given a prey to dismal solicitude, and quiet must be lost for ever." Yet after thus stating the secular disadvantages of thinking too much about troubles that may await us, Johnson proceeds to a discussion of the religious dangers attendant upon such improper concern with the future and concludes by warning that

in proportion as our cares are employed upon the future, they are abstracted from the present, from the only time which we can call our own, and of which, if we neglect the apparent duties, to make provision against visionary attacks, we shall certainly counteract our own purpose, for he, doubtless, mistakes his true interest, who thinks that he can increase his safety, when he impairs his virtue.

Johnson here stresses the pernicious effect improper fears can have upon our virtue when they make us neglect religious obligations ("apparent duties"). Conversely, in the *Rambler*, No. 110, he stresses the religious importance of properly directed fears by observing that "sorrow and terrour must naturally precede reformation; for what other cause can produce it?" This observation clearly reveals Johnson's conviction that dread of God, no less than sorrow for past misdeeds, is essential if we are to make our actions conform to the obligations imposed upon us by revelation. The proper direction—or suppression—of fears is thus treated by Johnson as an indispensable adjunct of piety as well as a necessary part of wisdom.

His discussion of the judicious regulation of hopes for the purpose of securing as much earthly happiness as possible is similarly complemented by a careful consideration of their proper religious role. In the *Rambler*, No. 69, for example, Johnson observes that

piety is the only proper and adequate relief of decaying man. He that grows old without religious hopes, as he declines into imbecility, and feels pains and sorrows incessantly crowding upon him, falls into a gulph of bottomless misery, in which every reflection must plunge him deeper, and where he finds only new gradations of anguish, and precipices of horrour.

Here religious hopes are viewed not only as the one source of happiness remaining during our last moments in this life but also as the only proper source of happiness. By describing such hopes as fitting, Johnson implies that they are demanded as part of our religious obligation. This chilling passage is reinforced by an equally strong affirmation in the *Rambler*, No. 203:

It is not . . . from this world, that any ray of comfort can proceed, to cheer the gloom of the last hour. But futurity has still its prospects; there is yet happiness in reserve, which, if we transfer our attention to it, will support us in the pains of disease, and the languor of decay. This happiness we may expect with confidence, because it is out of the power of chance, and may be attained by all that sincerely desire and earnestly pursue it. On this therefore every mind ought finally to rest. Hope is the chief blessing of man, and that hope only is rational, of which we are certain that it cannot deceive us.

Although, as I have pointed out, Johnson explicitly sanctions some forms of irrational hopes because they serve the secular purpose of making life happier ("hope itself is happiness . . ."), he also insists that we "ought finally to rest" our minds upon anticipation of heaven as the only completely rational hope available to us. His use of the word *ought* in this context surely carries the weight of religious obligation. He thus implies that it is not only supremely injudicious but sinful as well to fall into despair.

The uses, for the moral discipline of the mind, of properly directed religious hopes and fears are most clearly summarized and reiterated by Johnson when he discusses death. He asserts in the *Rambler*, No. 17,

A frequent and attentive prospect of that moment, which must put a period to all our schemes, and deprive us of all our acquisitions, is indeed of the utmost efficacy to the just and rational regulation of our lives; nor would ever any thing wicked, or often any thing absurd, be undertaken or prosecuted by him who should begin every day with a serious reflection that he is born to die.

Johnson goes on to show how daily reflection on mortality may help counteract "the disturbers of our happiness in this world" by convincing us of "the lightness of all terrestrial evil, which certainly can last no longer than the subject upon which it acts." He discusses not only the miseries caused by obsessive desires similar to those described by Cupidus and the inevitable disappointment encountered by scholars or statesmen who attempt more than they can possibly complete in one lifetime, but also the more sinful passions of envy and prolonged grieving over the loss of friends or possessions. Yet Johnson's emphasis here is upon the secular advantages of reflecting "with the father of physic, 'that art is long and life is short,' " as a method of avoiding needless misery in this world.

But in the *Rambler*, No. 78, Johnson strongly emphasizes the religious importance of reflecting upon death and final judgment as a means of preventing wicked as well as absurd conduct. "The great incentive to virtue," he notes, "is the reflection that we must die." Nevertheless, he also remarks, with characteristic appreciation of those practical difficulties which often stand in the way of the counsel of perfection, that "a perpetual meditation upon the last hour, however it may become the solitude of a monastery, is inconsistent with many duties of common life. But surely the remembrance of death ought to predominate in our minds, as an habitual and settled principle, always operating, though not always perceived." This remark is possibly misleading to a modern reader because it seems to anticipate Freud's conception of unconscious motives which always operate on our conduct even though they are never readily available to casual introspection. All Johnson probably means, however, is that preference for virtuous rather than sinful actions ought to become so habitual that we instinctively recoil from wickedness even when we do not pause to analyze our reasons for doing so. He would undoubtedly have said that such "habitual and settled principles" (unlike Freudian unconscious motives) are perfectly plain to us when we do take the trouble to think about why we respond virtuously. In any case, he provides a straightforward suggestion on how we may best instill such perpetual, even though often unperceived, remembrance of death: "It will . . . be useful to accustom ourselves, whenever we see a funeral, to consider how soon we may be added to the number of those whose probation is past, and whose happiness or misery shall endure for ever." This advice is similar to that provided in the *Idler*, No. 43, where Johnson points out that "unremitted vigilance of caution, and activity of virtue" might be usefully encouraged by considering the succession of day and night as well as the seasonal variation of winter and summer as emblematic of the passage of life and thus reminders of our own mortality.

Another use of religious hopes and fears which Johnson frequently points out is that of freeing us from excessive dependence upon other men's opinions. Johnson remarks in the *Rambler*, No. 127,

He that never extends his view beyond the praises or rewards of men will be dejected by neglect and envy, or infatuated by honours and applause. But the consideration that life is only deposited in his hand to be employed in obedience to a master who will regard his endeavours, not his success, would have preserved him from trivial elations and discouragements, and enabled him to proceed with constancy and cheerfulness, neither enervated by commendation, nor intimidated by censure.

In other words, to the extent that we can direct hopes of future approbation and fear of future disapproval towards heaven, we will find more happiness here on earth because we will see worldly successes or failures in the proper perspective of eternity. Johnson was too realistic, however, to propose that we simply suppress our desire to be praised while alive and remembered with applause by men when we are dead. "The love of fame," he affirms in the *Rambler*, No. 49, "is to be regulated rather than extinguished; and . . . men should be taught not to be wholly careless about their memory, but to endeavour that they may be remembered chiefly for their virtues, since no other reputation will be able to transmit any pleasure beyond the grave." Johnson here suggests that hopes of heaven and fears of hell, far from making us despise the applause of this world, should rather make us properly mindful of it and willing to struggle for a virtuous reputation. In itself, such fame is of no more significance than any other worldly possession which must be left behind when we die. Johnson is not saying that posthumous fame will directly "transmit any pleasure beyond the grave" by making us happier in heaven as our reputation spreads around the earth. He is merely affirming that all the virtuous acts we perform with an eye on our reputation will be duly rewarded by God, for it is only in this indirect sense that our reputation is able to "transmit any pleasure beyond the grave." Johnson's concern with the moral discipline of the mind thus leads him to suggest a useful way of harnessing secular hopes in the service of religious obligations for the immediate purpose of encouraging virtuous conduct. But there is, in his opinion, the further advantage that once love of fame has been properly regulated by hopes of heaven, it may serve to keep alive those religious hopes when they might otherwise, to our eternal detriment, fade out of mind. Johnson cautions that "if . . . the love of fame is so far indulged by the mind as to become independent and predominant, it is dangerous and irregular."

He goes on to suggest that it nevertheless "may be usefully employed as an inferior and secondary motive and will serve sometimes to revive our activity, when we begin to languish and lose sight of that more certain, more valuable, and more durable reward, which ought always to be our first hope and our last."

There is no mistaking Johnson's primarily religious concern with the future. A perfectly conventional Christian preoccupation with the "four last things"—death, judgment, heaven, and hell—clearly underlies his advice on the methods of continually reflecting on death so that such reflections will operate as the settled principles which, whether perceived at any given moment or not, guide our actions. The same Christian concern with religious obligations underlies his warning against the dangers of allowing morbidly exaggerated fears to distract us from virtuous attention to "apparent duties," just as it underlies his reminder that "terror must naturally precede reformation" and his advice on the proper regulation of our love of fame.

Yet within this firmly religious framework appears a noteworthy amount of concern with largely secular ends and many suggestions that mainly appeal to our desire for happiness on this earth. Stoic indifference, prudence as a guiding principle of life, and "an inveterate disease of wishing," for example, are all condemned because, though they are not necessarily sinful, they prevent us from being as happy as we might be in this life. We are warned to avoid such injudicious attitudes for this reason alone. Similarly, Johnson suggests the secular advantages of hoping for success in our endeavors even though such hope continually proves delusory, of magnifying the advantages we expect to gain from our efforts, and of rationally considering the possible obstacles that may impede our plans. He even devotes a paper in the *Rambler* to suggesting that daily reflection on death—without any consideration of final judgment, heaven, and hell—will in itself suffice to make our lives much happier by helping to cure envy, grief, and obsessive desires as well as by dissuading us from attempting impossibly ambitious, and thus inevitably disappointing, projects. Therefore, while it is true that Johnson's general suggestions on the moral discipline of our thoughts about the future are, like his suggestions on the moral discipline of our thoughts about the past, primarily religious, this is far from the whole truth. It is necessary to recognize the great number of specific suggestions which, while perfectly compatible with Johnson's underlying religious concern, are not explicitly related to the task of making our thoughts (and subsequently our conduct) more pious.

❧ 5 ❧

It is hardly possible to separate the religious and secular aspects of his advice on any part of the moral discipline of the mind without seriously distorting our vision of Johnson's achievement. I have called attention to the secular cast of Johnson's endeavor to promote self-knowledge by the rational method of pointing out the various artifices of self-deceit. Yet it has been equally important to note that behind his various exhortations to overcome self-deceptions by "assigning proper portions of . . . life to the examination of the rest" lies Johnson's awareness that self-examination is in fact a religious duty "recommended by divines, as the first act previous to repentance." Even his descriptions of self-delusion are strongly shaped by concern with the dangers of pride and the importance of that humility which is described by Johnson as "the basis of Christianity." Similarly, I have called attention to the secular cast of Johnson's proposal of an art of forgetfulness and his advice on the methods of promoting good humor and avoiding indecision, ill-humor, envy, boredom, vain imagination, stoic indifference, excessive prudence, and "an inveterate disease of wishing." Yet it has been equally important to note Johnson's primarily religious concern with the moral discipline of thoughts regarding the past and the future, just as it has been essential to note that even though his suggestions on the moral discipline of thoughts regarding the present are largely secular, he nevertheless suggests religious cures of impatience and suspicion and condemns indecision, ill-humor, envy, and vain imagination as sinful or dangerously conducive to sin as well as misery. There is, therefore, some difficulty in deciding whether the secular or the religious aspect of Johnson's advice is, ultimately, the more noteworthy.

Perhaps, after all, Johnson's own statement provides the best solution of this dilemma, for in the final essay in the *Rambler* he remarks that "the essays professedly serious, if I have been able to execute my own intentions, will be found exactly conformable to the precepts of Christianity, without any accommodation to the licentiousness and levity of the present age." This remark clearly suggests the main problem which Johnson had to deal with as a moralist writing periodical essays for a worldly audience rather than sermons for a captive congregation. Each genre presents its own purely literary difficulties. But the writer of sermons can introduce religious precepts without automatically alienating his audience. A congregation will expect dogmatic instruction and be willing to have elegance sacrificed to that end. Those who purchase periodical essays, poems, apologues, or biographies, on the other hand, will insist that even what is "professedly serious" be not only elegantly written but highly relevant to the affairs of this life. It is easy to frighten away such a worldly audience merely by introducing religious exhortations of any kind. Consequently, even a Christian moralist, when writing in secular genres, must be tempted to confine his advice to that part of morality which is independent of religion. Johnson, however, resisted this temptation. Most of his specific suggestions on the moral discipline of the mind are clearly dictated by a profoundly Christian concern with directing thoughts into lawful as well as judicious channels and away from sinful or potentially sinful attitudes. Even when his immediate concern is worldly happiness, it is usually possible to discern the ultimately religious importance of Johnson's various suggestions on the direction of our thoughts as they regard the past, the present, and the future. Considering, therefore, the secular genres which Johnson chose as a vehicle of moral instruction and, what he made corollary to that choice, his extensive reliance upon naturalistic explanation of the anatomy of the mind, it is probably most noteworthy that his advice on the moral discipline of the mind is so often conformable to what he regarded as the more important precepts of Christianity. Unobtrusively, yet unmistakably, Johnson did precisely what he set out to do.

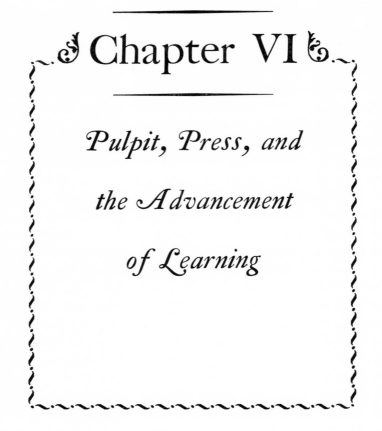

Chapter VI

Pulpit, Press, and the Advancement of Learning

BEFORE TURNING to the general conclusions that emerge from my analysis of Johnson's "dictatorial instruction," I should perhaps emphasize once again the scope and limitations of this book. It has been almost exclusively concerned with Johnson's consideration of "the arduous province of preserving the balance of the mental constitution"—with, in other words, his suggestions on how we may govern our thoughts in ways that "promote the increase of virtue." After explaining his underlying assumptions about the anatomy of the mind, I have classified almost all of his explicit advice on the proper methods of regulating thoughts and have discussed the reasons—religious and secular—which prompt him to make the various kinds of suggestions which we find throughout the moral essays. My analysis has thus been confined to Johnson's directions for the moral regulation of our inward responses to the world around us. I have not attempted to discuss the different, though of course closely related, subject of his directions for the moral regulation of our outward conduct. I have not, for example, considered his warning against giving vague directions to servants, his condemnation of rudeness to servants, or his stern censure of those authors who dedicate their books to wicked men. Nor have I considered his equally vigorous condemnations of such evils as slander, vivisection, servile flattery, forcing daughters into financially desirable marriages, imprisonment for debt, capital punishment for robbery, and mistreatment of American Indians. Nor, finally, have I discussed his warnings against the hazards involved in soliciting confidences, revealing secrets, affected behavior, social climbing, card playing, and talking down to people.

Many of these topics, as well as Johnson's other suggestions on proper moral conduct, have received their due share of discussion in recent scholarship. There still persists, however, the notion that in his consideration of the ethical aspects of our inner life Johnson did little more than pass on age-old wisdom given new vigor by his marvelous prose style. That his innovations as a prose stylist add much to the arresting quality of his accomplishment as a moral essayist can hardly be denied. But just as he shaped the familiar materials of our language into patterns whose novelty has been accounted for only after the most extensive analysis, so too did he combine the thought of his predecessors into a distinctive pattern that is significantly more than merely the sum of its parts. It has been my task in this book to show the major strands of intellectual material which Johnson wove into that unique pattern.

There now remains the necessity of closing with a reminder that those strands are of interest apart from their context only because Johnson put them together and in so doing transformed them. Thus, if familiar Lockean notions seem to have undergone a sea change when we encounter them in the midst of an extended effort to teach the moral discipline of the mind, that is because they have indeed become enriched in their new environment. Yet the nature of that transformation has unavoidably been obscured to some extent in the process of calling attention to the disparate materials that have undergone a Johnsonian metamorphosis. Perhaps, however, what is most characteristic about the pattern of Johnson's career as a public moralist can be summed up and thrown into sharp relief by considering how Johnson's moral essays differ from his sermons, for the extent of that difference provides some measure of how very well Johnson succeeded in doing exactly what, over a century before, Bacon had insisted that all future moralists must do.

Ever since Mandeville dismissed Addison by calling him a parson in a tiewig, there have been occasional attempts to suggest an affinity between periodical essays and sermons. The most amusing example is Taine's condemnation of Addison, Steele, and Johnson. "The *Spectator*, the *Tatler*, the *Guardian*, are mere lay sermons," he complained before proceeding to deal with the *Rambler* by wondering "who could have been the lovers of *ennui* who have bought up thirteen thousand copies." After raising this question Taine provided a famous answer by reminding himself "that sermons are liked in England and that these essays are sermons." [1] More recently and less tendentiously, Richardson has noted the existence of "what may be called the essay sermon"; and Mitchell has observed that during the seventeenth century "the purely hermeneutic and the literary converge, and the sermon, which in earlier times had been an oration, came to be regarded almost as an essay." [2] But no one has taken the analogy between sermon and moral essay seriously enough to attempt a precise

1. H. A. Taine, *History of English Literature*, trans. H. Van Laun (Edinburgh, 1874) III, 161, 323–24.

2. Caroline Francis Richardson, *English Preachers and Preaching 1640–1670* (New York, 1928), p. 86; W. Fraser Mitchell, *English Pulpit Oratory from Andrewes to Tillotson* (London, 1932), p. 349. See also Peter

statement of the formal properties shared by the two genres. Nor has there been any attempt to show whether the *Spectator* and the *Rambler* are in fact equally close to English homiletic practice.

In the *Idler*, No. 91, however, Johnson obliquely suggests the importance of purely homiletic works to the realm of periodical essays when he boldly asserts that morality "is comprehended in practical divinity, and is perhaps better taught in English sermons than in any other books ancient or modern." This statement implies that any moral essayist ought to look first and hardest at English pulpit literature for models of content and possibly form as well. Anglican sermons, the *Spectator*, and the *Rambler* all deal with such topics as pride, charity, self-knowledge, prayer, habits, flattery, envy, and idleness. If, however, Addison provides a greater number of merely entertaining essays than Johnson does, the *Spectator* also contains a higher proportion of explicitly religious essays than can be found in the *Rambler*. In the large number of papers where the two essayists are comparably serious in tone, it is, generally, the *Spectator* which is more sermon-like in subject.

But content alone is seldom the best measure of genre and will hardly carry us very far in this case, since the subject matter of Anglican sermons was no more limited than that of periodical essays. As genres, however, they differ structurally. Despite the wide variations of doctrine and prose style displayed in those English sermons which Johnson praised so highly, they invariably share in one crucial respect the same organizational archetype: each is constructed so that transitions from topic to topic are impossible to miss.[3] Though preachers might treat vastly different subjects or the same subject in vastly different ways, no alert auditor could possibly lose the thread of any homilist's discourse. Usually some text was explained, and that

---

Smithers, *The Life of Joseph Addison* (Oxford, 1954), p. 218; and Melvin R. Watson, *Magazine Serials and the Essay Tradition 1746–1820*, Louisiana State University Studies, Humanities Series No. 6 (Baton Rouge, 1956), p. 4.

3. Cf. Richardson, *English Preachers and Preaching 1640–1670*, pp. 70–71.

explanation was then followed by a consideration of the practical uses
to which each member of the congregation could put the doctrine thus
unfolded for his edification. But whatever the sequence of ideas or the
logic of their connection, some conspicuous device makes clear the
points of transition from one part to the next. Most often simple
enumeration is employed, as, for example, in Johnson's perfectly
typical twelfth sermon:

Let us diligently consider, FIRST: In what sense we are to understand that all is vanity. SECONDLY: How far the conviction, that
all is vanity, ought to influence the conduct of life. THIRDLY: what
consequences the serious and religious mind may deduce from the
position, that all is vanity. When we examine, first, in what sense we
are to understand that all is vanity; we must remember . . . since this
uncertainty and imperfection is the lot which our Creator has appointed for us, we are to inquire, SECONDLY: how far the conviction, that all is vanity, ought to influence the conduct of life . . . and
that this is the disposition which becomes our condition, will appear
when we consider, THIRDLY: What consequences the serious and
religious mind may draw from the position, that all is vanity . . .[4]

The chief hallmark of a sermon, then, is that it is an explicitly and
unmistakably methodical discourse usually devoted to explaining
some general doctrine and its uses or particular application. As one
influential Anglican preaching manual put it after defining method as
"an Art of contriving our discourses in such regular frame, wherein
every part may have its due place and dependence" and pointing out
that there are several methods that might be prescribed: "That which
our gravest Divines by long experience have found most useful for
ordinary and populous Assemblies, is this of *Doctrine* and *Use*." The
author of this advice took care to emphasize the fact that method is
not only useful for those who compose sermons but also "for the
benefit of the *Hearers* likewise, who may understand and retain a
Sermon with greater ease and profit, when they are before-hand

4. *The Works of Samuel Johnson, LL.D.* (9 vols.; Oxford, 1825), IX,
397–403. (Cited hereafter as *Works.*)

acquainted with the general heads of matter that are discoursed of. 'Tis but a bad Rule in *Alsted*, at least for vulgar Auditories, when he advises to conceal, and alter the method, for variety sake." [5]

When they came to discuss the important topic of method, secular rhetoricians and logicians were inclined, like Alsted, to urge concealment. In the textbook of logic long adopted as standard by English universities, for example, Isaac Watts points out that

Those *Writers* and *Speakers,* whose chief Business is to amuse or delight, to allure, terrify, or persuade Mankind, do not confine themselves to any *natural Order,* but in a *cryptical* or *hidden Method* adapt every Thing to their designed Ends . . . They place *the first* Things *last,* and the *last* Things *first,* with wondrous Art, and yet so manage it as to conceal their Artifice, and lead the Senses and Passions of their Hearers into a pleasing and powerful Captivity. It is chiefly *Poesy* and *Oratory* that require the Practice of this Kind of *arbitrary Method.*[6]

Watts never denies the importance of first thinking through one's subject methodically. Most of his chapter on method is devoted to explaining the necessity and means of doing so. But since his discussion is not specifically concerned with the problems and techniques peculiar to pulpit oratory, he dwells on the virtues of concealing

5. John Wilkins, *Ecclesiastes: or A Discourse Concerning the Gift of Preaching, As it falls under the Rules of Art* (6th ed.; London, 1679), pp. 6–7. Wilkins also remarks that the method of Doctrine and Use is "very *Logical,* putting *homogeneous* things together; handling generals first, and particulars after" (p. 7). Towards the conclusion of his chapter on method (pp. 6–39) he affirms that application, which he defines as "all the Uses that are inferred from the Doctrine," is "the life and soul of a Sermon; whereby these Sacred Truths are brought home to a man's particular conscience, and occasions, and the affections engaged unto any truth or duty" (p. 29).

6. Isaac Watts, *Logick: or, the Right Use of Reason in the Enquiry after Truth* (8th ed.; London, 1745), p. 348. It was from this textbook that Johnson drew his *Dictionary* definition of *method;* and according to Lewis Freed, "The Sources of Johnson's Dictionary" (diss., Cornell University, 1939), Johnson cites Watts' *Logick* 193 times in Volume I alone of his *Dictionary.*

method and departing from "natural" order when presenting material. He also remarks toward the conclusion of his chapter that "it renders the Discourse much more agreeable, when proper and graceful Expression joins the Parts of it together in so entertaining a manner, that the Reader knows not how to leave off till he hath arrived at the End." [7] Thus for Watts all gracelessly explicit transitional formulas would be suspect because even though they may show where a work is going they also make it easier to spot those points where one can conveniently "leave off." For those works which, unlike sermons, cannot depend upon a captive audience, Watts prefers to sacrifice the simple utility of obvious method in favor of those elegant transitions which help maintain readers in "a pleasing and powerful Captivity."

Addison, the parson *manqué* turned essayist, makes his position on method equally clear. Before his speculation on laughter he remarks: "When I make Choice of a Subject that has not been treated of by others, I throw together my Reflections on it without any Order or Method, so that they may appear rather in the Looseness and Freedom of an Essay, than in the regularity of a Set Discourse." [8] Novelty of content is thus one principle liberating a composition from the obligation to be—or at least appear to be—methodical. Moreover, it is such freedom which in Addison's view transforms a composition from some other thing into an essay. And Johnson seems to have shared this view, for unlike most earlier lexicographers he defines the genre in terms of its irregularity rather than in terms of its brevity: *essay* is defined in his *Dictionary* as "A loose sally of the mind; an irregular indigested piece; not a regular and orderly composition." [9]

7. *Logick*, p. 364.

8. *Spectator*, No. 249. All quotations from Addison's essays are taken from *The Spectator*, ed. Gregory Smith (Everyman Edition, 4 vols.; London, 1958).

9. Edward Phillips, *The New World of Words: or a General English Dictionary* (3rd ed.; London, 1671) defines *essay* as "A Short discourse on a subject." Nathan Bailey, *Dictionarium Britannicum* (London, 1730) defines *essay* as "A short discourse or treatise on some subject." And Benjamin Martin,

Addison does not specify the other occasions, in addition to novelty of content, which may allow him to break away from "the regularity of a set discourse," but he does suggest that it is important to be methodical when treating a complicated topic, thus implying that simple subjects may be discussed in an irregular manner.[10] He also acknowledges that many of his papers have been irregular:

Among my daily Papers which I bestow on the Publick, there are some which are written with Regularity and Method, and others that run out into the Wildness of those Compositions which go by the Name of *Essays*. As for the first, I have the whole Scheme of the Discourse in my Mind before I set Pen to Paper. In the other Kind of Writing, it is sufficient that I have several Thoughts on a Subject, without troubling myself to range them in such Order, that they may seem to grow out of one another, and be disposed under the proper Heads. *Seneca* and *Montaigne* are Patterns for Writing in this last Kind, as *Tully* and *Aristotle* excel in the other.

Addison devotes the rest of the *Spectator*, No. 476, to arguing that "method is of Advantage to a Work, both in respect to the Writer and the Reader." But what is most noteworthy about this speculation is his observation that in those papers, whatever they are, that are not essays, Addison feels obliged to arrange his material so that it will *seem* to the reader to be "disposed under the proper Heads." No doubt Addison does not mean to suggest that all such papers must provide explicitly listed topics and subtopics; but to make such

---

Lingua Britannica Reformata: Or, a New English Dictionary (London, 1749) defines *essay* as "A short discourse upon a subject." Thus Johnson's definition does not merely echo those provided by his predecessors. On the other hand it is not a completely new departure either, for Ephraim Chambers, *Cyclopaedia, or an Universal Dictionary of Arts and Sciences* (7th ed.; London, 1751), defines *essay* as "A peculiar kind of composition; whose character is to be free, easy and natural; not tied to strict order or method, nor worked up, and finished, like a formal system."

10. See, e.g., *Spectator*, No. 257, which Addison begins by saying: "That I might not lose myself upon a Subject of so great Extent as that of Fame, I have treated it in a particular Order and Method."

provision is certainly the best way of insuring that a paper will appear methodical to its reader—whose perception of the work perused is thus for Addison what primarily determines how that work is to be classified, since a paper that *appears* immethodical may be called an essay. It is certainly true, in any case, that, insofar as the heads of a discourse are made explicit so that it appears unmistakably methodical, a given paper becomes less of an *essay* as Addison understands this term and takes on an important formal characteristic of the sermon.

This is not to say that in every case where Addison provides explicit topical heads he is merely, or even primarily, approaching the typical homiletic form as he departs from that of the essay. He is not doing so, for example, every time he helps readers to follow the order of a complicated and lengthy discussion by providing occasional summaries of what has been treated in preceding papers together with brief topical outlines of what is to follow, as he does in the series on *Paradise Lost* and in the eleven papers on the Pleasures of the Imagination.[11] However, Addison does display his most striking affinities to Anglican homiletic practice in those essays whose method is made unmistakably clear by the inclusion of enumerated propositions which are then amplified.

Consider, for example, the *Spectator*, No. 447, on the moral uses of habits. The first paragraph of this paper comments on the powerful effects of custom (i.e., habits) on the body and mind. The second paragraph announces the particular topic which will be considered, namely, the power of habit to render customary behavior pleasant. This power is, in effect, the paper's "doctrine," and it is amplified in two paragraphs of explanation and example, after which Addison remarks that although "others have often made the same Reflections, it is possible they may not have drawn those Uses from it, with which I intend to fill the remaining part of this Paper." Thus we are

---

11. *Spectator*, Nos. 267 ff., 411–21. See also *Spectator* Nos. 58 and 59, on "True and False Wit."

explicitly informed that the second part of the paper will be given over to "uses" of the doctrine which had been explained, and it is evident that by this term Addison means prescriptive recommendations grounded on the doctrine explained in the first part. Moreover, the heads of the second part are made clear by enumeration: "In the first place . . . In the second place . . . In the third place . . . to enforce this consideration we may further observe . . . In the fourth place . . . the last Use which I shall make of this remarkable Property in Human Nature, of being delighted with those Actions to which it is accustomed, is to shew . . ." [12]

Apart from the series on *Paradise Lost* and the Pleasures of the Imagination, there are eighteen of Addison's *Spectator* papers disposed wholly or partly into enumerated heads, but of these only six are also unmistakably arranged in the pattern of doctrine followed by use, and the word *use* only appears once.[13] Thus Addison was more inclined to break away from than to rely heavily upon the formal pattern provided by the ideal Anglican sermon. Nevertheless, the presence of such typical homiletic structure in even a handful of papers whose method is simultaneously made explicit provides one concrete measure of the fact that Addison's periodical essays are more closely affiliated in form as well as in content to Anglican sermons than are those in either the *Rambler* or the *Idler*.

For Johnson never enumerates the topical heads under which his

12. Cf. *Spectator*, No. 210, by Hughes, in which the term *use* also appears in its homiletic sense: ". . . there is no one who has observ'd any thing but may observe, that as fast as his Time wears away, his Appetite to something future remains. The Use therefore I would make of it is this, that since Nature (as some love to express it) does nothing in vain, or to speak properly, since the Author of our Being has planted no wandering Passion in it, no Desire which has not its Object, Futurity is the proper Object of the Passion so constantly exercis'd about it."

13. Those disposed wholly or partly into enumerated heads are *Spectator*, Nos. 111, 177, 257, 381, 399, 447, 459, 465, 471, 487, 507, 565, 571, 574, 590, 615, 624, 631. Of these, the papers unmistakably arranged in the pattern of doctrine followed by use are Nos. 257, 381, 447, 471, 565, 571.

paragraphs are grouped, nor does he ever call attention, as Addison does in the *Spectator*, No. 447, to the division of his papers into a section of general doctrine followed by a section devoted to the particular application or use of that doctrine. To be sure, the *Life of Savage*, one of Johnson's earliest works, close in time to the *Spectator*, does conclude with a paragraph beginning: "This relation will not be wholly without its use, if those, who languish under any part of his sufferings, shall be enabled to fortify their patience, by reflecting . . ." Here the word *use* clearly signals the exemplary turn which Johnson gives to the biography. And many of his moral essays are in fact loosely organized in the form of generalizations followed by recommendations arising from the initial considerations. The frequent appearance of this pattern may well represent some degree of significant affinity to Anglican homiletic practice.[14] But if so, the affinity is more remote in Johnson's case because he, unlike Addison, was always careful to do what the Anglican preachers had been cautioned against, namely, "to conceal, and alter the method, for variety sake." That Johnson could heed this caution when he felt the occasion warranted it, however, can be seen by consulting his sermons. In them the method is never concealed, nor is it much altered from sermon to sermon. This in turn shows that whatever the influences exerted upon him by Anglican homiletics, Johnson was more inclined than Addison to consider the sermon and the periodical essay as distinct genres. Certainly this inclination does not account for all the differences between Johnson's secular works and his sermons; but it

14. See, e.g., the *Rambler*, Nos. 13, 25, 40, 41, 43, 48, 49, 155, 164, 203, as well as the *Idler*, Nos. 4, 37, 43, 58, 89. These are the essays in which Johnson seems most closely to parallel the ideal homiletic structure of doctrine followed by use. For essays in which the parallel, though discernible, seems more remote, see the *Rambler*, Nos. 31, 50, 54, 58, 63, 66, 70, 72, 78, 99, 136, 159, 166, 185, as well as the *Idler*, Nos. 11, 27, 38, 74, 80, 102. In these papers Johnson concludes either with explicit prescriptive suggestions put in the form of imperative sentences or else with implicit prescriptions put in the form of affirmative statements asserting some truth whose recognition implies the necessity of a particular course of action.

may at least partly explain why those sermons are his least original, least subtle, and therefore least characteristic achievement.

❦ 2 ❦

The homilies of Donne and South sufficiently demonstrate that Anglican sermons could be as artfully subtle as any other form of discourse. But with the shift throughout the Restoration and early eighteenth century to a plainer style of preaching, the one formal requirement of homilies—that method be made explicit—would have loomed larger in shaping their content. With such complicating stylistic devices as highly figurative language and variation of method frowned on, there would have been increasing pressure toward simplification of content when, formally, the main positive requirement was that of making explicit the transitions and divisions between parts of discourses most often devoted to explaining some doctrine and then spelling out its uses. Endeavoring to achieve maximum clarity by conforming to a simple, obvious, and traditional formula for the benefit of auditors would not make complication of content impossible—indeed, no one could maintain that Johnson's sermons are either simple-minded or artless—nevertheless, complicated arguments would not be thereby encouraged. And in the absence of any other notable encouragement of complexity the formal requirement pushing sermons toward simplicity would acquire a greater power.

No doubt whatever new prominence this requirement had was at first mainly symptomatic of shifting homiletic fashions—a consequence, rather than an instigator, of change. But, given the variously caused fact of that shift, even a symptom would often if not invariably become a contributing cause, hastening a process whose initial impulse was not purely formal. In any event, the sermon was becoming a more constrained genre formally just when the periodical essay, going in the other direction, was becoming increasingly free—and was being defined by its leading practitioners in terms of its irregularity. It may therefore be more than coincidental that all of Johnson's best works, apologue, biography, and poetry alike, share with his essays one formal trait setting them decisively apart from his sermons: greater liberty to vary and conceal method.

The non-homiletic works also share a different kind of audience, for they are designed to be read, not listened to. Moreover, this audience of readers was not captive: it is always easier to put down a book than it is to leave church during a sermon. And according to Watts's *Logick* it is concealment and variation—that is, complication—of method that helps create where necessary "a pleasing and powerful Captivity." Watts adds that it is "chiefly *Poesy* and *Oratory*" that require such complication. He evidently refers to secular rather than pulpit oratory. Implicit in his statement is an injunction to complicate not only poetry and oratory but also any works that must captivate an audience whose presence is not guaranteed by some outside obligation. The preacher alone is free from this particular need to conceal and complicate his method.

Johnson certainly understood the importance of varying his rhetorical appeals to suit the nature of his audience. He well knew that any effective author must conform to the pressures generated by the situation or character of those for whom he writes. In Johnson's view Shakespeare did so to a fault by inclining to fabulous plots because in a nation "yet struggling to emerge from barbarity . . . The publick was gross and dark." [15] A less deplorable instance that attracted Johnson's comment is the simplicity of Addison's critical essays:

That he always wrote as he would think it necessary to write now, cannot be affirmed; his instructions were such as the character of his readers made proper. That general knowledge which now circulates in common talk, was in his time rarely to be found. . . . he, therefore, presented knowledge in the most alluring form, not lofty and austere, but accessible and familiar. . . . An instructor like Addison was now wanting, whose remarks being superficial, might be easily understood, and being just, might prepare the mind for more attainments.[16]

15. "Preface to Shakespeare," *Works*, V, 124–25.
16. "Life of Addison," *Works*, VII, 470.

This reveals Johnson's approval of simplifying content where the audience is not well informed, so long as what is said remains merely superficial and does not become inaccurate. He is perfectly willing to justify superficial treatment of a secular topic.

That Johnson regarded simplification equally appropriate if the topics are religious is implied in a letter which he wrote advising "a young clergyman in the country" how best to compose sermons and provide pastoral care for an uneducated flock. In this important letter, which, as Boswell says, "contains valuable advice to Divines in general," Johnson tells an exemplary anecdote about a stratagem employed by his friend Dr. Wheeler:

One woman he could not bring to the communion; and, when he reproved or exhorted her, she only answered that she was no scholar. He was advised to set some good woman or man of the parish, a little wiser than herself, to talk to her in language level to her mind. Such honest, I may call them holy artifices, must be practiced by every clergyman; for all means must be tried by which souls may be saved.[17]

Language according to Johnson's *Dictionary* means (in the relevant sense) "Stile, manner of expression," and therefore he is primarily suggesting here simplification of diction and other dress of thought rather than content; but since the parishioner enlisted to aid Wheeler's "holy artifice" was only a "little wiser" than the reluctant communicant, the exhortations she received would inevitably have been simpler in content as well as style than those unsuccessfully provided by the scholarly Wheeler. Explaining one day to Boswell why the Methodists were such effective preachers, Johnson was more explicit:

Sir, it is owing to their expressing themselves in a plain and familiar manner, which is the only way to do good to the common people, and which clergymen of genius and learning ought to do from a principle of duty, when it is suited to their congregations . . . To insist against drunkenness as a crime, because it debases Reason, the noblest faculty

17. James Boswell, *The Life of Samuel Johnson*, ed. G. B. Hill, rev. L. F. Powell (Oxford, 1934–1950), III, 436–38.

of man, would be of no service to the common people: but to tell
them that they may die in a fit of drunkenness, and shew them how
dreadful that would be, cannot fail to make a deep impression.[18]

Here Johnson makes it quite plain that alteration of "manner" in the
direction of simplicity includes shifting the logical grounds of argu-
mentation away from subtlety.

In the letter to a young clergyman Johnson also touches on the
relationship between content and homiletic form when he remarks by
way of encouragement that "The composition of sermons is not very
difficult: the divisions not only help the memory of the hearer but
direct the judgment of the writer; they supply sources of invention,
and keep every part in its proper place."[19] If, as Johnson implies

18. *Ibid.*, I, 458–60.
19. *Ibid.*, III, 437. Under *divisions* in his *Dictionary* Johnson quotes from
Swift's *Letter to a Young Clergyman* the sentence "Express the heads of your
divisions in as few and clear words as you can, otherwise I never can be able to
retain them." Throughout his *Letter*, Swift urges simplicity as a means of
achieving clarity. He asserts that "a Divine hath nothing to say to the wisest
Congregation of any Parish in this Kingdom, which he may not express in a
Manner to be understood by the meanest among them." Here Swift is
primarily concerned with simplicity of diction, as he is when he concedes that
there is properly a "Difference between elaborate Discourses upon important
Occasions, delivered to Princes or Parliaments, written with a View of being
made publick, and a plain Sermon intended for the Middle or lower Size of
People." But perhaps in Swift's view the more "elaborate discourses" aimed at
a more knowledgeable audience and intended for publication would display
greater complexity of argument as well as a more recondite vocabulary than
would be appropriate for ordinary sermons ("A Letter to a Young Gentleman, Lately entered into Holy Orders," *The Prose Works of Jonathan Swift*,
ed. Herbert Davis [Oxford, 1948], IX, 66–67).
Cf. also *Spectator*, No. 476, in which Addison affirms a constant relationship between method and invention regardless of genre: "Method is of
Advantage to a Work, both in respect to the Writer and the Reader. In
regard to the first, it is a great Help to his Invention. When a Man has
plann'd his Discourse, he finds a great many Thoughts rising out of every
Head, that do not offer themselves upon the general Survey of a Subject. . . .
The Advantages of a Reader from a methodical Discourse, are correspondent
with those of the Writer. He comprehends every Thing easily . . ."

here, sermons are easier to compose than other kinds of writing, that is because explicit divisions, once made, generate what is said in addition to determining the order in which it is presented. He does not make clear why this should be the case in sermons more than in other genres, nor does he explain how, exactly, the author's judgment and the content of what is invented will be molded by the presence of divisions. But clearly the presence and explicit statement of those divisions, a formal property of sermons, does in Johnson's view determine in large measure homiletic content. And whatever the influence on his own sermons of formal pressures acting together with attention to the situation of his audience, it is equally clear that even where differences would seem least probable, Johnson's sermons are in many ways highly unlike his other works.

Sermon XII, for example, is on Ecclesiastes 1:14 "I have seen all the works that are done under the sun; and behold, all is vanity and vexation of spirit." The theme is certainly typical enough, and so in the main is the prose style: there are doublets, triplets, Latinate words, long sentences, parallel clauses, and rhetorical figures such as the chiastic "Our endeavours end without performance, and performance ends without satisfaction." There are fewer hard words and less learned imagery drawn from the natural sciences than in many of those *Rambler* essays in which Johnson endeavored to familiarize "the terms of philosophy, by applying them to popular ideas." [20] But this relative simplicity of diction is really a superficial difference, as is the absence throughout Johnson's sermons of elaborate character sketches and exemplary narratives organized as satires or apologues. The extended *exemplum* was infrequent in contemporary sermons, and it is not surprising that Johnson avoided difficult words when writing for auditors rather than readers. What is remarkable, however, is that in Sermon XII Johnson does not treat his theme as he characteristically does in *Rasselas* and *The Vanity of Human Wishes* and as he might well have done in a sermon.

20. *Rambler*, No. 208.

Both apologue and poem concentrate on illustrating the proposition that human wishes for enduring happiness in this world are vain. Though *Rasselas* calls attention to the soul's immortality and in other ways implies that there is comfort to be derived from considering the limitations of human life, the book is nevertheless deservedly most famous for its "Conclusion, in which nothing is concluded." After visiting the catacombs and listening to Imlac's discourse on the nature of the soul, Nekayah does say that for her "the choice of life is become less important," and she hopes "hereafter, to think only on the choice of eternity." [21] But as Joseph Wood Krutch rightly maintains, this concession to orthodoxy is "only the formal rather than the effective moral." [22] Another way of putting this is to say that throughout *Rasselas* Johnson focuses most of our attention on what is in Sermon XII only the first consideration: "In what sense we are to understand that all is vanity." So too in *The Vanity of Human Wishes* Johnson is primarily concerned with illustrating that first consideration; only in the last twenty-six lines does he turn to explicit concern with those topics that comprise the second and third divisions of Sermon XII: "How far the conviction, that all is vanity, ought to influence the conduct of life . . . What consequences the serious and religious mind may deduce from the position, that all is vanity." At the end of the poem it is stated that "petitions yet remain,/ Which heav'n may hear"; from this possibility of comfort Johnson proceeds to the somewhat Popean assurance that whatever God gives "he gives the best." Finally, the poem concludes with an optimistic affirmation that by granting faith, patience, a resigned will, obedient passions, and "love, which scarce collective man can fill," heavenly wisdom "calms the mind,/ And makes the happiness she does not find." [23] Here, as in *Rasselas*, the more optimistic considerations, however effective, are rhetorically overshadowed by the greater number of

21. *Rasselas* (*Works*, I, 308).

22. *Samuel Johnson* (New York, 1944), p. 183.

23. Samuel Johnson, *Poems*, ed. E. L. McAdam, Jr. with George Milne (New Haven, 1964), pp. 108–9.

lines devoted to amplifying a negative and disquieting proposition. Critics may agree that the poem's sanguine and comforting conclusion fits logically with what has led up to it. Critics may also argue that in many subtle ways the conclusion fits emotionally as well. But there has not been much overt emotional preparation for this radical shift in tone, compared with the preparation supplied in Sermon XII. In other words, both *Rasselas* and *The Vanity of Human Wishes* are primarily devoted to the presentation rather than to the solution of a difficult problem.

A large part of Sermon XII, on the other hand, is devoted to explaining how we must cope with that problem. Johnson thereby reassures his audience at relatively great length that the problem does have a solution. Shortly after the sermon's halfway point, for example, he states that although in carrying out lawful and necessary labor "we shall often have occasion to remember the sentence denounced by the preacher upon all that is done under the sun," we nevertheless "must still prosecute our business, confess our imbecility, and turn our eyes upon Him, whose mercy is over all his works, and who, though he humbles our pride, will succour our necessities." [24] The sermon might logically have ended with this comforting exhortation. It partly resolves our perplexities over the omnipresence of disappointments by affirming that such troubles are more apparent than real since it is only our pride which is humbled, while our necessities *will* be provided for. Moreover, we are firmly directed to keep going about such business in this world as does not involve the pursuit of vanities. Though often "our industry is permitted to miscarry," there is to be no retreat toward cultivation of a more private and spiritual garden. [25] This possibility is not raised, much less considered with the complexity of Johnson's dialogue in *Rasselas* on the value of monastic life. [26] Even the reassuring conclusion of *The Vanity of Human Wishes* leaves us in more doubt insofar as it does not explicitly direct

24. Sermon XII (*Works*, IX, 400).
25. *Ibid.*, p. 399.
26. *Works*, I, 303–4.

us to "prosecute our business" as usual. Without such direction all the
grim examples of worldly careers which have come to nothing remain
to haunt our reflections on the poem and make us wonder whether we
should continue even our permissible wordly affairs. Told that we
must not "deem religion vain," we may wonder momentarily whether
everything *but* religion comes under the head of vanity. No Christian
audience need remain long troubled on this issue, of course, for the
solution provided in Sermon XII is quite orthodox and could easily
be arrived at by any believer after brief reflection. In the poem,
though, Johnson does invite rather than supply that reflection. And
while the sermon's exhortation to turn our eyes heavenward is paral-
leled in the poem, *The Vanity of Human Wishes* ends on this note,
whereas the sermon proceeds to further amplification.

After three paragraphs which describe the uncertainty and vanity
of those pleasures which depend in some way upon "the help of
others," Johnson asserts that "conviction of this unwelcome truth"
should influence our conduct by teaching us "humility, patience, and
diffidence." [27] Arguments against pride are supplied in a brief paragraph followed by reiteration of the assertion that "we are not to
admit impatience into our bosoms." The reason supplied by Johnson
affords some comfort: "To live in a world where all is vanity, has
been decreed by our Creator to be the lot of man—a lot which we
cannot alter by murmuring, but may soften by submission." [28] This
reassuring possibility of softening what cannot be altered is succeeded
by a long paragraph outlining the advantages "necessarily" produced
by "full persuasion that all earthly good is uncertain": the man so
persuaded will display

inoffensive modesty, and mild benevolence. . . . he will not refuse
assistance to the distressed. . . . He . . . will seldom think any
possibilities of advantage worthy of vehement desire. . . . his endeavours will be calm. He will not fix his fond hopes upon things which

27. Sermon XII (*Works*, IX, 401).
28. *Ibid.*, p. 402.

he knows to be vanity, but will enjoy this world as one who knows that he does not possess it.[29]

There is no hesitation or qualification here. Persuasion that earthly goods are uncertain *will necessarily* produce the saintly frame of mind which is described. Since he is trying to induce this disposition by pointing out and dwelling on its advantages, Johnson does not pause to emphasize or even suggest how difficult it may really be to achieve the persuasion upon which those advantages depend. Instead, he proceeds to conclude Sermon XII by turning in a lengthy final paragraph to his third topic.

As a parting consideration Johnson suggests that, far from murmuring at our lot, we should be grateful that it is not better: "Instead of lamenting the imperfection of earthly things, we have reason to pour out thanks to Him who orders all for our good; that he has made the world, such as often deceives, and often afflicts us . . . that we have such interruptions of our pursuits, and such languor in our enjoyments, such pains of body and anxiety of mind . . ."[30] Taken even slightly out of context this passage seems unlike Johnson. It smacks more of what he found most irritating in Soame Jenyns' bland attempts to explain away evil. And of him Johnson complains that "This enquirer . . . has told us of the benefits of evil, which no man feels."[31] The same objection could well be made to Sermon XII, though with somewhat less justification. Johnson's statement there is more restrained and, in context, its logic is more compelling than that of the *Free Enquiry*. But even when put back into its context Johnson's remark still seems off-center emotionally in its treatment of the notion that painful afflictions "repress desire, and weaken temptation," thus making it easier for us to think on heaven, which is to be

---

29. *Ibid.*, pp. 402–3.
30. *Ibid.*, p. 403.
31. "Review of *A Free Enquiry into the Nature and Origin of Evil*," (*Works*, VI, 64).

obtained "By the contempt of worldly pleasures." [32] Of course the idea
that afflictions are blessings in disguise because they may engender a
salutary *contemptus mundi* turns up elsewhere in the canon and
cannot be dismissed as un-Johnsonian.

In the *Adventurer*, No. 120, for example, Johnson asserts that "it
is by affliction chiefly that the heart of man is purified, and that the
thoughts are fixed upon a better state." In the *Idler*, No. 89, Johnson
argues along very similar lines that without physical evil there would
be little temperance, justice, charity, or piety in the world. He sums
up this argument by asserting that "of what virtue there is, misery
produces far the greater part. Physical evil may be therefore endured
with patience, since it is the cause of moral good; and patience itself is
one virtue by which we are prepared for that state in which evil shall
be no more." Logically the arguments in these essays are almost
identical with the argument in Sermon XII. But there is a great
difference emotionally. In the sermon Johnson suggests that we
should be grateful for afflictions; in the *Idler* he merely urges patient
endurance of them. And in the *Adventurer* he concludes that "While
affliction thus prepares us for felicity, we may console ourselves under
its pressures, by remembering, that they are no particular marks of
divine displeasure; since all the distresses of persecution have been
suffered by those, 'of whom the world was not worthy'; and the
Redeemer of mankind himself was 'a man of sorrows and acquainted
with grief.'" Here too emphasis is on endurance of pressures that are
felt as sorrows and grief rather than on the reasons for pouring out
thanks for them. The tone is different in the secular essays, and so is
the rhetorical situation. Stirring an audience to feel gratitude for the
existence of evil is not quite the same task as persuading them that
Christian resignation is essential.

Insofar as their persuasive goals do overlap, moreover, the essays
display greater subtlety than the sermon. It is simpler to affirm
openly that "we have reason to pour out thanks" for afflictions and

32. Sermon XII (*Works*, IX, 403).

then present arguments designed to compel assent to this affirmation. It is more artful to show that physical evils do serve a highly useful purpose and then to leave thoughtful readers in a position where only one inference is possible: that in our fallen state we should be grateful for whatever—including evil—incites us to virtue, to the imitation of Christ, and thus to eternal happiness. What is explicit in the sermon is implicit in the essays. The sermon does everything for us, whereas the essays, like *The Vanity of Human Wishes* and *Rasselas,* force or at least invite some further mental activity on the reader's part. "Thought-provoking" may be an overworked term—nevertheless, it describes one quality of Johnson's work at its best. He never really supplies conclusions in which nothing is concluded. Nor, on the other hand, does he often (outside the sermons) explicitly resolve all problems in ways that simplify issues and tend to snuff out further consideration of their complexities. The paradoxically titled concluding chapter of *Rasselas* is only the most famous of the many devices by which Johnson teases us into thought.

He frequently does so by directing attention primarily to what is painful or problematic in life. Clear advice is offered, but panaceas are avoided. In *Rasselas,* for example, Nekayah is made to remind us that all virtue "can afford is quietness of conscience, a steady prospect of a happier state; this may enable us to endure calamity with patience; but remember, that patience must suppose pain." [33] Throughout Johnson's secular works, the tone of Nekayah's reminder prevails: though remedial directions for softening our lot are never lacking, they do not usually imply that calamities only seem unpleasant on superficial consideration. The sermons are more optimistic.

Johnson argues in Sermon V, for example, that "it is not certain that poverty is an evil. . . . poverty, like many other miseries of life, is often little more than an imaginary calamity." [34] He goes on to describe the happiness of primitive societies living in a state of nature:

33. *Rasselas (Works,* I, 257).
34. Sermon V (*Works,* IX, 336).

There is more tranquillity and satisfaction diffused through the inhabitants of uncultivated and savage countries, than is to be met with in nations filled with wealth and plenty, polished with civility, and governed by laws. It is found happy to be free from contention, though that exemption be obtained, by having nothing to contend for; and an equality of condition, though that condition be far from eligible, conduces more to the peace of society, than an established and legal subordination. . . . it is better to have no property, than to be in perpetual apprehensions of fraudulent artifices. . . . Thus pleasing is the prospect of savage countries, merely from the ignorance of vice . . . thus happy are they, amidst all the hardships and distresses that attend a state of nature.

Johnson's concession that a state of nature has disadvantages only serves here to underscore the inferiority of extant civilization, for it is hard to give much weight to distresses that do not prevent greater satisfaction than is derived from wealth, polished manners, established laws, settled property, and social hierarchy. The sermon does not dispose us to give much thought to hardships accompanying such satisfaction. The *Adventurer*, No. 67, on the other hand, is in a more typically Johnsonian vein. After showing that Indians may attain the necessities of life and thus live "in a state of plenty and prosperity," Johnson adds that "this picture of a savage life, if it shews how much individuals may perform, shews likewise how much society is to be desired. Though the perseverance and address of the Indian excite our admiration, they nevertheless cannot procure him the conveniences which are enjoyed by the vagrant beggar of a civilized country . . ."

From its rather un-Johnsonian account of the happy Indians, Sermon V proceeds to outline the utopian achievements possible to "a community generally virtuous," in which "all care and solicitude would be almost banished": it would be rich and powerful though not luxurious; it would be well-governed and filled with loyal, tractable citizens; consequently, though it might be attacked, *it could never be defeated* ("The encroachments of foreign enemies, they could not always avoid, but would certainly repulse"); its people would be industrious; their merit would always be rewarded; they would be eager to help one another; there would be no "envy, rivalship, or suspicion"; "all children would be obedient" and therefore loved by their parents; though "perhaps" grief at the death of those we love could not "be wholly prevented," it would be "much more moderate than in the present state of things, because no man could ever want a friend"; lawsuits would be rare and amicable; no disturbances would flow from differences of opinion "because every man would dispute for truth alone . . ." Whether the horses would be rational, Johnson does not say. But he firmly denies that "this prospect of things" —including, presumably, the eerily obedient children and the military invulnerability—can be dismissed as merely a "visionary scene, with which a gay imagination may be amused in solitude." He affirms that, on the contrary, "nothing has been maintained which would not certainly be produced in any nation by a general piety." [35] Perhaps. But to show how far this is from Johnson's more typical and convincing moments, I hope it is only necessary to set beside it a sentence from *Rasselas:* " 'Whether perfect happiness would be procured by perfect goodness,' said Nekayah, 'this world will never afford an opportunity of deciding.' " [36]

Johnson concludes Sermon V by turning to the question of "How much, in the present corrupt state of the world, particular men may, by the practice of the duties of religion, promote their own happiness." [37] Here, finally, in a cheerful context of tranquil savages and perfectibilian thought, is the question answered so bleakly in *Rasselas* by Nekayah's reminder of how little happiness virtue can afford us in this world. Sermon V is not so likely to depress our hope that for the righteous all may yet be as well here as it surely will be in the hereafter. At the end of a paragraph devoted to showing that "The man who considers himself as a being accountable to God . . . will not be very solicitous about his present condition," Johnson provides

35. *Ibid.,* pp. 338–40.
36. *Works,* I, 257.
37. *Works,* IX, 337–40.

the indisputable, if tautological, assertion that no man can ever "be miserable to whom persecution is a blessing; nor can his tranquillity be interrupted, who places all his happiness in his prospect of eternity." If there are difficulties in achieving such contempt of the world, Johnson does not indicate them. If we are powerfully tied down to the present life by our senses, our appetites, and our passions, Johnson does not say so here. Instead, he quickly winds up his discussion by stating the conclusion toward which the logic of Sermon V has led: "Thus it appears, that by the practice of our duty, even our present state may be made pleasing and desirable . . ." [38]

This is only the most extreme of Johnson's various homiletic departures from his more characteristic attitudes. He remarks in Sermon VIII, for example, that:

It has been observed by those who have employed themselves in considering the methods of Providence and the government of the world, that good and evil are distributed, through all states of life, if not in equal proportions, yet in such degrees as leave very little room for those murmurs and complaints, which are frequently produced by superficial inquiries, negligent surveys, and impatient comparisons. [39]

Since none of Johnson's writing is intended to provoke or support complaints against the dispensations of Providence, this remark is not at variance logically with the doctrines embedded in such works as *Rasselas* and *The Vanity of Human Wishes*. But its blandly reassuring tone is emotionally far from, say, Johnson's disturbing picture of the wise Swift expiring "a driv'ler and a show" and thus exemplifying how "few there are . . . / Who set unclouded in the gulphs of fate." That a peaceful old age is rare, that even on the virtuous "her load Misfortune flings," may leave more than "very little" room for

---

38. *Ibid.*, p. 341. See also Sermon XIV (*Works*, IX, 421): "He, therefore, that trusts in God will no longer be distracted in his search after happiness, for *he will find it* in a firm belief, that whatever evils are suffered to befall him will finally contribute to his felicity; and that by staying his mind upon the Lord, he will be kept in peace" [italics added].

39. *Works*, IX, 359.

complaint even if it does not ultimately justify impatience.[40] The apparent reasons for complaint are at least not glossed over or minimized in the poem. And equally far removed in tone from the remark in Sermon VIII is Imlac's dour statement of what *Rasselas* is designed to illustrate: "Human life is everywhere a state, in which much is to be endured, and little to be enjoyed." [41]

Even the satisfactions afforded by thinking about a future state are presented differently outside the pulpit. Thus, in the *Idler*, No. 42, published within a week of his mother's death, Johnson concludes that grief forces "the mind to take refuge in religion," because "Real alleviation of the loss of friends, and rational tranquillity in the prospect of our own dissolution, can be received only from the . . . assurance of another and better state, in which all tears will be wiped from the eyes and the whole soul shall be filled with joy." Here faith is described as engendering a reasonable contentment beyond the reach of unaided intellect, but joy is reserved for heaven. Johnson ends the paper by drawing a familiar contrast between the consolations of philosophy and revelation: "Philosophy may infuse stubbornness, but religion only can give patience." And patience only, the paper implies. Johnson goes further in a sermon written for his wife's funeral, though never preached:

So much is our condition improved by the gospel, so much is the sting of death rebated, that we may now be invited to the contemplation of our mortality, as to a pleasing employment of the mind, to an exercise delightful and recreative, not only when calamity and persecution drive us from the assemblies of men, and sorrow and woe represent the grave as a refuge and an asylum, but even in the hours of the highest earthly prosperity, when our cup is full . . . for, in him who believes the promise of the Saviour of the world, it can cause no disturbance to remember, that this night his soul may be required of him . . .[42]

40. "The Vanity of Human Wishes," *Poems*, pp. 105–6.
41. *Works*, I, 226.
42. Sermon XXV (*Works*, IX, 520–21); see also *The Life of Samuel Johnson*, I, 241.

There is no need to list the times when Johnson himself found it less than "delightful and recreative" to contemplate mortality. Perhaps it is even superfluous to cite a more characteristic passage from the *Rambler*, No. 78: "Surely nothing can so much disturb the passions, or perplex the intellects of man, as the disruption of his union with visible nature . . . and, what is above all distressful and alarming, the final sentence, and unalterable allotment." Whether or not this passage is logically at variance with that from the funeral sermon, their emotional contradiction seems irreconcilable.

There is certainly no distance logically between the evaluations of marriage in *Rasselas* and in Sermon I, which argues that "nothing but vice or folly obstructs the happiness of a married life." Early in the sermon Johnson concedes that marriage "does not always produce the effects for which it was appointed . . . it sometimes condenses the gloom, which it was intended to dispel, and increases the weight, which was expected to be made lighter by it." But the sermon's main point is that "religion appears, in every state of life, to be the basis of happiness, and the operating power which makes every good institution valid and efficacious." Johnson does not promise that religion will create perfect happiness. He only concludes, in the sermon's final sentence, that if we properly follow "the means which God has ordained"—marriage—we will "surely find the highest degree of satisfaction that our present state allows." [43] Exactly what degree of satisfaction that might be Johnson does not there consider in any way that could undercut his praise of matrimony. In *Rasselas* marriage is also recommended, but in other terms: to live unmarried "is not retreat, but exclusion from mankind." No endorsement could be stronger. Who would willingly exclude himself from the human race? The next sentence, justifiably so famous, wittily complicates the endorsement: "Marriage has many pains, but celibacy has no pleasures." [44]

43. Sermon I (*Works*, IX, 292, 294, 300).
44. *Rasselas* (*Works*, I, 255).

If this thoroughly Johnsonian aphorism drolly complicates the evaluation of marriage, it nevertheless does not in any way negate the endorsement provided in the preceding sentence and in Sermon I. It merely shifts the grounds of that endorsement: avoidance of a state with "no pleasure" in favor of its only alternative, marriage, seems as necessary as what is the converse process psychologically, seeking for the "highest satisfaction" possible, marriage, in order, of course, to avoid the situation most devoid of pleasure. While amplifying the proposition that to live unmarried is to be cut off from all social comfort and pleasure, the aphorism reminds us that marriage (like other virtues) does not exclude pain. If this reminder is implicit in the conclusion of Sermon I, it does not signal its presence. By the end of the sermon attention has been shifted entirely to the advantages attainable in wedlock. At the conclusion of the debate on marriage in *Rasselas,* however, the complication of Nekayah's aphorism is maintained. After explaining the drawbacks of early and late marriages, she finishes the discussion by rejecting the Prince's suggestion that an ideal marriage might combine the mutual affection of young lovers and the pleasure derived from children by elderly couples: "There are goods so opposed that we cannot seize both, but, by too much prudence, may pass between them, at too great a distance to reach either. . . . no man can, at the same time, fill his cup from the source and from the mouth of the Nile." [45] Because it reminds us that sufficient satisfaction can be found, there is comfort in this injunction to seize the advantages that are possible in marriage; but there is also a disturbing reminder that in doing so it is necessary to make a choice that is also an exclusion. While there is nothing here that contradicts the conclusion of Sermon I, the sermon does not compel us to dwell on the pains or limitations that may trouble even "the highest degree of satisfaction that our present state allows."

By so frequently allowing or inviting us to escape from dwelling on what is troublesome in life, Johnson's sermons do not fall short of

45. *Ibid.,* p. 263.

achieving their purpose. Quite the contrary. The homilist may certainly provide comfort by supplying more answers than questions, and perhaps the questions that turn men to the church are best raised outside the pulpit. Yet by relying so heavily on this rhetorical strategy of consolation throughout his sermons, Johnson has shifted their emotional center of gravity away from that of his other works. To describe all the rhetorical devices employed in Johnson's variously shaped secular calls to a devout and holy life, however, is a task for another book. In showing that his sermons are set apart by their form no less than by their tone from Johnson's other works, I have not meant to suggest that those works all share any formal characteristic other than freedom to conceal and vary method. Neither have I meant to imply that their formal properties are irrelevant. Johnson's works are anything but "pure content" or mere systematic philosophizing, nor is their tone ever unaffected by the forms through which their concepts are bodied forth. But insofar as the intellectual historian may characterize a single work or a body of works by abstracting its typical attitudes and underlying assumptions, it remains true that the sermons are atypical of Johnson's work in content as well as form.

For my present purpose, it only remains necessary to note a conspicuous omission: nowhere in the sermons does Johnson explain in significant detail the nature of our mental anatomy. Advice on the moral discipline of the mind is not lacking and often parallels that provided by him elsewhere. Nor does Johnson avoid his familiar topic of self-delusion. But emphasis is placed on the mind's operations rather than on its nature. Morally proper and improper modes of thought are described without any searching attention to the mental mechanisms which circumscribe the channels in which thoughts are inclined to flow. From the sermons alone it would be impossible to understand fully how Johnson conceived of the relationships between appetites, passions, and higher faculties or what, in his view, is done for and to us by memory, imagination, reason, judgment, and will. Lack of attention to these topics cannot of course be charged as a fault of the sermons. But it is nevertheless a major omission, and the decision to avoid such matters was crucial. That it was not an inevitable decison is proved by the fact that the bearing of mental anatomy on moral conduct was considered in some depth (though in different ways) by Robert South, one of the many Anglican divines with whose sermons Johnson was thoroughly acquainted.[46] It was by making this decision, however, that he confined his homiletic writing to the entirely appropriate subject of divinity, whereas by enlarging the scope of his secular works to include persistent concern with mental structure Johnson earned a distinctive place in the history of moral philosophy.

✎ 3 ✎

So at least it would have seemed to the first important English essayist. Moral philosophy is one branch of knowledge which Francis Bacon considered insufficiently developed when, in *The Advancement of Learning,* he carried out his "attempt to make a general and faithful perambulation of learning, with an inquiry what parts thereof lie fresh and waste, and not improved and converted by the industry of man." To explain what he found lacking, Bacon first observes that "the main and primitive division of moral knowledge seemeth to be into the exemplar or platform of good and the regiment or culture of the mind," which must, however, be mastered in order efficiently to make our conduct virtuous: "If before they had come to the popular and received notions of virtue and vice, pleasure and pain, and the rest, they had stayed a little longer upon the inquiry concerning the roots of good and evil, and the strings of these roots, they had given, in my opinion, a great light to that which followed."[47] This novel plea for consideration of "the regiment or culture of the mind" as it bears on morality seems, in retrospect, to

46. See my article "Robert South, William Law and Samuel Johnson," *SEL,* VI (Summer, 1966), 499–528.
47. Francis Bacon, *The Advancement of Learning,* ed. G. W. Kitchin (Everyman Edition; London, 1958), pp. 68, 154–55.

have set the task of English ethical speculation during the next two centuries. Hobbes, Locke, Shaftesbury, Mandeville, Butler, Hume, Adam Smith, Hartley, and many others endeavored to explore the relationship between moral conduct and the ways of managing those antecedent mental dispositions which govern our actions. These men hardly gave equal attention to this problem, nor did they agree with each other. But there was no longer any ground for complaint that the second division of moral philosophy was "not improved and converted by the industry of man."

Johnson's works alone went far towards supplying precisely the kind of "inquiry concerning the roots of good and evil" which had been recommended in *The Advancement of Learning*. Like Bacon, Johnson pointed out that although people had neglected to do so, "It is no vain speculation to consider how we may govern our thoughts, restrain them from irregular motions, or confine them from boundless dissipation. . . . To suffer the thoughts to be vitiated is to poison the fountains of morality." [48] Since Johnson's professed purpose was "to consider the moral discipline of the mind," he was in fact endeavoring to advance that hitherto neglected division of moral philosophy which, according to Bacon's classification, is concerned with "prescribing rules how to subdue, apply, and accommodate the will of man" to the practice of virtue. Bacon added that

if it be said that the cure of men's minds belongeth to sacred divinity, it is most true: but yet moral philosophy may be preferred unto her as a wise servant and humble handmaid . . . so ought moral philosophy to give a constant attention to the doctrines of divinity, and yet so as it may yield of herself, within due limits, many sound and profitable directions. [49]

Johnson certainly agreed with this recommendation since, as I have shown in Chapter V, his moral essays attend constantly to many "doctrines of divinity," and he explicitly states that his "own inten-

48. *Rambler*, No. 8.
49. *The Advancement of Learning*, p. 167.

tions" were to make the *Ramblers* "exactly conformable to the precepts of Christianity."

Bacon also remarks of "the culture and cure of the mind of man" that "in this, as in all things which are practical, we ought to cast up our account, what is in our power, and what is not; for the one may be dealt with by way of alteration, but the other by way of application only." [50] This realistic attitude was clearly shared by Johnson, in whose moral writings, as I have shown in Chapters I and II, it is possible to discern a remarkably elaborate and consistent set of explicit assumptions about the actual "anatomy of the mind" and consequently about "what is in our power and what is not." Johnson, as Bacon had urged, always endeavored to avoid the futility of advising people to alter what cannot be changed and must therefore be dealt with "by way of application only." Yet Johnson was also careful to point out those thoughts and actions which not only can but should be altered in order to prevent or cure the various "maladies of the mind" that often lead to immoral conduct as well as unhappiness. The importance of dealing with what Johnson referred to as "the arduous province of preserving the balance of the mental constitution" had also been stressed by Bacon, who found it "strange . . . that Aristotle should have written divers volumes of ethics, and never handled the affections, which is the principal subject thereof":

Another article of this knowledge is the inquiry touching the affections; for as in medicining of the body, it is in order first to know the divers complexions and constitutions; secondly, the diseases; and lastly the cures: so in medicining of the mind, after knowledge of the divers characters of men's natures, it followeth, in order, to know the diseases and infirmities of the mind, which are no other than the perturbations and distempers of the affections. [51]

As I have shown in this study, Johnson went far beyond Bacon's simple equation of mental diseases with distempered affections: the

50. *Ibid.*, p. 168.
51. *Ibid.*, p. 171.

importance of maintaining proper balance among the higher faculties
as well as the need for keeping appetites and passions duly controlled
is a recurring topic throughout Johnson's career as a moralist. In a
wide range of different literary contexts he suggests numerous methods of preserving such balance in order to prevent what Imlac refers
to as "disorders of the intellect." The greater complexity of Johnson's
analysis of "the diseases and infirmities of the mind," however, is
merely an extension of, rather than a departure from, the Baconian
view that such analysis is an essential aspect of "the regiment or
culture of the mind." Indeed, one of Johnson's most noteworthy
accomplishments is his extensive and detailed elaboration of that
branch of moral philosophy whose outlines were first sketched for
English readers in *The Advancement of Learning*.

Another equally noteworthy accomplishment, however, is Johnson's refusal to reject the essentially amoral methods of natural
philosophy simply because his aim was ethical instruction. To be sure,
he explicitly associated himself, as I have pointed out in Chapter I,
with the long tradition of Socratic humanism rather than with the
newer branches of natural philosophy whose pursuit he regarded as
sometimes necessary, though ultimately "less suitable to the state of
man" than consideration of the moral discipline of the mind. But as I
have also shown throughout the first two chapters and with particular
reference to Locke in Chapter III, Johnson was still willing to press
into the service of moral philosophy many theories and investigative
techniques characteristic of the new empirical naturalism. Moreover,
as I have shown in Chapters IV and V, his rich array of specific
suggestions for directing our thoughts into pious as well as judicious
channels is designed to complement rather than displace naturalistic
analysis such as that provided by his extensive discussions of self-
delusion, the dangerous prevalence of imagination, and the anatomy
of the mind. Johnson did not hesitate to fuse disparate, even potentially antagonistic, secular and religious elements into an imposing
intellectual edifice that combines a tough-minded theory of human

nature with a clear set of moral imperatives. In these respects, as in so many others, Johnson made choices which must be clearly understood in order to appreciate his unique accomplishment.

Increasing respect is accorded to Johnson's intellectual achievement as our own knowledge advances. A thoughtful critic of his political views, for example, concludes that "enough new information about Johnson and the political history of his times has become available for the continued currency of the simple old legend of Johnson the 'blind reactionary' to be an unnecessary handicap to serious students." [52] Other literary critics have been equally concerned to dispose finally of what one of them calls "the misconception of Johnson's relation to the world of ideas—that he was an entrenched conservative devoted to the established and the orthodox, set resolutely against all innovation." [53] Even the historians of science are beginning to discover how forward-looking Johnson's views often were: in a recent issue of *Medical History*, for example, *Rasselas* is described as "introducing a new understanding and a new dimension" to the study of the mind. [54] And as I hope this work has shown, our grasp of Johnson's effort as a moralist as well as our knowledge of how that effort is related to the newer empirical philosophy has now become so extensive that we can no longer maintain the simple old legend that Johnson was only a blindly conservative, though eloquent, sounding board for "traditional wisdom." Instead, we must recognize and attempt to refine our appreciation of the fact that while he is not to be ranked alongside such daring system-builders as Hume and Berkeley, Johnson's work nevertheless cannot be justly described as a mere repository of elegantly adorned commonplaces. In the *Rambler*, No. 108, Erasmus is

52. Donald J. Greene, *The Politics of Samuel Johnson* (New Haven, 1960), p. viii.

53. Herman W. Liebert, "Reflections on Samuel Johnson," *Samuel Johnson, A Collection of Critical Essays*, ed. Donald J. Greene (Englewood Cliffs, 1965), p. 18.

54. Kathleen M. Grange, "Dr. Samuel Johnson's Account of a Schizophrenic Illness in *Rasselas*," *Medical History*, VI (1962) 162–68.

numbered "among those who have contributed to the advancement of learning." Surely we may ungrudgingly add Johnson to that company. His was one of the most sustained and distinctive efforts to advance, as well as to apply, the English instauration of moral philosophy.

◦ Index ◦

Activity, 148
Addison, Joseph, 182, 183, 192; on
  method, 186–88, 194*n*. SEE ALSO
  Spectator, The
Adventurer, The, 97. SEE ALSO Essays
Advice, 143
Affectation, 127, 128*n*
Affliction, 199–200
Ambition, 15
Anglican rationalists, 107
"Animal appetites," 9–10
Animals, 46
Appetite, 10
Aristotle, 187, 211
Avarice, 15
Aversion, 12

Bacon, Sir Francis, 182, 209–12
Bailey, Nathan, 19*n*, 186*n*
Bate, Walter Jackson, 13, 25, 34*n*, 37,
  41*n*, 67
Beggar's Opera, The, 116
Benevolence, 156, 159. SEE ALSO Good
  humor
Berkeley, George, 213
Biography, 37–39
Boredom, 163
Boswell, James, 27, 39, 54, 121, 193
Burton, Robert, 8, 100–103

Butler, Joseph, 210

Chain of being, 48–49
Chambers, Ephraim, 187*n*
Chance, 112*n*
Change, 5
Character, 16
Charity, 40–43
Christianity, 54, 56, 64, 132–33, 160,
  176–79
Civilization, 16–17, 202
Clarissa, 114
Compassion, 39–43. SEE ALSO Pity
Consensus gentium, 89
Conservatism, 5
Cross, F. L., 50*n*
Cumberland, Bishop Richard, 57*n*
Curiosity, 15
Customs, 19–20

Davies, Godfrey, 34*n*
Death, 173, 205–6
Deism, 66
Democracy, 130
Desire, 11
Destiny, 46
Determinism, 13, 21, 25–26, 112,
  117–18
Distrust, 161

215

Doctrine and Use pattern, 184, 185*n*, 188–90
Donne, John, 191
Drama, 115–16
Duties, 148–49, 149–79 *passim*
Dyche, Thomas, 20*n*

Egalitarianism, 130
Empiricism, 108*n*
Environment, 19, 24–25, 89, 144–45
Envy, 15, 161–63
Epictetus, 163*n*
Erasmus, Desiderius, 213
Essay, defined by Johnson and others, 186–87
Essays, 182–209 *passim*; organization of Addison's and Johnson's, 190; and religious precepts, 177–79; rhetorical strategy in Johnson's, 49–53, 53–64 *passim*, 97, 107, 140, 178–79; secular treatment of imagination in Johnson's, 108
"Estimation," 29–31
Evil, 12–13

Faculty, 67
Faith, 47
Fame, 15, 175
Fear, 12, 168, 170–72
Fenwick, Sir John, 29
Fideism, 66
Flattery, 142, 144
Forgetfulness, 150. SEE ALSO Memory
Form, homiletic. SEE Sermons; Essays
"Four last things," 176
Fraser, Alexander Campbell, 12, 95
Freed, Lewis, 35*n*, 58*n*, 87*n*, 100*n*, 106*n*
Freedom of the will, 25–26, 80–84, 111–19 *passim*
Freud, Sigmund, 25, 94, 138, 174
Friendship, 15, 141

Future. SEE Thoughts
Futurity, 167

Gentleman's Magazine, 21
Glanvill, Joseph, 107
God, attributes of, 49–53
Good, 12–13
Good humor, 158
Grange, Kathleen M., 94, 213
Greene, Donald J., 28, 35–36, 88*n*, 213
Grief, 151–52
Guardian, The, 182

Hagstrum, Jean H., 9, 34, 54, 78, 79, 88*n*
Hallywell, Henry, 107
Hammond, Henry, 58–61
Happiness, 13, 57–58, 129, 148–49, 169, 202–4
Harth, Phillip, 107*n*
Hartley, David, 95, 210
Hatred, 11
Havens, Raymond D., 74, 76*n*
Historical method, 31–34
History, 34; intellectual, 85
Hobbes, Thomas, 13, 16, 26, 34, 87*n*, 95, 210; on pity, 39–43
Hooker, Richard, 45*n*, 62*n*, 72, 79, 82
Hoover, Benjamin B., 4*n*
Hope, 12, 122, 171, 172, 174–75
Hughes, John, 189*n*
Human nature: distinctive aspects of, 48; systematized knowledge of, 8; uniformity of, 5, 6, 17, 18, 19–21, 35–37
Humanism, 6–7
Hume, David, 210, 213
Humility, 132
Hypocrisy, 127–28

Idleness, 154. SEE ALSO Activity
Idler, The, 97. SEE ALSO Essays